D0932919

TO SEE WITH TWO EYES

TO SEE with TWO EYES

PEASANT ACTIVISM & INDIAN AUTONOMY in CHIAPAS, MEXICO

SHANNAN L. MATTIACE

UNIVERSITY OF NEW MEXICO PRESS ◆ ALBUQUERQUE

To MK
and
To Tomas: tanto tantísimo

© 2003 by the University of New Mexico Press
All Rights Reserved.
First Edition

LIBRARY OF CONGRESS CATALOGING-IN-PUBLICATION DATA

Mattiace, Shannan L.
    To see with two eyes : peasant activism and Indian autonomy
        in Chiapas, Mexico / Shannan L. Mattiace.— 1st ed.
            p.   cm.
Includes bibliographical references and index.
    ISBN 0-8263-2315-4 (pbk. : alk. paper)
        1. Indians of Mexico—Mexico—Chiapas—Government relations.
        2. Mayas—Mexico—Chiapas—Government relations.
        3. Chiapas (Mexico)—History—Peasant Uprising, 1994.
        4. Indians of Mexico—Mexico—Chiapas—Politics and government.
        5. Mayas—Mexico—Chiapas—Politics and government.
    I. Title.
    F1219.1.C45M376 2003
        323.1'19707275'09049—dc21
                                                                2003007239

DESIGN: Mina Yamashita

CONTENTS

LIST OF ILLUSTRATIONS

PREFACE

Prólogo
Estamos haciendo un libro,
testimonio de lo que no decimos.
Reunimos nuestro tiempo, nuestros dolores,
nuestros ojos, las manos que tuvimos,
los corazones que ensayamos;
nos traemos al libro, y quedamos, no obstante,
más grandes y más miserables que el libro.
El lamento no es el dolor.
El canto no es el pájaro.
El libro no soy yo, ni es mi hijo,
ni es la sombra de mi hijo.
El libro es sólo el tiempo,
un tiempo mío entre todos mis tiempos,
un grano en la mazorca,
un pedazo de hidra.
                    —Jaime Sabines (Tuxtla Gutiérrez,
                              Chiapas, 1932–98)

Prologue
We are creating a book,
a testimony of what was not said.
We gather together our moment in time, our pain,
our eyes, the hands we held,
the hearts we assayed;
we bring ourselves to the book, yet remain, nonetheless,
both greater and less than the book itself.
The wail is not the pain.
The song is not the bird.
The book is not me, nor is it my son,
nor is it my son's shadow.
The book is simply time,
an hour of mine among all of my ages,
a grain on the cob,
a branch of the hydra.
                    —Translation by Barbara D. Riess

Jaime Sabines, in "Prólogo," speaks of a book as a moment in time, among all the other moments the author has lived. In that spirit, I would like to begin this book by situating my "time" in Chiapas within other moments that shaped the project and me. I came to this project in 1995 with seven years of study and fieldwork experience in Mexico, convinced that this background would serve me well in Chiapas. Chiapas proved to be much more complicated than I expected. My original interest in Chiapas was sparked by my work on the Catholic Church in southern Mexico. In 1988, I conducted my first fieldwork in Yucatán as an undergraduate, examining the political attitudes and beliefs of parish priests. I later extended this study to Chiapas, as I became intrigued by the contrast between the social and political role of the Catholic Church in the diocese of Mérida, Yucatán, and the diocese of San Cristóbal de las Casas, Chiapas.[1] It was in the diocese of San Cristóbal where, from the late 1960s, Bishop Samuel Ruiz developed a pastoral mission centered around "Indian theology" *(teología india)*, a subset of liberation theology focused on the importance of validating Indians' culturally distinct manifestations of God's grace and salvation.

In graduate school at the University of Texas at Austin, I was exposed to Antonio Gramsci and the field of political anthropology, both of which would have a dramatic effect on the direction of my intellectual pursuits. Gramsci's understanding of culture as power, both in terms of shaping consensus as well as resistance, revealed the politics that lies outside formal, or institutional, realms. Although Gramsci did not theorize about ethnic and racial politics, his insistence on the interconnection between "the symbolic" and "the material" profoundly shaped my understanding of politics. When the Zapatista rebellion erupted on January 1, 1994, I was in the middle of developing a dissertation prospectus. Studying Indian politics in Chiapas seemed like an ideal way to combine my prior work in the diocese of San Cristóbal in 1988 and 1989 with my more recent interest in racial politics and cultural studies.

I arrived in Chiapas in early June 1995, two months after the government and the EZLN agreed on new rules for restarting a formalized process of dialogue.[2] That dialogue had been placed in serious jeopardy after the Mexican army entered Zapatista territory on February 9, 1995, in an attempt to capture the EZLN high command. In the weeks following, the army recaptured large areas of EZLN-controlled land within the "zone of conflict."[3] From December 1994 to February 1995, the EZLN amplified the territory that it had (at least partially) under its control from four municipalities to thirty-eight, creating what they called *"municipios libres"* (free municipalities, that is, land outside government control).

In August 1995, the first "table" *(mesa)* of dialogue on Indian Culture and Rights began. This table consisted of three phases of dialogue that took place between August 1995 and February 1996, culminating in the only accords that have been signed to date between the EZLN and the Mexican government: the San Andrés Accords on Indian Culture and Rights.[4] On the one hand, conducting fieldwork in Chiapas while the government and the EZLN were engaged in official dialogue was auspicious. Rules agreed on by both parties put limits on open military and police violence. Overt military action, for example, against indigenous peasants who occupied land in the "zone of conflict" was prohibited. On the other hand, it was during this period that a war of low intensity began. Until President Vicente Fox ordered the closure of several military bases in Chiapas in December 2000, the number of federal army troops in Chiapas was approximately seventy thousand, that is, one-third of its total force.

I deal extensively with questions of research methods in chapter 1, but suffice it to say here that this book lies at the interstices of political science and anthropology. Political science is centrally concerned with questions of power and representation. The study of power may be approached from a variety of different angles (for example, institutional, voting behavior, biography, and so forth); however, in this book I am primarily concerned with the power of meaning—particularly how cultural identities shape collective action. As one author put it, "The struggle over cultural meanings is integral to the logic of collective action, constituting people's motivations to act, their understanding of what they are doing, and the conclusions they draw from the results" (Hale 1994b: 25). Individuals and groups create meaning and interpret their world in context and in relationship to one another.

While in the field, I drew on the many anthropological studies that have been done about Chiapas's indigenous peoples. Anthropology's "thick description" helped me to uncover the layers of meaning, concepts, and events that guide the behavior of actors, helping me to get at the "why" of collective action (Ortner 1996).[5] As I was talking with indigenous peoples, I found that I first had to situate their words and behavior within their own cultural context before interpreting them back into categories recognized within social science. "Anthropology has always done best," Kay Warren argues, "at interpreting or unlocking the meanings of conflict and change in cultural and political systems in which symbolic languages, social realities, and conflicts are not easily translatable into conventional Western categories of social analysis, however Westernized the population appears to be" (Warren 1993: 8). As I learned more about the cultural contexts within which I was working, I found myself reworking many of the questions I put to my informants.

One of the main challenges I faced while engaged in this study was the tension between the need to be "objective" as a scholar and my interest in supporting concrete struggles for human rights and social justice. In 1995 and 1996, Chiapas was an intensely politicized place to do fieldwork. Although the lines between fact and value are porous and often blurred in social science, I do believe that scholars have to take some necessary distance in order to engage in analysis and critique. That distance does not make scholars necessarily objective observers, but it does differentiate our work from that of activists.

One of the scholar's main tasks is to criticize and critique honestly. In this study, I have pointed out the contradictions and tensions I observed in my work with peasant and Indian organizations in Chiapas and especially within the Tojolabal community. I hope such criticism does not overshadow the many positive and, at times, inspiring political moments that I observed within the Indian movement. One of the most memorable aspects of my fieldwork was to attend several EZLN-sponsored conferences where Indians and non-Indians came together to hope, dream, and speculate about a new Mexico they wanted to help create. I was struck by the plurality of these meetings: virtually anyone willing to spend several hours in line to get the appropriate credentials could attend. These conferences attracted people from all over Mexico and the world. Standing alongside me in line for accreditation at the National Indian Forum, for example, were bourgeois middle-aged women from Mexico City, intellectuals from Mexico and abroad, students of all stripes, representatives of human rights organizations and NGOs, artists, and, most importantly, Indians from independent organizations in Chiapas and throughout Mexico. The fraternity and solidarity present among participants at the forum seemed to speak of a new democratic impulse energizing those who had experienced few formal democratic rights.

As you read this book, I ask that you keep in mind the enormous diversity of indigenous peoples in Mexico. I will be drawing mostly from my work among the Tojolabal people and secondarily from work on Tzotzil, Tzeltal, Chol, and Mam Maya peoples of Chiapas. I do not pretend to speak for the Indian peoples with whom I spoke, nor is this study representative of all of Mexico's indigenous peoples. There are fifty-six different indigenous ethnicities in Mexico, and among these peoples, like peoples everywhere, there is a great deal of internal diversity. Some Indians strongly identify themselves as Indians, others as members of a particular Indian people, say, Tojolabal. Some call themselves campesinos (peasants) and others mestizos (mixed race). Of the almost seven million people the 2000 Mexican census identifies as Indian, all speak at least one indigenous language. Of these, about 60 percent speak Spanish as well (Mexico 2000: 30). There are many others not counted by the official census who may define themselves as Indian, yet speak no indigenous language.

Finally, unless otherwise noted, all translations are mine.

ACKNOWLEDGMENTS

Since I began this project in the fall of 1994, I have accrued many personal and professional debts. In acknowledging those people and institutions that have been so generous, I risk neglecting significant individuals. For that, I extend my apologies in advance. My gratitude, however, demands that I name some of the people who have accompanied me during this process.

I thank the García-Robles Fund and the U.S. Department of Education for the Fulbright fellowship that funded my work in Chiapas during the 1995–96 academic year. In Chiapas, the Centro de Investigaciones y Estudios Superiores en Antropología Social del Sureste (CIESAS-Sureste) welcomed me warmly as a visiting researcher. My colleague at CIESAS, Aída Hernández Castillo, became my closest friend there. Aída's intellectual intensity and passion for Chiapas were gifts, as were our endless conversations on that hill we shared with the Virgen de Guadalupe and a pack of wild dogs. I also thank Jan Rus, Ronald Nigh, and George Collier for generously sharing their knowledge and vast experience of Chiapas and its people. Aída, Jan, Ron, and George have been models to me of interdisciplinary exchange and enrichment. Thanks also go to María Teresa Sierra of CIESAS-Mexico, for many rich conversations about the EZLN and Indian politics in Mexico. I thank all those Tojolabals who generously shared with me their lives and their histories of organization and struggle. I especially thank Antonio Gómez Hernández of Veracruz, Las Margaritas, for the friendship and care he showed in introducing me to friends and family in Veracruz. Warm thanks also go to Araceli Burguete Cal y Mayor for the hours of conversation about politics in Chiapas. Araceli has been a model of collegial generosity and open intellectual exchange. My dear friend Suzanne Corley made two visits to Chiapas in 1996—in dry and rainy season—and together we viewed familiar landscapes with new eyes.

For support during the crucial write-up stage of the dissertation, out of which this book emerged, I am indebted to the Graduate School and the Department of Government at the University of Texas at Austin for a year of fellowship support. My thanks also go to the Center for U.S.-Mexican Studies at the University of California at San Diego for additional support and ten productive and enjoyable months in residence. Warm thanks go to the members of my dissertation committee: Henry Dietz, Michael Hanchard, Gretchen Ritter, Peter Ward, and Lawrence Graham. I especially thank Henry Dietz, for sharing with me his love for Latin America, and Mike Hanchard, for introducing me to social theory and to political anthropology, which became the intellectual foundations for this work. Profound thanks go to Roderic Ai Camp who first inspired my interest in Mexican politics at Central College in Pella, Iowa. I will always remember and cherish his cultivation of my early enthusiasm and intellectual curiosity.

In the crucial transition from dissertation to book manuscript, I thank the Academic Support Committee at Allegheny College for monetary support for additional time in Chiapas during the summer of 2000. I also thank Linda Mauro for administrative support during the final stages of the project. I am grateful to my colleagues in the Department of Political Science at Allegheny for their support and encouragement. Warm thanks also to my colleagues in the Latin American Studies program at Allegheny and to Barbara Riess in particular. Barbara has been my patron saint since the first day I arrived in Meadville; her loyal friendship has made my life in Meadville immeasurably richer.

In the transition from dissertation to book, Donna Van Cott's comments were indispensable. Donna's collegiality is exemplary; I thank her for her generosity and willingness to share her ideas and insights with me. I am indebted to my editor at the University of New Mexico Press, David Holtby, for encouraging me from the start and believing in the merits of this project. Throughout it all, I marveled at his cheerfulness, calm spirit, and immediate responses to my e-mail messages. Thank you, David.

Finally, my most heartfelt gratitude goes to my mother, Mary Kay, and to my husband, Tomas. Since the beginning, my mother guided and supported me through each step of the process with wisdom and discernment. This book is hers as much as it is mine. Tomas accompanied me through the crucial final phase of this process, restoring my faith and making me certain that self-doubt is no match for love.

GLOSSARY OF ACRONYMS

ADEPECH—Asamblea Estatal del Pueblo Democrático en Chiapas (State Assembly of the Democratic People in Chiapas)

ANIPA—Asamblea Nacional Indígena por la Autonomía (National Indian Assembly in Support of Autonomy)

ARIC—Asociación Rural de Interés Colectivo (Rural Collective Interest Association)

CAM—Congreso Agrario Mexicano (Mexican Agrarian Congress)

CAP—Congreso Agrario Permanente (Permanent Agrarian Congress)

CCI—Centros Coordinadores Indigenistas (Indigenist Coordinating Centers)

CCRI—Comité Clandestino Revolucionario Indígena (Clandestine Revolutionary Indigenous Committee)

CEOIC—Coordinadora Estatal de Organizaciones Indígenas y Campesinas (State Coordinator of Indigenous and Peasant Organizations)

CIOAC—Central Independiente de Obreros Agrícolas y Campesinos (Independent Central of Agricultural Workers and Peasants)

CNC—Confederación Nacional Campesina (National Peasant Confederation)

CND—Convención Nacional Democrática (National Democratic Convention)

CNI—Congreso Nacional Indígena (National Indigenous Congress)

CNJPI—Comisión Nacional de Justicia para los Pueblos Indígenas (National Commission of Justice for Indian Peoples)

CNOC—Coordinadora Nacional de Organizaciones Cafetaleras (National Network of Coffee Producers)

CNOP—Confederación Nacional de Organizaciones Populares (National Confederation of Popular Organizations)

CNPA—Coordinadora Nacional de "Plan de Ayala" (National Coordinating "Plan de Ayala" Network)

CNPI—Consejo Nacional de Pueblos Indígenas (National Council of Indian Peoples)

COCEI—Coalición de Obreros, Campesinos, y Estudiantes del Istmo (Coalition of Workers, Peasants, and Students of the Isthmus)

COCOPA—Comisión de Concordia y Pacificación (Commission of Conciliation and Pacification)

CONAI—Comisión Nacional de Intermediación (National Commission of
    Intermediation)
CONASUPO—Compañía Nacional de Subsistencias Populares (National
    Company for Popular Subsistence)
COPLAMAR—Coordinación Federal del Plan Nacional de Zonas Deprimidas
    y Grupos Marginados (General Coordination of the National Plan for
    Deprived Zones and Marginal Groups)
COPULMALI—Coordinadora del Pueblo Maya en Lucha (Struggles of the
    Maya People for Liberation Network)
CTM—Confederación de Trabajadores Mexicanos (Confederation of
    Mexican Workers)
CUD—Convenios Unicos de Desarrollo (Agreements for Local Development)
EZLN—Ejército Zapatista de Liberación Nacional (Zapatista Army of
    National Liberation)
FERTIMEX—Fertilizantes de México (Fertilizers of Mexico)
FIPI—Frente Independiente de Pueblos Indios (Independent Front of
    Indigenous Peoples)
FZLN—Frente Zapatista de Liberación Nacional (Zapatista Front of National
    Liberation)
ILO—Organización Internacional de Trabajo (International Labor Organization)
IMF—International Monetary Fund
INI—Instituto Nacional Indigenista (National Indigenous Institute)
INMECAFE—Instituto Mexicano del Café (Mexican Institute of Coffee)
ISI—Import Substitution Industrialization
ISMAM—Indígenas de la Sierra Madre de Motozintla (Motozintla Sierra
    Madre Indigenous Peoples)
LP—Línea Proletaria (Proletarian Line)
MAP—Movimiento de Acción Popular (Movement for Popular Action)
MLN—Movimiento de Liberación Nacional (National Liberation Movement)
NAFTA—North American Free Trade Agreement (in Spanish often referred
    to as the Tratado de Libre Comercio, or TLC).
NGO—Nongovernmental Organization
NSM—New Social Movements
OCEZ—Organización Campesina Emiliano Zapata (Emiliano Zapata Peasant
    Organization)
ORIACH—Organización Indígena de los Altos de Chiapas (Indian Organization
    of the Highlands of Chiapas)

PAN—Partido Acción Nacional (National Action Party)

PRD—Partido de la Revolución Democrática (Party of the Democratic Revolution)

PRI—Partido de la Revolución Institucional (Institutional Revolutionary Party)

PROCAMPO—Programa Nacional de Apoyos Directos al Campo (National Program for Support of the Countryside)

PRODESCH—Programa de Desarrollo Socioeconómico de los Altos de Chiapas (Program for Socioeconomic Development in the Highlands of Chiapas)

PRONASOL—Programa Nacional de Solidaridad (National Solidarity Program)

PROCEDE—Programa de Certificación de Derechos Ejidles y Titulación de Solares Urbandos (Certification of Ejidal Rights and Titling of Urban House Lots)

PSUM—Partido Socialista Unificado de México (Unified Socialist Party of Mexico)

PT—Partido del Trabajo (Workers Party)

RAP—Regiones Autónomas Pluri-étnicas (Multi-ethnic Autonomous Regions)

SEP—Secretaría de Educación Pública (Ministry of Public Education)

SER—Servicios del Pueblo Mixe (Services of the Mixe People)

UCEZ—Unión Campesina Emiliano Zapata (Emiliano Zapata Peasant Union)

UU—Unión de Uniones (Union de Ejido Uniones and Solidarity Peasant Groups of Chiapas)

XEVFS (radio station in Las Margaritas)—Voz de la Frontera Sur (Voice of the Southern Border)

Map 1. Chiapas and the area of Zapatista rebellion. From Collier, George A. with Elizabeth Quaratiello, *Basta! Land and the Zapatista Rebellion in Chiapas* (Oakland, Calif.: Food First Books, 1999). Courtesy of George Collier.

INTRODUCTION

On January 1, 1994, rebels calling themselves the Zapatista Army of National Liberation (EZLN) took over and briefly occupied seven towns in eastern and central Chiapas, Mexico (see map 1). They were Indians, with the exception of their spokesperson, subcommander Marcos, but their demands were spoken in the name of all Mexicans lacking access to the most basic of needs: adequate food, housing, and health care. The name of this Indian army highlights the movement's ties to one of Mexico's renowned revolutionary heroes, Emiliano Zapata.[1] While the Mexican government sought to paint the rebels as separatist, the Zapatistas insisted that they were recovering Mexico's revolutionary legacy. Observers had trouble categorizing the EZLN. Was the movement best understood as a new social movement? A revolutionary vanguard? A foreign-led guerrilla group? Within a few days after the uprising, the Zapatistas began to speak of Indian autonomy and the protection of Indian rights, such as the right to land and the official recognition of Indian languages. When the EZLN began peace negotiations with the federal government in February 1994, the first topic EZLN delegates set for discussion was Indian culture and rights. Since then, the Zapatistas' focus on Indian rights and autonomy has generated the strengthening and consolidation of a national Indian movement in Mexico.

The emergence of the EZLN on January 1, 1994, drew enormous national and international attention to the "plight" of Mexico's indigenous peoples.[2] Indigenous ethnic organizations in Mexico—organized on regional and local levels since the mid-1980s—took advantage of the space opened up by EZLN. The visibility that the EZLN gave to indigenous peoples was so important for the development of a national Indian movement in Mexico that it is no exaggeration to say that 1994 marked its birth.

The 2000 Mexican Census counted 6,950,567 Mexicans who spoke an indigenous language—the measure by which the government defines a person as indigenous. Although the government's statistics are below the 10 to 15 percent figure commonly cited by Mexican anthropologists, Mexico has the largest absolute number of indigenous peoples in the continent (Mexico 2000: 21–23, 30, see table 1). Before the 1970s, there was little communication and coordination

Table 1. Percentage of Mexican population five years or older that speaks an Indian language, by state.

Yucatán	37.32
Oaxaca	37.11
Chiapas	24.62
Quintana Roo	22.98
Hidalgo	17.22
Campeche	15.45
Guerrero	13.87
Puebla	13.04
San Luis Potosí	11.70
Veracruz-Llave	10.35
Estados Unidos Mexicanos	7.13
Nayarit	4.56
Tabasco	3.73
Michoacán de Ocampo	3.50
México	3.26
Chihuahua	3.21
Tlaxcala	3.15
Sonora	2.85
Morelos	2.31
Sinaloa	2.22
Querétaro de Arteaga	2.06
Durango	1.97
Baja California	1.87
Distrito Federal	1.83
Baja California Sur	1.43
Jalisco	0.71
Tamaulipas	0.71
Colima	0.64
Nuevo León	0.46
Guanajuato	0.26
Aguascalientes	0.15
Coahuila de Zaragoza	0.15
Zacatecas	0.15

From Mexico, Instituto Nacional de Estadística, Geografía e Informatica, *XII Censo General de Población y Vivienda 2000*. Tabulados básicos y síntesis de resultados de los Estados Unidos Mexicanos.

among Mexico's fifty-six Indian peoples. Indians were geographically dispersed throughout the country and access to transportation was limited.

Politically, the government organized Indians into national and state peasant confederations, which focused on class demands more than on ethnic or racial ones.[3] Indians who were not organized into peasant confederations were placed under the tutelage of the National Indigenist Institute (INI), which targeted indigenous ethnicities as separate and discouraged organization among Indian peoples.[4] Indians have resisted domination by non-Indians since the time of the conquest, yet it has only been within the last twenty-five years that Indians have constructed a foundation for political struggle based on common oppression and discrimination and on a positive sense of Indian identity. Organization based on this sense of Indian-ness has been difficult to construct, because historically Indians and non-Indians have viewed Indian identity as shameful and inferior.[5]

The EZLN and the national Indian movement in Mexico represent a growing trend in the Americas toward collective action based on pan-Indian identity. Concomitantly, the literature on Indian movements and the politicization of Indian identity in Latin America has grown exponentially (see Assies, van der Haar, and Hoekema 2000; Lucero 2002; Pallares 2002; Selverston-Scher 2001; Van Cott 1994, 2000a; Warren 1998; Yashar 1998, 1999). The Indian movement in Mexico emerged later than Indian movements in Ecuador, Bolivia, and in neighboring Guatemala.[6]

Research Question and Book Outline

If indigenous peoples lived in what is now Mexico long before Cortés "discovered" them in 1519, why did it take until 1994 for them to join together on the national level around a common cultural identity? The principal research question that motivates this book centers on the politicization of Indian identity. In the last twenty-five years, Indians have organized collectively as Indians and have become significant political actors in their own right. This study focuses on why and how an Indian movement emerged in Chiapas, Mexico. On arriving in Chiapas in 1995, my preliminary hypothesis was that ethnic mobilization had replaced class, or peasant, mobilization among indigenous peoples in the state. After the Zapatista uprising, Indian demands for "autonomy" had become a watchword and a central axis around which indigenous peoples were mobilizing.[7] Over time, my focus narrowed to examine Indian demands for autonomy as a way of testing my hypothesis.[8] "Autonomy" seemed to encapsulate the aspirations of many indigenous peoples to govern themselves on local and regional levels and

to combine local and "traditional" mechanisms of conflict resolution with respect
for human rights. (By "traditional," I am not suggesting that Indian practices
are static. "Traditions" reflect constant adaptation by communities to changing
circumstances.) I began to pose questions such as: To what extent do demands for
autonomy represent the demands Indians have had for years and are now couched
under different names? Are demands for autonomy new? Are indigenous
movements challenging existing definitions of democracy? Do these movements
promote democracy in practice? Although demands for autonomy draw on a
long history of indigenous organization, not until 1994 did indigenous
organizations begin to organize explicitly around autonomy.

During the process of dialogue between the government and the EZLN in
1995 and 1996, advisors to both parties spoke of three basic autonomy models:
communal, municipal, and regional. Indigenous communities in Oaxaca best
represented the communal model. The Zapatistas—at that time—had most
fully developed the municipal model. The Tojolabal-Maya peoples of southeastern Chiapas (residing principally in the municipalities of Las Margaritas,
Comitán, La Trinitaria, and La Independencia) best represented the regional
model. Soon after arriving in Chiapas in May 1995, I was struck by the active
participation of Tojolabal-Maya leaders in the many forums and organizational
meetings on autonomy that I attended. Much of my subsequent fieldwork
focused on the Tojolabal-Maya experience of regional autonomy.

The bulk of the fieldwork for this project was done during fifteen months
from June 1995 to August 1996, although I also made brief trips in July 1999 and
during the summer of 2000. The four principal sources of data I used to conduct
this study were newspaper accounts, organization documents, open-ended
interviews, and participant-observation in national, regional, and local organization meetings. First, for information about the EZLN and general information
about peasant and Indian organizations in Chiapas and in the rest of Mexico, I
did a content analysis of *La Jornada,* a left-leaning Mexico City daily newspaper,
from January 1, 1994, to August 1996. For more specific information about regional and local events in Chiapas, I regularly consulted two daily newspapers,
Expreso Chiapas and *Cuarto Poder,* published in Tuxtla Gutiérrez, the state capital.

Second, I relied on internal organization documents from various sociopolitical groups active among the Tojolabal people, such as the CIOAC (Independent Central of Agricultural Workers and Peasants) and its member organizations
(Unión de Ejidos y Pueblos Tojolabales, Yajk'achil B'ej, and Tierra y Libertad).

Third, I conducted approximately sixty formal and informal open-ended interviews between October 1995 and July 1996 with political activists and persons who had worked extensively with and in the Tojolabal community.[9] I found that personal interviews were the best source of information about the Indian movement in Chiapas, which—despite the long history of Indian resistance in the area—is a highly informal movement whose leaders often move outside formal, institutional channels. The Indian movement in Mexico has grown exponentially in membership and affiliations since the EZLN uprising of January 1994; while I was conducting fieldwork, it was just beginning to define a formal platform of demands and a set of proposals.

Fourth, during these months I participated as an observer in numerous conferences and forums on Indian culture and rights, many of which the EZLN convened. My attendance at these gatherings was an invaluable source of information about the level of grassroots support organizations enjoyed, the relationship between leadership and base, internal debates within organizations, tensions between peasant and Indian organizations, and alliances made among organizations. For example, I attended a statewide meeting of the Asamblea Estatal del Pueblo Democrático en Chiapas (State Assembly of the Democratic People in Chiapas, ADEPECH) held in San Cristóbal in October 1995; a national meeting of the Asamblea Nacional Indígena para la Autonomía (National Indian Assembly in Support of Autonomy, ANIPA) held in San Cristóbal in December 1995; several regional meetings of the Frente Independiente de Pueblos Indios (Independent Front of Indigenous Peoples, FIPI) in San Cristóbal; several EZLN-sponsored forums in Oventic (Aguascalientes II), Chiapas; two National Indigenous Institute (INI) conferences; and the Foro Nacional Indígena (National Indigenous Forum) held in San Cristóbal in January 1996.

While the Tojolabal people received little attention from scholars before 1994, they have attracted increasing attention since the Zapatista uprising for two principal reasons. First, Tojolabals living in Las Margaritas make up a significant portion of the EZLN's grassroots support. The principal Zapatista headquarters—Guadalupe Tepeyac and later La Realidad—are Tojolabal communities. Second, Indian activists have pointed to the Cañada Tojolabal (a canyon area that connects the cities of Altamirano and Comitán, see map 2) as a model for the creation of regional autonomous zones.

Chapter 1 provides a theoretical framework within which to situate the case study presented in this book. In the 1930s when anthropologists began studying indigenous peoples in Chiapas, their focus was on the local community. Anthropologists, many of whom were North American, examined indigenous

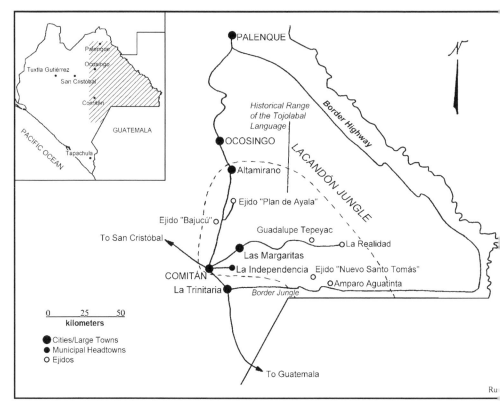

Map 2. Communities in the Tojolabal region. From Mattiace, Shannan L., Rosalva Aída Hernández, and Jan Rus, eds. *Tierra, libertad y autonomía: impactos regionales del zapatismo en Chiapas* (México, D.F.: CIESAS, 2002). Original map in Spanish. Courtesy of Jan Rus.

communities as worlds unto themselves, minutely documenting different dimensions of political, socioeconomic, and cultural life. Anthropologists were not much interested in the larger regions within which these communities were located. This changed in the 1970s as Marxist scholars from Mexican universities began to focus their attention on the Mexican countryside and the indigenous peoples who lived there. In contrast to much North American anthropological scholarship, which examined local cultural practices, Marxists focused on the "big" picture, paying little attention to the particularities of different Indian ethnicities. From the 1930s through the 1970s, scholarship produced by both North American and Mexican scholars on indigenous peoples tended to speak for Indians; Indians, for the most part, were the subjects of analysis. This changed in the 1970s as Indians began to meet together and organize into larger, regional associations. Indians were becoming political actors. By the 1980s, indigenous peoples in Chiapas and throughout Mexico joined larger national and international communities to make demands for ethnic autonomy, to insist that the state fulfill its obligations to indigenous peoples as citizens, and to assert their collective rights as peoples. Indians had moved "from tribal village to global village" (Brysk 2000). Chapter 1 traces this political history.

The question of how Indians became political actors in Mexico in the 1990s cannot be explained without examining a much longer history of regional and local political organization. Demands for Indian autonomy among the Tojolabal people drew on a history of agrarian struggle within an independent peasant, or agrarian, organization, the Independent Central of Agricultural Workers and Peasants (CIOAC). This regional history and experience will be taken up in chapter 2, where I examine how years of agricultural crisis and declining state support for rural areas weakened support for official (that is, corporatist) peasant politics in Mexico, opening up spaces for independent organization and struggles for autonomy. Tojolabal Indians who were at the forefront of a national movement in support of Indian autonomy in the 1990s, acquired valuable experience within independent peasant organizations in the 1970s and 1980s.

Throughout much of the twentieth century, the Mexican state was actively involved in making public policies aimed at assimilating indigenous peoples into mainstream, or mestizo, society. These policies, which are often referred to in their entirety as *indigenismo,* are examined in chapter 3. As an official policy, assimilation was abandoned in the 1970s and replaced by "participatory" indigenismo, which involved indigenous peoples more actively in the policies designed for them. Participatory indigenismo provided opportunities for many indigenous peoples to organize themselves *as Indians,* which contributed to the development of the incipient Indian movement in Mexico during those years. Chapter 3 examines the tensions that emerged between the INI and independent Indian organizations, particularly over the question of territory and political rights. Despite many policy changes, INI programs have consistently emphasized Indian culture and have skirted issues of power and resource distribution.

In chapter 4, I turn to the Tojolabal region of eastern Chiapas, which includes part of the Lacandon jungle area. In the 1980s, Tojolabal Indian leaders spearheaded the development of a regional Indian government, which became an early model for Indian autonomy in Chiapas and in Mexico. I became interested in this region and the Indian movement that emerged there because the Tojolabal were viewed as having "lost" their culture and community traditions and customs years before.

In the mid-nineteenth century, communities were broken up as Tojolabals became sharecroppers on large farms that dominated the region. It was not until the 1940s and 1950s that Tojolabals began to recover some of this land in the form of *ejidos*. In this chapter, I contrast the Tojolabal experience with regional government to two other autonomy models (communal and municipal).

The emergence of the EZLN on January 1, 1994, provided a tremendous boost to the Indian movement in Mexico. In chapter 5 I examine the relationship between the Indian movement in Mexico and the EZLN. In the peace negotiations between the EZLN and the government in 1995 and 1996, Indian rights and culture emerged as the first topic of discussion. For the first time in Mexico, questions of collective rights and ethnic autonomy were discussed as issues of national importance. In this chapter, I situate the discussion of Indian culture and rights at San Andrés Larraínzar (the site of the dialogue between the EZLN and the government) in larger conversations about Mexico's democratic transition.

In the book's concluding chapter, I broaden the discussion of ethnic autonomy regimes to Latin America. I contrast Mexico's failed attempt to establish an ethnic autonomy regime to successful attempts in Panama, Nicaragua, and Colombia. I also look at some of the challenges Indian movements in the Americas confront today, from neoliberal economic policies that privilege the protection of private property (making the protection of collective rights, especially to land, difficult) to the perennial question of representation: Who speaks for indigenous peoples?

Interspersed throughout the book are four vignettes, or short essays, about some of the people and issues I refer to in the text. My purpose in including these vignettes is to enliven some of the more abstract ideas and references found in the book chapters, giving these ideas a human face and making them more palpable for readers. The abstract ideas addressed in the text, such as agricultural crisis or national-level policy changes within the National Indigenist Institute, have an impact on real peoples' lives, a sense that you do not get, for example, from solely reading the statistics on the percentage of land devoted to maize during a twenty-year period.

Until the EZLN rebellion, little scholarly work had been done on the rise of Indian politics in Chiapas, because scholars did not typically view ethnic identity as a basis for "real" organization. Both class and ethnicity theorists, while disagreeing on a host of other topics, often unwittingly concurred in viewing indigenous peoples as premodern and incapable of independent organization, especially on the national level. There is a substantial body of scholarship written by Mexican social scientists about Indian people, mainly concerned with the question of whether indigenous people would survive in the modern world as class identity eclipsed ethnicity. Some class theorists predicted that peasants would eventually disappear as urbanization spread and as agricultural profits for small producers fell. Others claimed that capitalism required a large pool of low-paid rural workers to harvest crops for export on seasonal plantations.[10] Scholars of ethnicity, especially anthropologists working on Mesoamerica (southern Mexico and Central America), focused on closed Indian communities (Wolf 1957); they defined ethnicity largely as a set of ascribed characteristics (for example, language, dress, traditions, and customs). In these analyses, ethnicity was understood as more primordial than constructed. For these theorists, "culture" was expressed in terms of loss and preservation: Indians who moved outside their communities of origin to live in the city and who spoke Spanish regularly had "lost" their culture, while those participating in community rituals in "traditional" communities were preserving indigenous culture (see Warren 1992).

The EZLN uprising put a final nail in the coffin of ethnicity and class-based theories of Indian organization. Since the uprising, thousands of rallies and marches of support for Indian rights have been held across Mexico. The slogans that appear on the large banners carried high by the marchers include demands for land as well as for rights and respect for indigenous culture. Justice, respect, and rights have long been an implicit part of peasant organizations' demands (Harvey 1998), yet in recent years they have been more explicitly tied to Indian culture. The first topic of discussion between the EZLN and the Mexican government during the Dialogue of San Andrés was not land and land reform, but "Indian Rights and Culture." While Chiapan peasants continue to participate in land invasions and insist that the government resolve their long-standing and pent-up demands for additional land, they have increasingly framed their demands in cultural terms. This focus on culture among Indian peoples dovetails with a general trend visible on the international level—a shift from class-based movement activity to membership in "new" social movements, a theme that I take up in chapter 1.

CHAPTER ONE

THE POLITICS OF CULTURE

Beginning in the 1930s, North American anthropologists arrived in highland Chiapas. The highlands region seemed like an ideal field site: it was close to San Cristóbal, a quaint colonial city situated in a valley surrounded by mountains and by Indian villages where "traditional" indigenous peoples lived—Indians who continued to speak autochthonous languages and practice customs visibly different from national, mestizo culture. With few exceptions, anthropologists who came to the highland region of Chiapas from the 1930s to the 1970s studied these Indian villages as "closed corporate communities" isolated from the rest of Chiapas and Mexico.[1]

By the 1970s, however, this work came under increasing scrutiny. From a methodological standpoint, Marxist scholars questioned anthropologists' focus on local communities and insisted that these communities be placed within larger regional, national, and international contexts. Also by the 1970s, Indians themselves began organizing into regional associations, joining with Indians in other parts of Chiapas and Mexico to face common problems, such as land reform and lack of credit. By the 1980s and 1990s Indians used the international arena to get support for their demands for Indian rights and autonomy.

Indian communities in Chiapas have progressively moved from "the local" to "the global." Most recently, social movement scholars have viewed Indian movements in the Americas as part of a global trend of social mobilization and grassroots organization based on culture. These "new social movements," as some scholars have dubbed them, have increased quite dramatically in number during the last thirty years. Three different approaches to the study of social movements have emerged: new social movements, resource mobilization, and political opportunity structures. Each sheds light on the politicization of Indian identity in Mexico in the 1990s.

Anthropologists and the "Closed Corporate Community"
The anthropologist Sol Tax first brought functionalist social anthropology to the study of highland Chiapas in the 1930s. A student of Robert Redfield from

the University of Chicago, Tax followed Redfield's lead in focusing on isolated Indian communities to get at the "fundamental structures" of "simple" societies. Functionalist anthropologists analyzed social interaction and change in terms of balanced reciprocity, employing an analogy of society as an integrated human organism and eschewing historical research in favor of synchronic studies largely carried out on local levels (Hewitt 1985). In the highlands of Chiapas, Tax produced a monograph on Zinacantán that attempted to take into account all the principal elements of community life and to relate them to a meaningful whole (Tax 1943).[2]

A couple of decades later, anthropologists from Harvard University launched an ambitious project that generated a prodigious volume of scholarly work on highland Indian communities in Chiapas. The Harvard project, directed by Evon Vogt, began in the 1960s and took its theoretical cues from structural-functionalism.[3] The work of the anthropologists and historians involved in this project continued the work of previous anthropologists in the region, focusing on "traditional" life within indigenous communities. However, instead of focusing on the life of the community in all of its dimensions, they focused on particular characteristics of discrete indigenous groups, such as religion, patterns of land tenure, or medicine, for example. These scholars continued to study indigenous communities in isolation from one another, arguing that the boundaries among ethnic groups were "culturally determined" and, thus, relatively fixed. Much of this work assumed an absolute correspondence between the local community and its culture.

Although structural-functionalism informed much of the work done during this period in all of Mesoamerica, research on Chiapas was especially notable in this respect. As Wasserstrom (1983) points out, anthropologists have typically emphasized the community-as-tribe and the town-as-social/moral-universe, claiming that indigenous identities were culturally programmed to respond in a certain limited fashion to outside stimuli. Indigenous identity, in this view, is confined to local villages and communities, with little possibility of interethnic cooperation or organization. Silverts, for example, in describing indigenous communities in the highlands of Chiapas, wrote that "each village is a self-contained unit and the tribesmen see no alternative way of dealing with people in this world except commercial interaction with ladinos on unequal terms, and ceremonial communication and small scale trading on equal terms with other Indians at patron saint feasts" (Silverts 1969: 115).[4] More than any other feature, this notion of Indian communities as "closed, corporate communities" is what distinguished the work of Tax and his students, as well as the work done by anthropologists who participated in the Harvard Project.

To a certain degree, this view of indigenous communities as isolated from the outside world and of indigenous identity as largely community-based accurately described the situation that existed in Chiapas and other largely indigenous states from the colonial period until the middle of the twentieth century. Indigenous identity during this period largely reflected the system instituted by the Spanish to establish economic and political control over indigenous communities. Spanish colonial officials used local leaders to exact tributes and to institutionalize local control over the indigenous at the municipal level. In the nineteenth century, Chiapas state officials utilized local religious-civil festivals—the *cofradía*, or cargo, system—to maintain political and social control. The local cofradía was based on religious brotherhoods founded to honor important patron saints (Wasserstrom 1983: 262). In addition to being a civil-religious hierarchy, the cofradía was also the repository of local political power and a primary mechanism through which status was defined within the community (Hewitt 1985: 55).[5]

Although the state has historically sought to divide and control indigenous communities, indigenous peoples utilized these "imposed" structures to resist pressure from the outside world—including the state. The identities that were created within local communities, however, were not based solely on resistance to the outside world; local communities, in effect, became repositories for Indian culture and identity until they began to break apart in the 1970s as a result of multiple pressures. In the highlands region of Chiapas, then, this entrenched political system of divide-and-rule led anthropologists to conclude that indigenous identity was community-based, representing microcosms of identity that were strongly corporatist in nature (Favre 1973).

Indians were never as isolated from regional and national markets as the functionalist view implied, however. Beginning in the 1970s, a handful of anthropologists working with the Harvard Project pointed to the limitations of the "closed community" approach to studying Indian culture (Favre 1973; Rus 1977; Wasserstrom 1983). These scholars placed indigenous peoples within larger regional and national policies and politics. Working with Tzotzil oral testimonies, Jan Rus, for example, examined the use of temporary Indian labor in the southern Soconusco region of Chiapas from the 1880s to the 1970s; Indians were contracted (almost always under conditions of exploitation) in the highlands and brought to the coast as cheap labor to harvest crops for export (Rus et al. 1986). Rus, Wasserstrom, and Favre all argued that while the local community played a significant role in the construction of Indian identity, the communities themselves did not exist in isolation. Rather than viewing the local community as a vestige of the past, these scholars situated communities within larger political and economic histories. Indian communities, they argued, are the result of political strategies used by Spanish colonial rulers and later by postindependence leaders fearful of Indian rebellion, on the one hand, and, on the other hand, of Indian responses to an often hostile and repressive world. Gavin Smith's description of Indian communities in the Andean region is an apt one to describe similar communities in the highland region. The Indian community, Gavin claimed, "has been both a means for inserting Indians into the larger economy and society and a means for expressing a local identity in contradistinction to that economy and society" (Smith 1989: 29).

An earlier challenge to North American functionalism was Mexican anthropologist Aguirre Beltrán's work during the 1960s on regional (under)development in Chiapas. Drawing from his experience as the director of the National Indigenist Institute's Tzotzil and Tzeltal Coordinating Center (CCI) in San Cristóbal, Aguirre Beltrán (1967) argued that if the state wanted to promote the development of Indian communities, it could not focus exclusively on the community level. He insisted that Indian communities were part of backward, neglected regions within Mexico and that these regions were on the periphery of the nation-state. In some regions, he noted, social patterns and relations were characteristic of the colonial period. Aguirre Beltrán's regional focus was a first step in making important connections between local communities and national-level policies and politics, but he did not pursue the notion that these underdeveloped regions often existed adjacent to regions of intense commercial agricultural development. Aguirre Beltrán limited his criticism to regional ladino (non-Indian) oligarchies that extracted surplus from surrounding indigenous communities (Knight 1990b: 83). As an employee of the National Indigenist Institute (INI), Aguirre Beltrán, not surprisingly, was hesitant to critique national economic policies (Rus 1977).

If North American anthropologists—on the whole—quite accurately described Indian communities in Chiapas's highland region from the 1930s through the 1960s, by the 1970s several factors emerged that challenged the usefulness of their theories. First, the spread of Protestantism caused growing religious cleavages within communities, leading to the expulsion of thousands of highland Indians from their communities beginning in the early 1970s and increasing throughout the decade. Second, the incipient but growing presence of opposition political parties and independent peasant organizations outside the National Peasant Confederation (CNC) gave rise to political cleavages within communities. Finally, beginning in the 1970s land pressures—particularly in the highland region where land was scarce and marginally arable—provided the impetus for Indians to try their luck in the Lacandon forest, where they settled in newly formed communities and joined pan-ethnic regional cooperatives. All of these factors contributed to making functionalists' assumptions about Indian communities in the highlands outdated and not representative of Indian peoples in the state as a whole. Class analysis emerged in the 1970s as a response to structural-functionalism; rather than examine individual indigenous communities as structural-functionalists did, scholars situated Indians within larger regional and national networks of socioeconomic exploitation.

From Caste to Class

Class analysis has been widely used by Mexican political leaders, scholars, and activists to explain the subordinate position of indigenous populations within Mexican society and the character of their political struggles. This usage is due, in large part, to the prominent role Marxist thought played in Mexican universities during the twentieth century, particularly in the 1970s and 1980s. Marxist scholars viewed Indians as part of a dominant capitalist mode of production—exploited because of their status as peasants and as seasonal workers. Stavenhagen (1989) described this approach as one that attributed the fundamental poverty of indigenous communities to the economic exploitation they had been subjected to since colonial times. While most of the authors who employed this approach recognized that the exploitation of indigenous peoples was doubly harsh because of factors other than narrowly defined economic ones, such as social and cultural discrimination, these factors figured as secondary and derivative in their argument. Scholars subsumed differences among indigenous groups under class analysis, while the principal cause of exploitation was the social discrimination that accompanied capitalist relations of production (Medina 1982; Pérez 1982; Pozas and Pozas 1971). Because the class paradigm was based on the assumption that Indians could overcome socioeconomic and cultural subordination by working within national proletarian or peasant organizations, Indian demands for territorial and political autonomy and bilingual education, for example, were subsumed under the larger class project. In short, class analysis centered on the idea that the historical process emerges from the economic antagonisms arising out of production or market relations.

If structural-functionalists paid too much attention to "culture" and not enough to the unequal power relations that kept Indians in a subordinate relationship to the non-Indian world, Marxist activists and scholars, by contrast, gave short shrift to culture. The limitations of the Marxist perspective on the role of culture in organizing Indians was seen clearly at a 1974 Indian congress, the Congreso Indígena, sponsored by the diocese of San Cristóbal—a gathering that is widely heralded as marking the beginning of pan-Indian organization in Chiapas. The Mexican anthropologists present at the 1974 congress, many of whom were Marxist, were surprised by Indians' insistence in putting cultural demands on the table (see Morales 1992).[6]

Throughout the 1970s, many scholars and policymakers in Mexico continued to argue that the greatest potential for "successful" indigenous collective action rested on Indians' unity with other Mexican peasants, both indigenous and mestizo. Presumably this unity would be achieved by accelerating the process by which Indians moved from a condition of caste to one of class (Aguirre Beltrán 1976). Although some scholars acknowledged that class exploitation would continue to be a problem as the indigenous joined peasant ranks, they believed that the indigenous would benefit by abandoning the isolated communities that kept them bound in "primitive conditions of cohesion" to join the class struggle (Aguirre Beltrán 1976).

Another influential current of leftist thought critiqued Marxist scholars who claimed that ethnicity would disappear as the class struggle advanced and those who argued that ethnic identity should be secondary to class identity.[7] In opposition to the view of some Marxist analysts, Díaz-Polanco (1985) contended that ethnicity should not be viewed as insignificant to class analysis because every social group possesses its own ethnicity, which is an essential component of class identity. But because ethnicities are local rather than national, he argued, they cannot be the basis for struggles of liberation. According to Díaz-Polanco (1987), ethnic differences among the indigenous were a vestige of the colonial period and acted as an obstacle to understanding that the true interests and liberation of indigenous peoples lay with the national peasant and proletarian classes. He urged the left to welcome the indigenous in their struggles, even if the latter did not yet see themselves as proletarians. The job of revolutionary or mass-movement leaders, in Díaz-Polanco's view, was to link the indigenous to the revolutionary movement and direct them toward anticapitalist positions (Díaz-Polanco 1985; 1987).

Leaders of the Institutional Revolutionary Party (PRI), however, were adamantly opposed to any revolutionary or independent mass-movement initiative. The PRI sought to stymie future revolutions from emerging among the popular sectors through the creation of sectoral organizations.[8] During the administration of President Lázaro Cárdenas (1934–40), a system of linkages between the state and the popular sectors was forged through the creation of national-level peasant (National Peasant Confederation, CNC) and worker (Confederation of Mexican Workers, CTM) confederations. These confederations had parallel organizations on the subnational and local levels.[9]

How did Mexico's indigenous people fit into this system? In general, the state encouraged Indians, the overwhelming majority of whom were peasants or agricultural workers, to join the National Peasant Confederation (CNC). Those Indians who either would not or could not easily assimilate—such as Indians living in the highlands of Chiapas—would be supervised by the National Indigenist Institute (INI). In effect, the creation of the CNC and the Confederation of Mexican Workers (CTM) greatly diminished the likelihood, as one author put it, "that specific labor or peasant organizations would hold undue power" (Davis 1994: 83). The creation of the CNC and the CTM greatly raised the cost of organizing class-based alliances between workers and peasants. It was not until the 1970s that independent peasant confederations began to make inroads into the Mexican countryside after years of economic crisis and in the face of the CNC's decreasing legitimacy among peasants.

State corporatist rule came under increasing pressure after 1968 when the Mexican army gunned down hundreds of student protestors in Tlatelolco Plaza—located in downtown Mexico City—on October 2. Tlatelolco was a watershed political moment in Mexico in which the PRI openly distanced itself from the ideals of the revolution it sought to represent. Increasingly after 1968, students, urban popular sectors, peasants, and workers turned to alternative movements through which to channel their demands for free universal education, decent housing, and land reform and distribution, among other demands (see Aguayo 1998; Montemayor 2000).

A changing demographic profile of Indian communities in Chiapas over the last thirty years gave rise to a new generation of Indian leaders, many of whom organized independently from state-based corporatist organizations. After January 1, 1994, Indian "autonomy" became an umbrella demand for this generation of Indian leaders.

Indians as New Actors

During the last thirty years in Chiapas, Indian communities have undergone enormous change. Even the most "traditional" indigenous communities of the highland region are no longer the closed corporate communities Tax and Vogt described. They increasingly resemble Indians in the rest of the state, taking day jobs in San Cristóbal, speaking Spanish, operating cargo trucks and taxis, and worshipping in Protestant churches. The structural-functionalism of North American anthropologists who concentrated on local Indian communities, defining them as synonymous with Indian culture, is no longer useful in dealing with these increasingly urban Indians.

If we define "peasant" as one who makes his or her living off the land, then there are very few peasants in Chiapas. For decades, indigenous peoples supplemented agricultural work with seasonal wage labor, the making and selling of handicrafts, cattle ranching, and migration—seeking work in the burgeoning maquiladora industry on the northern border and in the United States as dishwashers, gardeners, and construction workers. Declining productivity on their lands forced many Indians to abandon corn farming and to seek wage income in urban areas. In the highland Indian community of Zinacantán, for example, Frank Cancian noted that 96 percent of male-headed households seeded corn in 1966; by 1983, 40 percent had no fields (Cancian 1992: 13).

Indians, despite predictions to the contrary, have not disappeared. Not only have Indians not disappeared with modernity, but they have become new political actors in their own right. In the past three decades in Chiapas, and in Mexico more broadly, Indians have increasingly united around Indian identity, demanding rights as citizens and as Indians. Whereas Marxist theorists predicted and even encouraged native organization across local communities, they assumed that Indians would organize around common class—that is, material—interests. Yet, Marxists' assumptions about progress as a linear evolution from tradition to modernity assumed that Indians would disappear as they became more "modern." Structural-functionalist anthropologists also believed that in time, indigenous culture would be "lost" in the face of growing urbanization. The anthropologist Robert Redfield, for example, even while he romanticized rural, indigenous life, believed that "folk" culture would increasingly give way to more urban and "sophisticated" customs and practices (Redfield 1941). Certainly, the "folk" culture Redfield described in Tepoztlán, Morelos, and in the Yucatán Peninsula has been dramatically altered by changing land-tenure patterns, industrialization, and migration in the more than five decades since he wrote. These changes have not resulted, however, in culture "loss" or in the disappearance of Indian peoples.

It was possible for social scientists such as Sol Tax, Evon Vogt, Robert Redfield, and Gonzalo Aguirre Beltrán to study Indians as objects, but today the "field" has changed substantially. Indians are now producers of knowledge about themselves and their communities. They are increasingly demanding that non-Indian scholars collaborate with them in producing work that both parties deem useful (see Stephen 2002). Before I was granted interviews with leaders of the Independent Central of Agricultural Workers and Peasants (CIOAC) in Comitán, Chiapas, for example, I promised the head of the organization that I would present transcripts to those I interviewed, giving them a written version of the organizational history I was writing. This promise was made in the context of a conversation I had with CIOAC leaders about how I could work with them to provide information that the organization wanted and needed.

While it was not until after 1994 that a national Indian movement began to coalesce in Mexico, since the early to mid-1970s Indians have asserted their own definitions of culture on the margins of North American structural-functionalism and Mexican Marxist analysis. The aforementioned 1974 Indian congress held in San Cristóbal marked a watershed moment in Indian political organization. This congress put pan-Indian and cultural demands on the table, even if community- and class-based organization would dominate throughout the 1980s. It sparked a wave of social and political organization of indigenous peoples in the state, drawing on the organization of regional conferences in preparation for the event as well as the spark that the congress itself provided. The diocese of San Cristóbal actively supported Indian organization through its program of training indigenous community leaders as catechists who would function as lay leaders in their home communities—running Bible studies during the week as well as representing the church on the local level. Although diocesan catechists were not political leaders per se, the diocese emphasized the importance of Indian unity in overcoming common problems, many of which had been raised by Indians themselves at the congress.[10] Indian participants at the 1974 congress did not explicitly raise cultural demands. Yet, they reflected and commented on the cultural dimensions of their common problems. Land, for example, was discussed as having both material and spiritual dimensions.

The church wasn't the only institution or organization to be galvanized by the 1974 congress. Non-Indian activists, many from the north of Mexico and active in organizations such as the Maoist Política Popular, built on the congress's momentum, spearheading the creation of producer organizations that would function much like economic cooperatives and pressuring the state for credit. While non-Indian advisors played a dominant role in organizing Indians in the wake of the Indian congress, by the 1980s and 1990s, Indians became increasingly autonomous and independent in organizing themselves. Political activists working in the Lacandon jungle created producer cooperatives that Indians used to market their goods, particularly coffee. These organizations were not explicitly cultural, but they organized Indians across community boundaries, allowing Indians of different ethnicities to see themselves as members of a larger community. The largest of these producer-based organizations was the Union of Unions (UU), formed in 1980.

Indians living in the Lacandon jungle area were, in many respects, autonomous from the state. State presence in this region had always been sparse, particularly in terms of social services.[11] The producer and cooperative organizations formed during the 1980s in the Lacandon region filled a gap that the state had left empty. Similarly, during the 1980s, Tojolabals living on the edge of the jungle in Las Margaritas created peasant organizations independent of the CNC, such as Lucha Campesina and the Independent Central of Agricultural Workers and Peasants (CIOAC). In this area of more traditional Tojolabal settlement—the valley stretching from Comitán to Altamirano known as the Tojolabal Canyon—state presence was limited to the CNC and the National Indigenist Institute's Tojolabal Central Coordinating Center, opened in 1974. Indians in these areas developed alternative forms of social and political organization not only in confrontation with state officials but also in their absence.

Indian autonomy was not only a strategy of resistance against the state (although it certainly was that), it also functioned as a mechanism for survival. Even in areas where state presence was more intense, such as the highlands region, Indians' search for alternatives to state-sponsored and state-sanctioned organization accelerated throughout the 1970s and 1980s. By the mid-1970s and after decades of neglect, Mexican rural areas were in deep crisis. For Indians in the Chiapan highlands, jobs that they had worked seasonally for years in the central valleys and on the southern coast dried up. Land density, already the highest in the state, pushed some Indians to search for a new start in the Lacandon area. Those who stayed sought day jobs in San Cristóbal; thousands moved permanently to San Cristóbal and to the state capital, Tuxtla Gutiérrez.

By the 1980s, closed corporate communities had "exploded" (see Nash et al. 1995), and a diminishing number of Indians worked the land. The demographic profile of Indians had changed significantly from the 1970s and 1980s when

structural-functionalism and Marxism provided different visions of Indian organization and culture. By the 1990s, in the wake of the Zapatista rebellion,
autonomy became a watchword for Indians in different regions of the state.
After 1994, Chiapan Indians made demands for autonomy that can be situated
within a larger international context of indigenous self-determination.

Indian Autonomy and State Sovereignty

If, on the most basic level, autonomy is defined as the right of an individual or
group to use their own discretion to act independently, that is, on their own,
Mexico's Indian peoples have practiced different forms of Indian autonomy for
decades. This de facto autonomy is the result of community resistance to outside influences, governmental neglect, and local practices (that is, traditions
and customs). Indian autonomy has been, in part, a tool of resistance against a
political, economic, and cultural system dominated by non-Indians. Indian
autonomy has also been a way for Indians to survive the consequences of
governmental abandonment. Indigenous areas of the country often lack basic
services typically provided by the state—such as health care clinics and elementary
schools equipped with teachers to staff them. After the EZLN rebellion, however,
indigenous peoples and organizations began to demand de jure autonomy,
arguing that constitutional and legislative reforms were needed that recognized
and legitimized de facto autonomous practices. After 1994, "autonomy" has
become a kind of umbrella demand, encompassing a host of cultural, political,
economic, and social grievances.

Indian demands for autonomy, though sharing some essential characteristics,
are diverse and varied. This diversity can be attributed in part to the local character
of Indian autonomy practices: ritual practices and traditions in indigenous
communities are not uniform. Demands for Indian autonomy in Chiapas include
a wide range of political, economic, cultural, and social rights. Political rights
involve the use of local customary practices to elect officials (typically outside
political party slates), as well as Indians' participation in formal political institutions
(for example, legislatures) at state and national levels. Economic rights include
the right to develop and to manage natural resources on indigenous land, which
Indians increasingly refer to as territory, implying substantial areas of land possession
and management. Cultural rights include the official recognition of Indian
languages for political, administrative, legal, and cultural purposes, as well as
the recognition of indigenous customs, traditions, and spirituality (Sierra 1995:
244). Social rights encompass the right to education (in indigenous languages

as well as in Spanish), possession and control of telecommunications technology and the media, as well as a welfare system funded, at least in part, by the state.

Some aspects of Indian autonomy demands are unique to Indian communities—such as the exercise of Indian law. Others overlap quite extensively with demands articulated from within Mexican civil society. Demands for greater control over municipal funds and powers of taxation, for example, coincide with calls made by non-Indian citizens and organizations to national government officials to devolve administrative, political, and economic resources to state and municipal governments.

Whereas indigenous communities exercise a wide range of autonomous practices on the local level, these practices do not include independence or external self-determination (that is, the right to exercise sovereignty vis-à-vis other states).[12] Even the most far-reaching international legislation protecting Indian rights, such as the ILO's Convention 169, has been careful to protect states' right to territorial integrity. During the course of the twentieth century, the international community has interpreted the "right" to self-determination (declared by President Woodrow Wilson in the aftermath of World War I) as applying only to former colonized areas, primarily in Asia and Africa. Not surprisingly, states have jealously protected their sovereignty from claims made by indigenous peoples living within national boundaries.[13] According to Hurst Hannum, whose work on self-determination and sovereignty is de rigueur for students interested in these issues, United Nations and state practice since 1960 "provides evidence that the international community recognizes only a very limited right to external self-determination" (Hannum 1990: 34).[14]

If de facto autonomy was commonplace within Indian communities long before the Zapatista uprising, why was it only after 1994 that autonomy became a central demand for indigenous organizations and communities throughout Mexico? In a nutshell, the EZLN uprising provided a space for Indian and non-Indian activists and intellectuals to discuss and debate the issue of Indian rights and culture in Mexico. Beginning in the 1980s, a number of Mexican Indian and non-Indian intellectuals and leaders began participating in international forums where issues of autonomy, sovereignty, and multiculturalism were discussed extensively with indigenous peoples and experts on the topic from around the world. The EZLN uprising, and the gatherings that ensued in its wake, introduced a new generation of regional and local Indian leaders to the language and discourse of Indian rights. Although Indian leaders with experience on the international level—such as Antonio Hernández Cruz, Margarita Gutiérrez, Margarito Ruiz, and Genaro Bautista—had been talking about the ILO's Convention 169 since it was first promulgated in 1989 (Mexico ratified the convention in 1990), local leaders became familiar with its terms when the Mexican government and the EZLN sat down to talks on Indian culture and rights in 1995 and early 1996 during the first "table" of peace negotiations. Several of the non-Indian advisors invited by the EZLN to this first "table" had extensive experience with Indian autonomy. In the mid-1980s, for example, Héctor Díaz-Polanco and Gilberto López y Rivas advised the Sandinista government of Nicaragua in crafting a regional autonomy agreement with the Miskito Indians of the Atlantic coast.

When the EZLN and the Mexican government sat down at the negotiating table in 1995 to discuss Indian rights and culture, interest in Indian rights at the international level was on the rise. In the wake of the momentum generated after Rigoberta Menchú won the Nobel Peace Prize in 1992, the United Nations declared an International Decade of the World's Indigenous People (1995–2004), which aimed to strengthen "international cooperation for the solution of problems faced by indigenous people in such areas as human rights, the environment, development, education and health" (http://www.unhchr.ch/indigenous/ind_sub.htm#decade). In 1993, the United Nations–appointed Working Group on Indian Populations (formed in 1982) finished drafting a Declaration on the Rights of Indigenous Peoples and a permanent forum was created to facilitate the representation of indigenous peoples and organizations in the United Nations. During the same period, regional- and national-level Indian organizations in the Americas grew in number and strength, both in countries with an indigenous population that comprised a majority of the total population, such as Bolivia, and countries with a much smaller indigenous population, such as Colombia.[15] Indians launched political movements (and in some cases, political parties) in Mexico, Venezuela, Colombia, Bolivia, Guatemala, and, perhaps most impressively, in Ecuador. By the mid-1990s, most countries in Latin America had incorporated the principles of nondiscrimination and multiculturalism into their legal frame-work, either directly in their constitutions or through the adoption of international human rights conventions with constitutional rank (Van Cott 2000a, 2001).

Although the EZLN uprising did not initiate the discussion of Indian rights and culture in Mexico, it did advance it greatly. The gatherings convened by the EZLN in the momentum generated by the uprising brought Indian and non-Indian activists and intellectuals together, fostered broader networks and movements in support of autonomy and Indian rights, and sparked the beginning of a national Indian movement in Mexico. At these meetings and in these discussions, "autonomy" emerged as a term broad enough to encompass a host of political, cultural, economic, and social goals. That autonomy became an umbrella demand does not mean that there were not conflicts among activists and leaders, particularly over the level at which autonomy would be practiced by Indian communities. The debate over the scope of Indian autonomy was heated and provoked quite serious fissures among EZLN advisors.

Discussions of Indian autonomy in Mexico and throughout the Americas overlapped with the deepening of neoliberal economic policies in the region and the dismantling of state corporatist regimes. According to Yashar (1999), the dismantling of corporatism in Latin America reduced Indian autonomy, thrusting indigenous peoples into the global economy. Yashar (1999) notes that, somewhat ironically, state corporatism guaranteed a certain measure of autonomy (that is, self-sufficiency) to indigenous communities. Latin American corporatist states tended to be overbearing, but they did include a measure of protection for Indian lands and some subsidies for agricultural products.[16] As corporatist states crumbled in the 1980s and 1990s, Indian communities lost some of the autonomy they had previously exercised. New political freedoms offered by the democracies that swept the region in the 1980s and 1990s might have compensated for this loss of autonomy. However, when Latin American states did not deliver on the promises made by political elites to their citizens, mobilization from within civil society, including indigenous communities and organizations, increased. Even in cases in which constitutional reforms were passed to protect Indian rights, such as Colombia and Bolivia, they were the result more of democracy's failure than its success. Examining the multiculturalist reforms made to the Colombian and Bolivian constitutions in the early 1990s, Van Cott argues that political elites in both countries agreed to constitutional reforms to protect Indian rights in an effort to buttress weak political institutions and to deepen democracy (Van Cott 2000a). Interestingly, by the 1990s, defense of indigenous rights and culture was in vogue in the international arena. Countries that recognized indigenous rights were viewed as more modern and, thus, more legitimate in the eyes of the international community than countries that did not. Defense of indigenous rights is part of a global trend of social mobilization based on culture.

Social Movements and Identity Politics

In both the developed and the developing world, cultural politics have come to the fore of public and scholarly discourse—particularly since the end of the cold war—as the centrality of class politics diminished. Although the problems that gave rise to class analysis have not disappeared, class analysis no longer occupies the predominant place it once did in scholarly and popular circles. In part, this is due to the decline of the organized labor movement, which began years before the end of the cold war, as the industrial economic base gave way to a postindustrial, service-oriented one. As labor union organization declined in membership, even while the membership of social movements such as the women's, environmental, gay rights, and ethnic-based movements rose, class-based analysis of social problems has also fallen out of favor. Today when individuals engage in social action, it tends to be in smaller, more specialized movements that target particular interests, rather than in organizations such as political parties or labor unions, which aspire to represent the general interests of broad-based constituencies. Finally, labor unions' decline over the last two decades is due not only to shifts in the economy but also to their unwillingness to engage gender- and ethnic-based demands. Despite the influx of women into the labor pool, for example, the leadership of the largest and most powerful unions in both the United States and Mexico continue to be male. In Mexico, two of the largest and most politically important official corporatist organizations, the Confederation of Mexican Workers (CTM) and the National Peasant Confederation (CNC), have been loathe to open up top positions to Indians or to women. More damaging, however, has been labor unions' refusal to recognize the ways in which racism and sexism compound the economic subordination experienced by the rank and file.

Since the late 1960s, labor unions have competed for political space with "new" social movement organizations.[17] Scholars of these new social movements claimed that they were a catalyst for a new style of doing politics (that is, less hierarchical than union or party politics and more focused on single issues and on the local production of meaning). Early work—written mostly by Western European scholars—characterized these post-1968 movements as "new" and centered on cultural demands, which they viewed as nonnegotiable, such as group respect and recognition (Melucci 1989; Touraine 1988). Social movement demands, these scholars argued, were different from those of labor unions, such as higher wages and increased employee benefits, which they saw as negotiable. In this view, labor unions made material demands while social movements focused on expressive politics.

New Social Movements (NSM)

Western European scholars sought to apply their new theories on social movements to concrete movement organizations, particularly in Latin America, where, beginning with the 1964 military coup in Brazil, formal channels of political participation closed as military rulers forcibly took power throughout the continent.[18] Because of their flexibility, local character, and capacity to quickly disband, social movements survived—and even thrived—during these years of military dictatorship. Social movements not only helped channel social and political discontent with military rule but also pressured military governments to gradually open— or liberalize—their regimes. From 1964 to 1990, social movement organizations played a far more important political role in Latin America than parties or labor unions, which were barred or severely restricted under military rule.[19]

For Western European scholars of social movements, such as Melucci (1989) and Touraine (1988), identity politics marked a rupture with class. To a certain degree, they were right. Class politics was based largely on the view that a single actor could represent groups of people with heterogeneous identities and demands. In the Latin American case, however, this distinction between old and new movements was not as critical, because collective action tended to be multiclass in nature and class identities more complex and fluid (Foweraker 1995: 30). The demands of many social movements in Latin America differ from movements in the advanced industrial world where citizens are already guaranteed access to citizenship rights. In Latin America, citizenship rights, while guaranteed by law, are not accessible to the majority of citizens. In terms of grievances, Latin American social movements continued to make demands for "material" goods, such as electricity, affordable housing, and land reform (see Foweraker and Craig 1990).

Thus far I have characterized the scholarly work on social movements as principally focused on new social movements, that is, on identity politics. This work came largely from Western European scholars writing in the 1980s who separated identity from material interests, which, they claimed, were being replaced by demands based on culture and by contests over meaning. Scholars working within the identity-politics framework were heavily influenced by their social and political context—Western Europe—where citizens' basic material needs were fulfilled and where the greatest threats to freedom appeared to be the growing bureaucratic structures that provided these burgeoning social services.

Resource Mobilization

On the other side of the Atlantic, in North America, social movement scholars tended to focus not on the expressive dimensions of social movement activity, but on their strategic elements (McCarthy and Zald 1977; Oberschall 1993).

Scholars such as McCarthy and Zald, for example, focused on the resources social movements needed to marshal in order to survive as a movement and get their demands met. Rejecting the work of psychological and individual-centered theories of collective action that preceded them (see Gurr 1970), resource mobilization scholars focused on how movements overcame the free-rider problem: the fact that many individuals benefit from the work of social movements without participating in or contributing to them (see Olson 1965). Resource mobilization scholars argued that political mobilization does not occur simply because individuals share similar grievances; common grievances are no guarantee that individuals will be able to unite successfully to solve their problems. For resource mobilization theorists, movement leaders must offer their members and potential members selective incentives to encourage individuals to join and to sustain their membership.

New social movement and resource mobilization camps examined very different aspects of social movement activity. The former focused its attention on the subjective dimensions of the social movement experience for participants, highlighting these movements' transformative possibilities. While the NSM literature tended to downplay differences between leaders and followers or to ignore them altogether, scholars working within the paradigm of resource mobilization examined the internal dimensions of movement activity. If NSM scholars romanticized social movement organizations, viewing them as contentious movements of resistance against the state and transnational capital, resource mobilization scholars focused on the instrumental or strategic aspects of these movements.

Political Opportunity Structures

Despite their differences, both new social movement and resource mobilization camps tended to neglect the *political* environment within which social movements emerge and are sustained. The first author to refer explicitly to a "political process model," Doug McAdam (1982: 39–40) described it as resting on the assumption that "social movements are an ongoing product of the favorable interplay of both [environmental factors and factors internal to the movement].... Movements develop in response to an ongoing process of interaction between movement groups and the larger sociopolitical environment they seek to change" (cited in Cook 1996: 30).

Beginning in the 1980s, a subsequent wave of scholarship focused less on individual incentives to join groups and the experiences of members within these groups and more on the institutional spaces that facilitated or blocked the emergence and sustainability of social movements (Cook 1996; McAdam, McCarthy, and Zald 1996; Tarrow 1994). They called these institutional spaces "political opportunity structures." One of the hallmarks of the political process model of social movements was its focus on the interaction between social movements and the state. In the Latin American context, this was crucial since the state played a much larger role in shaping social movement activity and incentive structures than in North America and Western Europe. From their inception, Latin American social movements—including Indian rights organizations—have been vitally concerned with pressuring their respective states to expand citizenship rights. Indian movements throughout the Americas have demanded access to citizenship rights enshrined in national constitutions *and* collective, or special, rights as peoples (Dandler 1999; Yashar 1999).[20] For indigenous peoples in Latin America, states continue to be the target of their demands, even while they have used transnational organizations and international legislation to buttress their cause.

Writing on changing political opportunity structures for Indian activists in the Americas, Donna Van Cott (2001) argues that in the last three decades indigenous leaders have been successful in mobilizing around cultural resources that had been available for centuries (for example, inherited cultural symbols and community-level political structures). She attributes this mobilization to three factors that have emerged in the last twenty years in Latin America: the imposition of neoliberal policies; the replacement of military regimes with elected civilians; and the transnationalization of indigenous movements. To put it another way, indigenous movements formed as incentives emerged that facilitated leaders' use of cultural symbols as strategic resources.

Other authors have pointed to the changed international context as a factor facilitating the growth of regional and national indigenous organizations in the Americas (see Brysk 1996, 2000; Keck and Sikkink 1998). Nongovernmental organizations (NGOs), such as the Copenhagen-based International Work Group on Indigenous Affairs (IWGIA) formed in 1968, and the U.S.-based Cultural Survival, formed in 1971, were crucial early actors in promoting the protection and organization of indigenous peoples throughout the world. International governmental organizations, such as the United Nations Work Group on Indigenous Populations, created in 1982, have also been instrumental in providing a space for indigenous activists around the world to meet and work together to craft a common political agenda.

Over the same period, pan-Indian organizations in the Americas grew exponentially. Early organizing efforts within Latin America were centered on the Indian Parliament of South America, which, since 1974, brought together indigenous parliamentarians across the continent with the support of the Inter-American Foundation and the World Council of Churches (Brysk 2000: 97). Indigenous peoples have formed regional confederations in South America (Consejo Indio de Sud América [Indian Council of South America, CISA]), Central America (Coordinadora Regional de Pueblos Indios de Centroamérica [Regional Coordinator for Central American Indians, CORPI]), and the Amazon Basin (Coordinadora Indígena de la Cuenca Amazónica [Indigenous Coordinator of the Amazon Basin, COICA]) (Brysk 1996: 45).

The Anti-Quincentenary, or 500 Years of Resistance Campaign, was a boon to continent-wide indigenous organization. Beginning in 1989, indigenous organizations across the continent joined together to plan and coordinate countercelebrations to the 1992 Quincentenary. While the movement's initial focus was on the five hundred years of discrimination indigenous peoples had experienced, it gradually expanded to include black and popular organizations (a women's sector was also added) (see Gabriel 1994). In some countries, 500 Years' organizations did not disband after 1992 and have remained active members of regional and national indigenous organizations. Such is the case of the 500 Years' organization of Guerrero, Mexico, now a member of the National Indigenous Congress (CNI).

Alone, identity-politics, resource-mobilization, and political-opportunity camps cannot fully explain recent Indian mobilization around culture; all three of these camps have something valuable to say about Indian mobilization and organization.[21] The identity-politics framework has been useful in distinguishing post-1968 social movements from labor-union organization, even while these authors have, at times, overstated this distinction. Resource-mobilization scholars have examined the use of culture as a strategic resource and not just as an expressive dimension of social life, encouraging us not to romanticize these movements but to view them as having instrumental dimensions. Scholars looking at social-movement organization through the prism of political-opportunity structures have focused on the state and the ways in which political structures at the national and international levels shape and influence the ways that local leaders frame their demands.

In my work with Indian leaders in Chiapas, I found that their use of ethnicity/ race as a mobilizing tool varied significantly depending on the level at which they worked. Leaders at the national level in Mexico tend to use ethnic frames more explicitly, while local leaders with more frequent and intensive ties to their home communities tended to use them less—focusing instead on older themes such as land reform, the marketing of goods, and access to credit. At the national level, Indian rights discourse is couched in the language of international law—specifically Convention 169 of the International Labor Organization.[22] National Indian leaders from Mexico such as Margarito Ruiz and Margarita Gutiérrez travel regularly to international congresses and forums on Indian rights, bringing their international experience to bear on the National Indian Assembly in Support of Autonomy (ANIPA), an organization that both of them have led. Indian leaders who spend the bulk of their time outside their home communities develop proposals and advance initiatives that are framed quite differently from those of their colleagues working full time in local communities. For example, a recent article written by Antonio Hernández Cruz—a former federal deputy (1996–99) and Tojolabal Indian leader—has argued in favor of placing community decision-making in the hands of Elder Councils, something Hernández claims was common practice in Tojolabal communities until "outsiders" destroyed the prevailing harmony (Hernández Cruz 1999). In contrast to Hernández, who had extensive leadership experience on the national level, Tojolabal leaders without this exposure were less interested in projects dealing with "tradition" and more interested in demanding the same goods for which they struggled for years: access to credit, subsidies to production, and land.

Indeed, peasant politics, both official (state-based) and independent, was a principal channel for indigenous organization from the late 1930s through the 1980s in the Mexican countryside. Although peasant identity and demands for land and for agricultural credits were at the center of these movements and the ethnic or racial identities of peasants explicitly downplayed or viewed as irrelevant, the search for organizational and political autonomy vis-à-vis the state did figure prominently within these organizations. Despite the fact that the power and membership strength of peasant organizations has waned in recent years, the experience garnered within its ranks continues to shape the contours of con-temporary Indian politics. The discussion of Indian autonomy that occurred in the wake of the Zapatista rebellion was also informed by the experience of many Indian activists and organizers active in peasant movements during the 1970s and 1980s.

CHAPTER TWO

"SOMOS CAMPESINOS"
Land and Agrarian Politics

If we define peasant in the classic sense—as self-sufficient producers living in rural communities—few remain in Latin America today. There is little dispute that the "golden age" of subsistence farming in Latin America is over.[1] Although subsistence farming is no longer a viable option for rural people, many continue to work the land on a part-time basis, combining agricultural work with other employment. Peasant organizations continue to occupy land, negotiate with the state over land regularization, and struggle for access to credit.[2]

Countless others are potential peasants, as Edelman points out in his work on Costa Rica, who continue to connect their future and their dreams for the future to the land. Throughout Latin America, Edelman argues, the lack or instability of waged employment "keeps alive and strengthens campesino aspirations" (Edelman 1999: 207). Arguing against the idea that there is no hope for peasant survival, Edelman claims that peasant migrants and informal-sector descendants of campesino parents or grandparents continue to crave the self-sufficiency and autonomy that their ancestors enjoyed. Migrants' insecure position in the urban labor market makes it unlikely that they will easily give up these dreams.

For much of the twentieth century, the Mexican revolutionary party/state—the PRI—organized indigenous peoples into the National Peasant Confederation (CNC). The CNC formed part of the PRI's system of corporate rule, which organized peasants and workers into separate national-level confederations, thus preventing peasant-worker unity by tying the CNC and the CTM (Mexican Workers' Confederation) vertically to the state. This system was corporatist in the sense that workers and peasants (and, to a lesser extent, urban dwellers after 1943) were organized into hierarchical groups based on occupation and linked directly to the state. All peasants, for example, were to be organized into local-level CNC branches that were tied to subnational and to the national-level organization. All credit from governmental agencies was to be funneled through the CNC and CNC affiliates were given preference over nonaffiliates in the distribution of land. This system kept workers, peasants, and urban dwellers separate by organizing them in distinct confederations, thus preventing the possibility of another revolution. Yet, it also kept popular sectors tied to the state and gave millions of Mexican citizens access to state largess.

The state "encouraged" peasants and workers to join the CNC and the CTM by employing both the carrot and the stick. That is, while the state offered positive incentives for peasants to join, such as credit and crop subsidies, if peasants did not respond to state overtures, party officials did not hesitate to use force to ensure compliance. This was especially true in Chiapas where state governors have historically been closely aligned with landowners, often using state power to ensure a docile, largely Indian workforce on the state's many large landholdings. Peasants who operated outside the CNC were subject to harsh reprisals by landowners and the state police. For example, one author documented 165 political assassinations that occurred in the state of Chiapas during a thirteen-year period (1974–87). These assassinations, the author argued, took place primarily in rural areas where poor peasants demanding land were the target of state-sponsored violence (Burguete n.d.: x). In exchange for access to credit and land, the PRI expected political loyalty from CNC affiliates. To put it simply, the state/party was the patron that delivered the goods (for example, subsidies, credit, land) and the peasants were the clients, who voted for the PRI on election day.

This corporatist system dominated twentieth-century Mexican politics, but it was never all-powerful.[3] Even at its heyday in the 1940s and 1950s, there were notable examples of open resistance to the CNC from within and without. From within, competing peasant organizations emerged, such as the Central Campesina Independiente (Independent Peasant Central, CCI) supported by Cárdenas and formed in 1961, and the Unión General de Obreros y Campesinos Mexicanos (General Union of Mexican Workers and Peasants, UGOCM) that organized as early as 1949 (A. Bartra 1985). Despite the fact that the CNC served as an instrument of assimilation—turning Indians into Mexicans—Indians and Indian culture did not disappear. In fact, while specifically Indian demands were not at the forefront of official peasant politics in Mexico, the experience that indigenous Mexicans gained within peasant organizations proved valuable as an antecedent to the pan-Indian organization of the 1990s.

Shifting state agricultural policies influenced the formation of independent ethno-peasant organizations throughout Mexico whose leaders increasingly sought wider forums for collective action (that is, regional and national network organizations). Demands expressed by peasant organizations did not remain stagnant over time, but expanded from a focus on land reform to include productivist issues (for example, credit and product commercialization) in the late 1970s and early 1980s. Since the late 1980s, some peasant organizations included the issue of Indian rights and autonomy as part of their agenda. Here I examine these shifts by focusing on the experience of one independent peasant organization, the Independent Central of Agricultural Workers and Peasants (CIOAC), active in organizing the Tojolabal-Maya people in eastern Chiapas. A crisis of Mexican agriculture came to a head in the early 1970s. This crisis resulted in a dramatic decrease in the CNC's legitimacy, driving many peasants to search for alternatives outside official channels.

The peasantry has not disappeared from Latin America, but its situation is increasingly complex, combining demands for land and credit with more explicitly cultural demands for Indian rights. In the face of these new political actors, whose struggles synthesize the cultural character of material demands and the material character of cultural demands, it becomes imperative to complement cultural studies with perspectives that analyze economic and political inequality.

Agrarian Politics and Agricultural Crisis

For more than fifty years after the revolution, the Mexican state attempted to incorporate indigenous peoples into national society, based on the idea that the country's modernization and development depended on Indians' assimilation as mestizos. Despite years of governmental policy incentives and targeted development projects, however, many Indians did not assimilate; they continued to live in their communities of origin, speaking their language and planting their milpa (plots of corn and beans for family consumption). As unassimilated Indians, their fit within the National Peasant Confederation (CNC) was uncomfortable. As Mejía and Sarmiento note, "Indians as such did not have a place within the organic structure of the CNC" (Mejía and Sarmiento 1987: 39). Although the professed goal of political leaders after the Mexican Revolution was to make indigenous peoples Mexicans (that is, turn them into mestizos), the government was wary of encouraging alliances between peasants and Indians that posed a threat to state control over rural areas. Thus, the state encouraged the organization of Indians into official peasant organizations. The state also tolerated unassimilated Indians who maintained their "culture" and "way of life" in a way that did not threaten state hegemony.

The years between 1940 and 1965 were boom years both for the regime and for the CNC. High growth rates and a booming economy helped maintain regime stability, in both urban and rural areas. By the end of the 1960s, however, this situation began to deteriorate as prices for basic agricultural products fell dramatically and Mexico began to import corn for national consumption. Referring to this period, Armando Bartra asserts:

> In many senses it [the 1970s] was a decade of rupture. With respect to the rural areas, these years seem to put an end once and for all to a long historical cycle. They end the era of institutional agrarianism that is transferred to the hands of the Indian movement. Finally, the agrarianism of the state returns to its structural causes—the exhaustion of the model of farming that was followed for more than 40 years. . . . and the crisis that announced the exhaustion of this model also questions, at its base, the relationship between the Mexican state and the rural classes. (A. Bartra 1985: 144)

Between 1971 and 1974, the amount of land dedicated to corn crops diminished by more than 1 million hectares (20 percent of the total) while the planting of beans was reduced by 600,000 hectares (31 percent of the total) (A. Bartra 1985: 100). The sector hardest hit was that of crops destined for the internal market, especially staple crops such as corn and beans. From 1950 to 1960, the production of corn and beans grew at an average of 5 percent, while total agricultural production grew at an average of 4 percent. When the production of these staples diminished, however, as occurred from 1970–76 when average growth dropped to four-tenths of a percent, total agricultural production declined to one-tenth of one percent (A. Bartra 1985: 95–96). Ironically, population census data from 1960 and 1970 reveal that ejido land area increased from more than 44 million hectares to almost 70 million during that decade; four thousand new ejidos were created, and the population employed on ejido lands increased by more than 1 million persons (R. Bartra 1993: 147). Although the total value of agricultural production and the importance of the ejido increased during the 1960s, the yield of the labor employed declined, owing to the increase in the massive presence of *ejidatarios* (agrarian reform beneficiaries) with very small plots of poor-quality land. Thus, the average area cultivated per ejido producer (plus family members employed in production) dropped from approximately 4 hectares in 1960 to 3 hectares in 1970, although the average total area increased from 16 to 19 hectares (R. Bartra 1993: 149).

President Luis Echeverría (1970–76) responded to the agricultural crisis by first enacting a series of national populist policies that greatly increased land distribution and then by creating additional federal agencies to increase the state's role as intermediary between peasants and commercial markets.[4] But years of neglect by the federal government could not be undone overnight, and peasants continued to demand deeper changes. Hostile farmer and business interests strongly repudiated Echeverría's populism and forced the president to moderate his stance. Armando Bartra argues that Echeverría failed to maintain this difficult balance between revitalizing agrarian politics and keeping key business sectors content:

> With the revitalization of agrarismo, Echeverría's plan of setting things right is complete. These are the objectives of the new agricultural politics: to contain the peasant movement and to revitalize the official organs of control, to overcome the economic crisis in benefit of the interests of capital as a whole, and at the same time to respect and promote private interests in the countryside. In all aspects this policy fails. (A. Bartra 1985: 115)

By the 1970s, CNC legitimacy had diminished markedly with the increasing violence in the countryside. Fox and Gordillo (1989) argue that the causes of the 1972–76 wave of peasant mobilization derive from a convergence of economic and political factors. They point first to a weakening of the agricultural model followed since the 1940s in Mexico that prioritized industrial development and emphasized irrigated export production. Second, the decades of conservative land redistribution policy began to undermine mass political legitimacy in the countryside. Finally, they note that during these years the pressures on the land dramatically increased (Fox and Gordillo 1989: 139). For all these reasons, peasants began to search for alternatives outside official peasant organizations.

The Rise of Independent Peasant Organization

In the mid-1970s, state and regional peasant organizations independent of official organizations such as the CNC began to emerge in Chiapas. The main political goals of the independent peasant movement can be distinguished by a look at the diverse organizational strategies of the Coordinadora Nacional Plan de Ayala (CNPA) and the Central Independiente de Obreros Agrícolas y Campesinos (CIOAC). For the CNPA, land reform was central to its struggle, which had an anticapitalist and radical character. Formed in 1979, the CNPA was the result of an incision among member organizations of the Consejo Nacional de Pueblos Indígenas (CNPI); politically independent organizations within the CNPI opted to join the CNPA, while the official and quasi-official organizations reorganized around a decentralized version of the CNPI, now called the Coordinadora Nacional de Pueblos Indígenas.[5] Some of the most radical peasant organizations in the country joined the CNPA, including the Coalition of Workers, Peasants, and Students of the Isthmus (COCEI) in Juchitán, Oaxaca; the Chiapas-based Organización Campesina Emiliano Zapata (OCEZ); and the Unión Campesina Emiliano Zapata (UCEZ) of Michoacán.

Although the COCEI, OCEZ, and the UCEZ are all militant, class-based peasant organizations, the majority of their members are indigenous. They all combined demands for land reform with respect for indigenous language and cultural practices. The COCEI, for example, in a decades-long struggle against regional caciques in alliance with other popular sectors, placed land reform and recovery at the center of its struggle along with a strong defense of Zapotec language and culture. These Zapotecs from Juchitán, Oaxaca, used a strategy of ethnic revitalization in their struggle for political power in the region (Campbell 1994; Rubin 1990). Similarly, in its platform of political demands, the UCEZ of Michoacán includes a defense of Purépechan language and culture. According to its founders, the UCEZ was created to "defend ourselves better, to understand ourselves better, to organize ourselves, to preserve our lands, our culture, our customs, and to reach the place that is rightfully ours in the society" (cited in Mejía and Sarmiento 1987: 145). Similar to UCEZ and COCEI in its general goals, Mejía and Sarmiento describe the demands of the Venustiano Carranza–based organization, the OCEZ: "Although their [OCEZ's] fundamental demands are common to the peasantry—land reform, municipal democracy, respect for human rights, and freedom for political prisoners—their defense of communal property and collective agriculture are based on a recognition of ethnic identity" (Mejía and Sarmiento 1987: 135).

It was not until the latter half of the 1980s when demands for ethnic or Indian rights emerged from within the ranks of the Independent Central of Agricultural Workers and Peasants (CIOAC). At first, CIOAC leaders in Mexico City reacted to these demands with hostility; these leaders were far removed from indigenous areas and fairly orthodox in their view of politics and political action. The CIOAC—with historic ties to the Mexican Communist Party—was formed in 1975 to unionize agricultural workers, who were considered the vanguard of the revolution and leaders of a vast peasant class (Rubio 1987: 177–78).

In 1980s, the CIOAC shifted its political strategy from the unionization of rural workers to struggles for land reform and distribution. In the late 1980s, a rift formed between those interested in pursuing the question of Indian rights and those who resisted.[6] These tensions were exacerbated in the early 1990s, both on the national level and on the Chiapas state level, as Arturo Luna, member of the executive committee of CIOAC Chiapas, describes:

> When we [CIOAC Chiapas] spoke in 1993 about the changes we had made with respect to the goals we decided to pursue as CIOAC, we began to include, or we were on the verge of including, the problem of Indian rights. I would be lying to you if I told you that we had clearly framed the question as one of Indian rights. No, we did not have it totally developed as Indian rights, but we did understand the necessity of demanding something that could be differentiated [from peasant demands]. . . . And it is true that CIOAC on the national level did not understand this. . . . Only later did they [CIOAC national] understand. We [CIOAC Chiapas] understood the proposal because we had been discussing it together in Comitán [Chiapas] and so it was easier to incorporate it, not in great detail, but in principle proposing that Indians have specific rights that make them different and that the demand for their own rights is legitimate.[7]

Even within organizations that were not exclusively indigenous—such as the CIOAC—Indian members acquired important political experience. In the Tojolabal region, leaders who would later be instrumental in the emerging Indian movement, such as Margarito Ruiz and Antonio Hernández Cruz, worked within the ranks of the CIOAC in Chiapas and on the national level. Struggles for land reform within this organization put Indian leaders in contact with other Indians and peasant leaders throughout the region and nation, providing an important base for the Indian politics that would later come to the fore.

Both Margarito Ruiz and Antonio Hernández got their first political experience in the CIOAC-Comitán that had its organizational base in the Tojolabal Canyon, a traditional area of Tojolabal settlement stretching from Comitán to Altamirano (see map 2 in the introduction). In this region, demands for Indian autonomy emerged from within the CIOAC.

Tojolabals in the Historical Record

Tojolabal, the word used to refer to a Mayan Indian people who live in south-eastern Chiapas, means "legitimate word" (*tojol*: legitimate) (*ab'al*: word), re-vealing the Tojolabal belief that they are the true or legitimate people situated at the center of their cosmological universe. The Tojolabal people live in the extreme south-center of the state. They are bordered on the west by the Pan-American highway (which runs through San Cristóbal south to Comitán), to the north by the municipality of Altamirano, to the east by the Jataté River, and to the south by the international border with Guatemala.[8]

Scholars have paid scant attention to the Tojolabal people. García Barrios (n.d.) speculated that they have not interested most anthropologists because they are viewed as having "lost" many traditional Indian customs such as native clothing, language (in some areas), and the practice of governing themselves through civil-religious, or cofradía, structures.[9] Tojolabals do not put on spec-tacular fiestas, nor are they organized into the corporate community structures that have been of enduring interest to anthropologists working with other Maya groups. Monolingualism in Tojolabal is also rare because of the relatively fre-quent contact between Tojolabals and non-Indians since the colonial period. In one of the early anthropological studies of the region, Montagú (1986) noted that the percentage of bilingual Tojolabals was remarkably high, even taking into consideration the exaggerated census figures. In her travels in the Tojolabal region in 1957, she observed that for many Tojolabals Spanish had become the principal language and that in a number of neighborhoods of Comitán "the people are virtually indistinguishable from the poorest ladino class." In com-parison to the Tzotzils, Tzeltals, and Ch'ols (Chiapas's three largest Maya groups), Tojolabals became much more acculturated linguistically and in terms of so-cial structure.[10]

In general, Mesoamericanists have tended to focus on indigenous people residing in small, isolated village communities; there has been little work done on ladinoized Indians and mestizos. This "closed corporate community" approach to the study of Indians has come under heavy scrutiny recently as anthropologists, in increasing numbers, have begun to study native people in larger regional and national contexts (Kearney 1996; Wolf 1982). Looking specifically at the Tojolabal region since the colonial period, the indigenous and growing mestizo populations developed and changed alongside one another and, to no small degree, in relation to one another. Ruz (1992: 18) notes that already by the end of the eighteenth century Comitán had become a city of mixed castes: "The world of the Tojolabals retreated to the periphery, or Indian belt, that began in the marginal neighborhoods of the old city of Balún Canán [Comitán], where it alternated with the *castas* in mixed neighborhoods, and, above all, to the region's constellation of farms and some ranches" (Ruz 1992: 18).

From the time of the arrival of the Spaniards, the area around Comitán was seen as a bountiful place for planting grains and sugar and raising cattle. Dominican priests first administered these rich lands, but by the mid-seventeenth century Spanish landowners had begun to encroach on Dominican "possessions" in the eastern part of the region. Eventually this encroachment forced many Indians off their land to join the growing number of *castas* (those of mixed race, neither Indian nor Spanish) who converged on Comitán by the end of the seventeenth century. Meanwhile, for Tojolabals living in the western portion of the region, it was not until the mid-nineteenth century that ladino landowners were able to force them to work as sharecroppers and indentured servants on land that had formerly been theirs (see Gómez and Ruz 1992).[11] Gómez and Ruz (1992) argue that Tojolabal identity—instead of being "lost"— was re-created on the fincas during this period (1850s to the 1940s).[12]

In my conversations with Tojolabals, economic subordination, race, and historical experience were often understood as interconnected and inextricable. "Somos pobres" [We are poor] was a repeated response Tojolabal leaders gave to my questions about the relationship between ladinos and Tojolabals in Las Margaritas or in Comitán. "Son ricos, ellos [los ladinos]; siempre han sido" [They (the ladinos) are rich; always have been], I was told; "El Tojolabalero vende barato y compra caro" [Tojolabals sell cheap and buy dear]. Urban ladinos disparage Tojolabal language and traditional dress, a fact that is linked in the minds of many Tojolabals with the economic marginalization of their communities. When I asked Tojolabals about the sources of this marginalization, past and present experiences often merged in their responses. Although forced labor on the large haciendas in the region had ended by the mid-1940s, the sons and grandsons of the *mozos* (entailed workers) still talk of the time of *baldiaje,* or debt labor, drawing on the stories of relatives who had worked on the fincas in the region.[13] Don Paulino Méndez Aguilar, founder of Nuevo Santo Tomás, an ejido in the *selva-fronteriza* (jungle-border) region of the rain forest, was part of the first contingent of Tojolabal men who emigrated to this area in the 1960s. Although he was just a boy when debt labor ended, he described those days as "very difficult because they didn't pay us anything. They had accounts for us at the company store. We walked without shoes in the mud with nothing to protect us from the

Figure 1. Despite years of agricultural crisis, many Tojolabals continue to plant corn and beans on small plots of land. Photo courtesy of National Indigenous Institute, Mexico City.

rain. We had an overseer on the fincas, and wherever we went there were bosses" (interview, September 22, 1995). (Figure 1 depicts Tojolabal farmers.)

The migration of many Tojolabal to the Lacandon jungle, which Don Paulino narrates above, along with the long years of sharecropping on the large fincas that dominated the area, shaped Tojolabal ethnic identity. In contrast to the highlands region of the state, which has been heavily studied by anthropologists, Tojolabal ethnic identity was based less on closed communities and more on a general sense of economic subordination and discrimination. The Tojolabal experience of sharecropping and migration fueled regionwide political organization beginning in the 1970s.

Rise of Regional Politics

Linked to the agricultural crisis in Mexico in the 1970s was a search by the rural poor all over the country for new forms of collective action. Independent regional organizations emerged among the Tojolabal people during this decade, culminating in the formation of a Tojolabal regional government in the late 1980s.

The agricultural crisis of the 1970s engendered growing discontent among indigenous peasants with the National Peasant Confederation (CNC), the state's

Figure 2. On their way to do some washing, Tojolabal region, Altamirano municipality. Photo courtesy of the photographer, Gemma van der Haar.

official peasant organization. One of the ways in which the administration of President Luis Echeverría (1970–76) attempted to deal with the crisis was by creating Consejos Supremos Indígenas (Supreme Indigenous Councils), regional organizations that would presumably channel indigenous activism in more approved directions.[14] What I want to emphasize here is that—against all expectations—many of these councils actually became sites for independent organization *in opposition* to the government. The Tojolabal council was such a case. By the early 1980s it was at the center of political conflict in the municipality of Las Margaritas. Although Don Francisco Alfaro, a prominent member of the CNC, served as the council's first president, a dissident group of bilingual teachers used it as an institutional base from which to advance radical demands for land redistribution in the municipal capital.[15] As Burguete (n.d.: xxxiv) notes, "Although the Tojolabal Supreme Council was a creation of the PRI [Institutional Revolutionary Party], it was in the hands of democratic teachers who imprinted on it a seal of service to Tojolabals identified with independent political struggle. This was an important experience that illustrated the potential for Indian organization and created a certain body of demands." The council also served as a base of support for the Tojolabal candidate for municipal president of Las

Margaritas in 1982, Alejandro Aguilar. Unlike the situation in other indigenous areas of Chiapas (for example, the highlands) and elsewhere in Mexico (for example, Oaxaca), Las Margaritas had never had an indigenous municipal president, despite the fact that the majority of its inhabitants were indigenous. Observers characterized the municipal election of 1982 as racially divisive: the majority of ladinos supported the PRI candidate, while Tojolabals rallied behind Aguilar. As another important Tojolabal leader later claimed, despite the "loss" of the election (participants in the campaign and Aguilar himself continue to insist that the election was stolen), it "was an important step that created a new consciousness and group identity, illustrating the possibilities for future Tojolabal organization and regional power" (interview, May 4, 1996).

In 1984, the CNC became worried that the leadership of the council had become too independent and called in the state police during an election for council president to force members to accept its candidate. The "democratic" teachers' faction subsequently split from the council to form its own ejido union, the Unión de Ejidos y Pueblos Tojolabales (Union of Ejidos and Tojolabal People), which later affiliated with the Independent Central of Agricultural Workers and Peasants (CIOAC). This break represented the beginning of an enduring division of the Tojolabal people into three political camps: the CNCistas, affiliated with the PRI; the CIOAC-Unión de Ejidos y Pueblos Tojolabales; and the ejido union Lucha Campesina (Peasant Struggle).

Of these three groups, the CNC and the CIOAC were essentially *agrarista* with respect to their political ideology and strategy; their demands centered on the historic struggles for land reform and redistribution. Lucha Campesina, in contrast, was productivist, focusing on such issues as access to credit and working collectively to achieve higher prices for its members' products. It had been one of the founding organizations of the Unión de Uniones Ejidales y Grupos Solidarios de Chiapas (Union of Ejidal Unions and United Peasants of Chiapas, UU), established in September 1980. The UU united three principal ejido unions of eastern and northern Chiapas: Unión de Ejidos Quiptic Ta Lecubtesel (in Tzeltal, "Applying Our Strength for a Better Future") in Ocosingo and Tierra y Libertad (Land and Liberty) and Lucha Campesina in Las Margaritas, Altamirano, and Chilón. The consolidation brought together 180 communities from 15 municipalities, representing 12,000 families (Harvey 1998: 84). Unlike the agraristas, UU leaders saw confrontation with the state government as counterproductive.[16] Instead of demands centered on land reform and distribution, the UU focused on ostensibly less controversial issues such as marketing (for instance, of coffee) and peasant access to low-cost agricultural inputs and credit.

This focus on productivism within the UU occurred in conjunction with policy shifts on the national level. From the beginning of the administration of President José López Portillo (1976–82), federal policy took a decisively productivist turn. Reacting against the populist policies of his predecessor, Luís Echeverría, López Portillo declared in 1976 that there would be no further land reform. Instead, the principal goal of agricultural policy would shift to raising production levels. Peasant organizations altered their strategies in response to this shift. The CIOAC enlarged its scope to include the formation of subsidiary organizations such as the National Union of Agricultural Credit, Forestry, and Agro-industry of Ejidatarios and Small Property Owners, which distributed subsidized fertilizer to CIOAC members that it acquired through government-owned corporations (interview, April 15, 1996). The UU went much farther than the CIOAC in adopting productivist strategies, since its founding members had united their forces for the express purpose of facilitating greater marketing power and access to larger credit lines through collective organization. The period in which UU emerged (1980) was characterized by state emphasis on productivist strategies. Thus, for the federal government, the UU did not pose as serious a threat as did organizations like the CIOAC, for example, and many UU demands were met through institutional and legal channels. Within the union, leaders decided that it would be more effective to pursue productivist initiatives in the short term that could serve as a future lever for resolving more difficult problems of land tenure (Harvey 1998: 85).

Although the formation from below of productivist organizations like the UU was not seen as a threat by the national government, the state government's response was immediately hostile. Governor Juan Sabines moved immediately to strengthen the government-controlled CNC, which had historically been weak in the UU regions, and attempted to co-opt UU leaders by offering monetary incentives to encourage defection. In the Tojolabal region, reports in July 1982 claimed that representatives of Lucha Campesina accused the regional secretary of the CNC, Aaron Gordillo Noriega, of coordinating attacks on members of the ejido "20 de noviembre" because they had refused to affiliate with the CNC. Lucha Campesina members denounced the CNC for the death of one of its members during the attack. They also accused Gordillo of fomenting division among rival peasant groups over disputed land and of advising other CNC activists on how to persuade the Tojolabal Indian authorities to give up holdings (Harvey 1998: 84–90). What explains the state and national government leaders' differing responses? Harvey suggests that the federal government was more flexible with the UU because the UU did not openly criticize the agrarian policy of the López Portillo administration and, in fact, called on state agencies such as Instituto Mexicano de Café (Mexican Coffee Institute, or INMECAFE) to help raise production (Harvey 1998: 84–90). The state government, in contrast, dominated by powerful local landowners, saw any independent peasant or worker organization as a threat and as potentially subversive.

The experience of the UU was part of a larger movement toward greater regional and national unity among independent peasant organizations, breaking the previous pattern of isolation. From 1977–83 in the center-south region of the country (Chiapas, Oaxaca, Veracruz, Hidalgo, and Puebla), where more than 40 percent of all organized protests occurred during the period, twenty national and regional forums took place, and peasants formed thirteen new regional organizations (Rubio 1987). Armando Bartra claims that peasants framed this search for unity not only in terms of independence from the state and from official peasant organizations, but as a position against the antiagrarista politics that characterized the López Portillo administration (A. Bartra 1985: 138). However, productivist alliances, such as the UU, also illustrated this new trend toward regional organization.

This trend in regional political organization was, to a significant degree, ethnically based. Tojolabal participation in agrarista organizations like the CIOAC, for example, was based on a connection to the land that was more than simply material—it was closely tied to the spiritual, material, and symbolic life of the larger community. Scholars have long recognized the centrality of land both in the cosmology of Mesoamerica's indigenous peoples and in their political claims to be the original inhabitants of the territory they presently occupy (Wolf 1959).[17] For traditional indigenous communities, living on the land was inseparable from peasant labor and identity. Although seasonal migration within the region has been common since the colonial period, most Indians continued to return to their communities at the start of each agricultural cycle to plant their milpas. Despite this change, however, Tojolabals continue to emphasize that they work the land, and that their relationship to the soil distinguishes them from mestizos who work at other occupations in the city. Yet Indians' relationship to the land is becoming increasingly tenuous as productivity rates for corn and beans fall, the percentage of ejido land used for cattle grazing rises, and migration within and outside Mexico becomes increasingly common.[18]

The fact that Tojolabals share many of the same demands as poor mestizo peasants yet continue to feel different from them and to perceive a distinct treatment by society shows the multiple layers of oppression and of discrimination Indians experience. Demands made by Tojolabal regional and local leaders make reference to race, material subordination, and geographic location. For example, the transportation of goods and people from the outlying areas of Las Margaritas to the municipal head town and to Comitán has historically been a concern for rural Tojolabals. Before they had their own ejido unions, regional caciques provided the only public transport available. On this high-priced transport service, Tojolabals claim, they suffered *maltrato* and *falta de respeto* (mistreatment and lack of respect). One Tojolabal from the ejido Tabasco, Las Margaritas, and member of the ejido union Tierra y Libertad, described the problem of transport for Tojolabal communities and the subsequent action that the community took:

> It was in 1978 or 1979. The ejidal commissaries from each community got together because at this time we had a grave problem with transportation: ejidal transportation, and public transportation. In those days there was a landowner who had his own bus and who worked in this region, but the people began to see that this bus was often in disrepair, stuck by the side of the road. And even when the bus was running, the people were badly treated; the passengers were beaten, for example. It was then that the people began to open their eyes; they saw that it would be good to form a union of ejidos and buy their own bus through the efforts of the community. Well this is how the union was formed. And in this way it advanced and cooperation between the people grew. The people themselves became members; they cooperated to buy a bus. And in 1980, on the 20th of April, the bus arrived. (Interview, January 2, 1996)

Another Tojolabal and former CIOAC-Comitán leader also spoke of the importance of transportation for Tojolabal communities and their fight to wrest control of the transportation concession (a route license granted by the state government without which it is illegal to carry passengers or cargo for pay) from regional caciques:[19]

> Well, at that time [circa 1980] we organized ourselves, and the moment finally arrived when we understood that it was the concession that we needed. But at this time the state government, the transit department, controlled granting such concessions. And I can tell you that they did

not understand our conviction that we needed a concession. Indians did not have a right to concessions or to have vehicles. To them, we were insignificant. But the moment arrived when we decided that at all costs they had to respect our rights. We organized ourselves and brought four hundred people to the entrance of the State Delegation for Transit. The police were going to run us out but we said, OK, if you do that we'll block the street. We then all laid down in the middle of the street. So then they had to talk to us. We brought pozol [corn gruel] and tortillas with the idea that we would have to put up with the discomfort and that eventually the authorities would have to negotiate. And that's how it turned out. The director of transit of the Tuxtla-Comitán region arrived to see what was happening, to see what we wanted. That was easy. We were simply demanding that they give us the concession for our own buses because we constituted an ejido transport union. And we want our own buses, our own mini-buses. What we wanted was for them to free the route so that we could work it. What we didn't want were mestizos running the buses because they mistreated the people. That concession later cost us a great deal. It cost us deaths, there were deaths and kidnappings after the authorization of the route. We, the leaders of the union, practically could not step foot in Comitán because there were people waiting for us to grab us, that is to say, to "disappear" us. (Interview, April 19, 1996)

The Tojolabal regional government that emerged in the Cañada Tojolabal in the late 1980s derived from the two organizational structures described above. The first was the Consejo Supremo Tojolabal, an organization created by the federal government in 1975 to control independent "ethnic" organization, but used instead by the Tojolabals themselves as a springboard for the formation of two further regionwide, independent organizations: Lucha Campesina and the Unión de Ejidos and Pueblos Tojolabales. The second can be traced to Tojolabal participation in independent peasant organizations like the CIOAC. Indian leadership within the CIOAC-Comitán privileged regional and local concerns specific to the area, such as the control of transport concessions. For many Tojolabals, founding their own bus line meant regaining dignity as well as guaranteeing the transport of products for sale in regional markets. Among the Tojolabal, ethnic identity has been used both as a mobilizing factor in making demands and as a lens through which to understand "economic" and "political" issues.

Gobierno Tojolabal

During the mid- to late 1980s, the Unión de Ejidos y Pueblos Tojolabales was at the forefront of the organization of a Tojolabal regional government, some of whose members, such as Margarito Ruiz, later inaugurated the Frente Independiente de Pueblos Indios (Independent Front of Indigenous Peoples, FIPI [see Ruiz 1994]). The fight for adequate transportation, described above, was taken up by the Unión de Ejidos y Pueblos Tojolabales when they formed in the mid-1980s. But the geographic marginalization of Tojolabals—which makes adequate transportation crucial—also reflects racial, or ethnic, marginalization. Outlying Tojolabal communities are on the margin of a peripheral state. Government services such as schools and health clinics often do not reach these communities, and when they do they are often in disrepair and grossly understaffed. Tojolabals speak of the government as neglecting and abandoning them and they associate it with urban, mestizo areas that sharply contrast with the rural areas where they live.

In a public ceremony held in the ejido Plan de Ayala (see map 2 in the introduction) in 1988, leaders of the Unión de Ejidos y Pueblos Tojolabales declared the formation of a regional government. In effect, this declaration served to formalize activities that were already being performed by the ejido union. Typically, regional ejido unions have helped resolve disputes among members if they cannot be resolved at the community level and, in effect, sometimes serve as regional tribunals. Ejido unions unite several communities in a particular region and represent them in larger coordinating organizations, such as the CIOAC. The Unión de Ejidos y Pueblos Tojolabales formalized these functions by subsequently issuing identification cards to its members on which was stamped "Gobierno Tojolabal" (Tojolabal government).

Referring to this regional government, Margarito Ruiz states that "the Indian government functioned as a parallel government in opposition to the municipal one, which was identified with the government of the rich" (Ruiz 1990). Araceli Burguete, advisor to the FIPI who worked in the region for several years, adds that the Tojolabal regional government of the 1980s served as an ethno-peasant movement that placed the self-determination of indigenous peoples at the center of its political demands. She claims that demands for access to political power at the municipal level and increased social control over Tojolabal territory were present at the formation of the Unión de Ejidos y Pueblos Tojolabales (Burguete n.d.) By the early 1990s, however, not much more was heard about Tojolabal regional government, although the Unión de Ejidos y

Figure 3. During a party, Tojolabal region, Altamirano municipality. Photo courtesy of the photographer, Gemma van der Haar.

Pueblos Tojolabales continued to function much as before, resolving intercommunity conflicts, representing their members in the region, providing bus service to and from Comitán, and managing small development projects in coordination with the CIOAC.

Nevertheless, although this experiment with Tojolabal regional government was short lived, it is often held up by Indian activists—both in Chiapas and in Mexico as a whole—as a concrete demonstration of the potential for regional autonomy, one of the central demands of Indian organizations since 1994. Indian autonomy has become a rallying call for the national Indian movement since the Zapatista uprising, and the regional autonomy project is one of three principal autonomy models being discussed by Indian activists nationally (the other two are communal and municipal). Margarito Ruiz, who was closely involved in the early stages of establishing Tojolabal regional government, illustrates the linkages between it and the RAP design:

> Now, in terms of time period, for us the concept of the RAP is quite old, basically because of the Tojolabal experience. We had been reflecting on the question of autonomy and how to make it a reality for a long

time. In elaborating an autonomy proposal our principal reference was always the Tojolabal experience, always, always. And if you notice, the proposal that I developed when I was federal deputy in 1989 had two main lines of argument: it was regional and it was multi-etnic. Why multiethnic? Because we had the Tojolabal experience that we had lived. It was multiethnic because there were Tojolabals living side by side with Tzeltals in Altamirano, for example. . . . And why regional and not communal? Because for us in the Tojolabal region, with our experience of the finca and the ejidos, the concept of the [corporate] community does not exist. For us, the community was a concept that we could not digest conceptually. (Interview, May 4, 1996)

This experience with regional governance proved to be a powerful antecedent to the regional autonomy models proposed after 1994 on the national level. Tojolabals Margarito Ruiz and Antonio Hernández were key proponents of this model as they contrasted it to a communal model of Indian autonomy. In retrospect, the Gobierno Tojolabal functioned as a kind of bridge between the peasant politics of the 1970s and 1980s and the struggle that emerged after 1994 for Indian self-determination and control over territory. In contrast to the state's policies for managing Indian people—indigenismo—the Gobierno Tojolabal can be said to mark the beginning of an incipient *Indianismo* in the region.

The Mexican state has been a key player in defining the shape and nature of Indian politics. The state's role has shifted across time, often in response to grassroots initiatives by Indian peoples as well as to leaders' changing perceptions of state needs.

NO MORE FEAR

On an afternoon in mid-December two years after the Zapatista uprising, I was having lunch in San Cristóbal when Charles Krauze, Latin American correspondent from the *Lehrer News Hour,* approached me. I had watched this program regularly for a number of years and recognized Krauze as he introduced himself. His visit to Chiapas, however, was not related to the News Hour; Krauze was on assignment with *National Geographic* magazine for a special issue on the Maya Route—that string of archeological stops and colonial towns stretching from Uxmal in the Yucatán Peninsula to Tulúm in Quintana Roo, passing through San Cristóbal. In addition to the picturesque photos of ancient Maya devotional sites and the obligatory shots of Indian women weaving on backstrap looms, the article would devote some space to the political situation in Chiapas and what had been accomplished in the two years since the uprising began. Krauze told me that he wanted to hear both sides of the issue of land invasions within the "zone of conflict": cattle ranchers whose land had been invaded and indigenous peasants who had invaded those lands. With some hesitation—I was concerned that talking to cattle ranchers in Comitán, where I had been working, would jeopardize the relationship I had forged with local peasant leaders—I agreed to accompany him. I had never met or talked to a cattle rancher, and I was curious to hear what they had to say.

Krauze already had some names of ranchers who belonged to local (Comitán) cattle-ranching associations. Our first interview was with César Robles. Robles did not own land in Altamirano, Ocosingo, or Las Margaritas, the three municipalities within the designated "zone of conflict." Nevertheless, he had strong feelings about the "situation."

It was clear from the start that César thought that Charles and I were at best naïve and, at worst, misinformed. In an effort to set us straight, he provided a simple, straightforward narrative. César was patient but firm. "In order to understand 'the conflict,'" he began, "you need to understand the cultural differences that exist here. Peasants reproduce like rabbits, and all they want is their own 5 hectares." He then proceeded to tell us why this land distribution was not possible.

"The reason is simple," he said, "Indians are lazy and don't work the land. They're not productive." He repeated, "The ejidatarios [those working on ejidos] are the ones with the most land, and they are the ones who don't work it." He told us that he spoke not just for himself, but on behalf of many cattle ranchers, and assured us, "We'd gladly withdraw all our claims to the land if we were confident that the land would be worked." This seemed to me to be an odd shift in the narrative, but I translated it to mean that Robles and his cattle ranchers would be perfectly happy to let the Indians have the land they demanded if they worked the land productively. From the point of view of Robles and his fellow ranchers, however, that outcome was not likely.

Soon, the conversation turned to the question of who was responsible for the unrest. The real problem, he said, was governmental manipulation of the Indians: "The government gives Indians subsidies, such as PROCAMPO, and they just want more."[1] I wondered: The government promises the Indians land and money, thus raising Indians' expectations? I struggled to understand Robles's logic. Before I could grasp this line of thinking, he shifted to another: "It's a different story in the north of Mexico where there is a different culture. People want to work more; they're closer to the U.S." The conversation then moved back to Chiapas where, he said, "wily leaders are manipulating the Indians." The sudden shifts between explanations left me dizzy.

One of the things that surprised me most about our conversation with César was the intensity of his dissatisfaction with the government—both national and Chiapas state. Cattle ranchers in Chiapas had long been angry with the federal government, which they saw as being distant, as hostile to rural interests, and as favoring peasants. Yet, cattle ranchers had always had a cozy relationship with Chiapas state government officials, who had historically been more conservative than the federal government and fiercely protective of ranching interests. Ranchers' relationship with state government officials had been so cozy, in fact, that it was nearly impossible to tell them apart in terms of their political views and economic interests. Things had changed since 1994, however, and the cattle ranchers were angry. The state government had offered ranchers an array of options to compensate them for their losses within the zone of conflict: compensatory rent packages, land in the neighboring state of Campeche, and land purchase programs. Still, ranchers were not satisfied. César Robles claimed that the compensatory rent package covered only three months, the pay-per-hectare amount of the purchase programs was too low, and only a fool would go to Campeche to live. These sentiments were echoed by Efrén

Bañuelos and his wife, María de Socorro Reyna, members of Comitán's Cattle Ranching Association and landowners whose farms had been invaded in October 1994.

The Bañueloses accepted Krauze's request for an interview and invited us both to their home. It was on the outskirts of Comitán and not easy to find. We almost turned back when we found a house that matched the address we had been given. The house was so run-down and ill-kept that we did not think it could belong to landowners—whom we imagined as being fairly prosperous. Both Krauze and I expected the family to be living a fairly comfortable, middle-class lifestyle. Instead, we found something very different from what we expected. The house was as dirty on the inside as it looked from the outside. The couple's children played on the floor with broken toys: everything looked run-down and cheap. If this was how the landowners lived, I thought, in what conditions must their workers be living? We would soon find out.

A few days later, Charles and I talked to the Tojolabal Indians who had formerly worked for Efrén and María de Socorro Bañuelos and who had "recuperated" their land after the uprising. They were members of the ejido union Tierra y Libertad (Land and Liberty), a member union of the CIOAC-Comitán (Independent Central of Agricultural Workers and Peasants). The land in question consisted of four farms in the municipality of Las Margaritas, about four kilometers from Nuevo Chiapas (see map 2 in chapter 1)—La Floresta, La Colmena, Medellín, and La Florecilla.

We asked José and Alberto Hernández (not their real names), local leaders of Tierra y Libertad, to describe their former boss: "He was decent, much more noble than the owner of the land before him, who would slaughter animals that wandered onto his property without giving it a second thought." José told us that Don Efrén Bañuelos would occasionally throw some good fiestas for his workers. Although Jose wasn't under any illusion about his boss's motives— "The fiestas," he said, "were for political gain, the owner wanted to gain the peoples' confidence"—José explained that Mr. Bañuelos "wasn't a bad guy, really. He was from out of state; he wasn't from Chiapas." This last comment struck me as interesting and was something I had heard before. Peasants perceived landowners who came from out of state as being more decent than native-born Chiapan landowners.

In contrast to Efrén and María de Socorro Bañuelos, almost desperate in their anger at losing their land, the Hernández brothers were matter-of-fact and calm as they described—from their perspective—the events that had transpired that year. Their rationale for invading the land, in addition to the fact that they had received no word from the government about the petitions for land submitted years ago, was that the land they "recovered" had been part of the original ejido allocation the government granted to them in the 1950s. The landowners, José claimed, through bribes and special dispensations, were able to buy out governmental officials and keep the best part of the land for themselves, giving peasants the part without rivers, the poorest land.

Krauze asked the Hernández brothers why they hadn't invaded the land before 1994. "Within a few days after the uprising," Alberto said,

> we saw that there was a little more respect. Even though the government put some pressure on us, it saw that there was another army here and that they [the government] had to be careful. The government saw that it wasn't convenient to run the Indians off the land we had occupied. It was as if the Zapatista force were protecting us. The people here began to feel very strong because another organization—an armed one—existed. And besides that, those who worked with a social organization, like the CIOAC—organizations that weren't official [governmental] but were with the opposition—began to feel strong.

In their home a few days before, the Bañueloses told us that in March of 1994 Tojolabals from Tabasco approached them about purchasing the four farms. Efrén was not interested in selling at the price that was offered, and he turned it down. On October 3, 1994, according to the Bañueloses' version of the story, intruders broke down the doors at La Floresta. The "intruders" were former workers of theirs from the ejido Tabasco, plus others from surrounding communities—three hundred in all. Those who were at the farm (Efrén and María de Socorro were not present) were taken hostage at gunpoint and later released.

The Hernández brothers preferred to stick to the larger picture; their version of events emphasized the moral rightness of their claims, rather than specific details: "After [the Zapatista uprising] the people took the land as a pressure on the government to resolve the agrarian crisis. Within a few days after the Zapatista uprising, we noticed that the presence of the Zapatistas protected us a lot. Because of them, for a year there were no land evictions by the government."

The most intense disagreement between the two parties was over the value of the property "taken" or "recovered" on October 3, 1994. The Bañueloses claim to have lost 3 million pesos. (At the time the land changed hands, the exchange rate was 3 pesos/1 dollar, but after December 1994, the exchange rate fell to 8 pesos/1 dollar.) In addition to the land, the Bañueloses claim to have lost 482 head of cattle. (They later claim to have recovered 42.)

We asked the Bañueloses for their opinion about who was responsible for the conflict. Although both Efrén and María de Socorro could name individual Tojolabal leaders, their anger was targeted at Archbishop Samuel Ruiz, the Independent Central of Agricultural Workers and Peasants (CIOAC), and the EZLN—whom they viewed as operating in cahoots: "The Tojolabals acted under orders from the bishop." In the next breath, Efrén blamed the government for favoring the Indians. "Where do you think the Indians raised money for their revolution?" he asked without pausing, quickly supplying the answer. "From programs such as PRONASOL [National Solidarity Program], and the INI [National Indigenist Institute], whose money was funneled to the EZLN."[2]

Our visit with the Bañuelos household unsettled me, and I tried to sort out the reasons for my consternation. I found the couple and their politics anachronistic: they were landowners who existed only because they had Indians living like serfs on their land. Their time was up—and I suspected they knew it as well. As they told us their story that afternoon with the television blaring in the background and kids underfoot, I got the sense that their narrative was less a descriptive account than a reflection of how they wanted to appear. They clung, almost desperately at times, to an image of themselves that could no longer be sustained. The linchpin of this self image was the presence of subservient Indians. But after January 1, 1994, the Indians were no longer subservient, and the world to which the Bañueloses clung no longer existed.

On the other side were the Hernández brothers and the Tojolabals from Tabasco. There is no question that those living in Tabasco have palpable material needs. The only governmental presence we saw was a primary school where classes were taught sporadically. With the help of the diocese of San Cristóbal, the community built and staffed a rudimentary health clinic that serves Tabasco's 450 inhabitants. The community has extensive ties with the diocese of San Cristóbal, which trained both Hernández brothers to be lay religious teachers—or catechists. The village lacks a sewage system, and people bathe in a nearby river. In addition to corn and beans, coffee is planted, along with some sugarcane and pineapple. In the last ten years, the community has accumulated some cattle as well.

Were the Tojolabals from Tierra y Libertad justified in seizing the Bañueloses' land? Morally, I think they were, but I wondered about the medium- and long-term political and economic consequences for Chiapas if investors pulled out of the state. What I found most compelling about this struggle was the fact that the Tojolabals of Tabasco were fighting for basic rights: for the right to education and the right to defend their rights. The demands that the Bañueloses and César Robles found so radical were, in the end, quite basic: the right to read and write, the right to political organization, and the right to basic infrastructure in their communities.

A couple of days later Charles and I had one last conversation and meal at the same restaurant where he had found me a month or so before. He promised to follow up on the story he was writing for *National Geographic*. A year later that issue did come out, but our story was not included. Krauze did not appear as author of any of the related stories on Chiapas, and I never found out what happened to him or to the story. As for the land conflict, thousands of hectares were invaded, or "occupied," throughout the state after 1994. To date, the land issue has not been resolved. The dialogue between the EZLN and the government was suspended in 1996, making any comprehensive resolution of land demands—particularly in the zone of conflict—unlikely, if not impossible.

CHAPTER THREE

STATE, NATION, AND
THE "INDIAN QUESTION"

An agricultural crisis and the declining legitimacy of the National Peasant Confederation (CNC) in the 1970s led to an increase in independent peasant organizational activity. Burgeoning ethno-peasant organizations emerged in this decade and served as antecedents to the Indian politics that would come to the fore in the 1980s and 1990s. Also by the 1970s, challenges to the state's policy of assimilationism—from within and without—opened up institutional spaces for Indian cultural politics inside the National Indigenist Institute (INI). Indian politics emerged in dynamic relation to the Mexican state. Thus, we must look closely at the state and at state policy to understand the subsequent emergence of Indian rights and autonomy demands.

It would not be an exaggeration to say that the chief concern of the Mexican state during most of the twentieth century was to promote unity among the country's diverse regions and peoples: to forge *patria* (nation)—as Manuel Gamio (1960) put it. For the Mexican state, nationalism meant progress and unity. That unity would come through racial homogenization—turning Indians into mestizos. Mexican leaders coming to power in the wake of the Mexican Revolution placed the mestizo at the center of a modern, progressive Mexico. The mestizo, while combining the best of the Spanish and Indian peoples, was quintessentially Mexican. Yet, while official state discourse suggested a seamless process of racial mixture, an examination of the National Indigenist Institute (INI) and its policy directives over time suggests that *mestizaje* was a process fraught with tensions and struggle. Within the state, there was disagreement among leaders about how best to deal with Mexico's indigenous population—whether to attempt full incorporation or whether to preserve some indigenous traits that were perceived as having value.

Over time, INI policies shifted from assimilationism, dominant during the 1950s and 1960s, to participatory indigenismo in the 1970s and 1980s. By the

1990s, the institute had declined in influence vis-à-vis other state agencies, overshadowed by an independent Indian movement, on the one hand, and a hostile national government that threatened to dismantle the institute, on the other. Although the INI was never powerful relative to other state agencies, in many areas of rural Mexico where state presence was thin, such as eastern Chiapas, the INI quite literally was the federal government. The institute was seldom radical, but it did inadvertently aid the development of an independent Indian movement in two important ways. First, it provided space for projects of cultural revitalization that were, in some cases, appropriated by indigenous participants. Second, INI officials represented a different kind of governmental presence—often more progressive than recalcitrant state governments. In 1992 in Chiapas, for example, state government officials arrested three top INI functionaries, including the state director! The governor at that time, Patrocinio González Garrido, called for the arrest of these INI officials for their work in assisting local, independent indigenous organizations.

Over time, indigenous peoples appropriated cultural spaces created by the state as sites for making independent political and economic demands. Although the Mexican state encouraged the expression of indigenous folklore through traditional dances, plays, and handicrafts that emptied Indian identity of political content, in the 1970s and 1980s Indians increasingly appropriated INI-administered cultural projects and programs for their own ends. By the end of the 1980s, President Salinas (1988–94) pushed to modernize Mexico by allocating additional funds to promote Indian culture while simultaneously privatizing indigenous communal land.

Subjects of the Crown and Liberal Citizens: Prerevolutionary Indigenismo

Since the colonial period, state-directed policies concerning indigenous peoples have been alternatively used to control, protect, and aid the indigenous population. During the colonial period, Spanish officials legally separated Indians and non-Indians into the Republic of Indians and the Republic of Spaniards, but after Mexico's independence from Spain in 1824, liberal administrations abandoned what they viewed as paternalist colonial policies toward indigenous peoples. Liberal notions of equal rights under the law eliminated racial categories that were de rigueur under Spanish rule.

Changes in law, however, had little impact on social attitudes toward the indigenous population from pre- to postindependence periods. Brading (1980) argues that during both periods the elite distrusted the capacity of Indian masses to contribute substantially to public debate, and more specifically, to the creation of a new regime. During the preindependence period, images of a romanticized indigenous past were used as a rallying cry by criollo leaders to create alliances with the Indians.[1] Using the figures of Cortés and Moctezuma, criollo elites combined these heroic narrations and images with the figure of the Virgin of Guadalupe as the basis for the creation of a nationalist movement to liberate New Spain from the Spanish. While the criollos were successful with their particular version of Mexico's Indian past, they made no effort to develop a political program that would include Indians within a new, postindependence regime; criollo romanticization of indigenous people consigned Indians to the past. The criollos' ideological basis for independence from Spain was largely negative. Their best theorists, men such as Bustamante y Mier, never developed a positive theory of nationalism that could effectively counter and critique classic liberalism, which would become dominant after independence (Brading 1980: 127).

Whereas criollo insurgent leaders romanticized Indians, liberals, who came to power after independence and who dominated Mexican political life during the period between 1824 and 1855, openly disparaged them. For liberals, Mexico's colonial past was a story of oppression and subordination of the Indian masses. They sought to eliminate this oppression and subordination by bringing Mexico into the modern world: the world of progress and Enlightenment thought. Liberals viewed the Indian population, together with the hacienda and the church, as an obstacle to this progress. It was to the liberals that the main task of constructing the Mexican nation was given. This was no mean task, as regional and local caudillos and caciques governed postindependence Mexico and did not look favorably on the possibility of losing their power bases to the new federal government. In addition to attempting to unify and consolidate the nation-state, Mexican liberals in the postindependence period focused on the exercise of civil liberties, popular sovereignty, and reason, which they thought would transform the old colonial system into a modern, civilized nation (López Cámara 1977: 262).[2]

After independence from Spain, it became imperative that the new nation distinguish and distance itself from Spain and the Old World. Mestizaje emerged during the period of nation-building in Latin America (1824–60) as an ideology capable of providing such a foundation. During this period, Latin American political elites sought to reconcile what they viewed as a serious tension between the majority presence of mestizos within their borders and liberal ideals in vogue at the time in Europe that only white, "pure" races could further progress

(Leys 1991; Wade 1993).[3]

The ideology of mestizaje, however, prevented neither elites nor the mestizo population in general from discriminating against Indians (and blacks).[4] Mexico's Indian past was glorified and constructed as a source of pride for Mexican leaders and citizens, yet elites viewed present-day Indians as an impediment to progress and development. This view was amply demonstrated during the long dictatorship of General Porfirio Díaz (1876–1910, dubbed the Porfiriato), during which time the Porfirian army brutally repressed Indian rebellions in the North (the Yaqui of Sonora) and the South (the Mayas of Yucatán). Once the inhabitants of large tracts of land organized by Indian governments in the precolonial and colonial periods, during the nineteenth century the Yaqui and Maya were forced off their traditional lands and contracted to work on export-oriented fincas. The central government never completely controlled the Yaqui and the Maya, however; throughout the nineteenth century both Indian peoples sporadically launched local and regional rebellions. These rebellions increased in intensity during the Porfiriato. One historian argues that Porfirio Díaz viewed Indians as an antinational element requiring prompt and, if necessary, forcible assimilation (Knight 1990b: 79). The fact that Díaz was "almost a pure Mixtec" Indian did not make him more sympathetic to Indians' place in his national plan of "progress" through export-led development.[5]

Indigenismo in the Wake of the Mexican Revolution

Like other social revolutions, the Mexican Revolution of 1910 had a significant popular dimension, which historians have highlighted (Gilly 1971; Hart 1987; Knight 1986). Yet despite Indians' considerable participation in the revolution (especially if a broad definition of Indian is adopted), they fought "in the absence of any self-consciously Indian project" (Knight 1990b: 76). Thus, according to Knight, policies enacted immediately after the revolution that dealt with the "Indian question" were not the product of direct Indian pressure. Similar to the situation faced by elites in the immediate postindependence period, revolutionary political leaders again needed to forge a nation. The liberal administrations of the nineteenth century had been weak, and outside Mexico City the power of regional caudillos had gone unchallenged. Díaz, although a stronger national leader than his predecessors, allowed regional leaders to maintain their power bases in exchange for unconditional personal loyalty. After the extraordinary social upheaval and physical devastation of the revolutionary period, leaders were under intense pressure to end these entrenched regional fiefdoms to "create" a nation.

The revolutionary leaders and political elites who came to power after 1917, again appropriated images of Mexico's Indian past to forge a sense of national unity. Perhaps more than anywhere else in Latin America, the revolutionary Mexican state held up the Indian as an integral member of the "revolutionary family" and as a vital part of Mexico's national patrimony. Political leaders used indigenist policies to garner legitimacy where myriad regional political cleavages hampered national integration. In contrast to the coercive, confrontational stance taken by Porfirio Díaz, after the revolution, political leaders wanted integration to be planned, enlightened, and respectful of Indian culture. As Manuel Gamio, the head of the Ministry of Agriculture's Direction of Anthropology during the first revolutionary government, described it: "Indian economic and intellectual development can proceed without the annihilation of the original [Indian] culture" (Gamio 1960).

The positive features of indigenous culture, according to Gamio, lay principally in its precolonial past. He worried that contemporary differences in culture among ethnicities, namely the country's indigenous and nonindigenous populations, were stumbling blocks in the way of national unity (Gamio 1960). That national unity was one of Gamio's central preoccupations is evident from the title of his classic work, *Forjando Patria* (Forging the nation). Other influential politicians and intellectuals saw the mestizo as the foundation of the revolutionary project and the nation-state. José Vasconcelos, a noted intellectual of the period who in the 1920s occupied the post of minister of education under President Obregón, argued that the mestizo character of the population would improve the defects of purer races (Vasconcelos 1976). The question remained, however, about what to do with the contemporary Indian population.

In general terms, a consensus formed among political elites that Indians, as mestizos, would be incorporated by noncoercive means into the nation-state.[6] However, beyond that minimal assertion, various positions competed for official attention on how this incorporation would take place. Moisés Sáenz, vice-minister of education in the 1920s, was an early defender of the total incorporation of indigenous peoples, but later became a staunch defender of cultural pluralism. His experience with failed community development projects designed in Mexico City and applied to Indian communities throughout Mexico convinced him that it was necessary to consider the differences among indigenous communities when making policy (Hewitt 1985). Vicente Lombardo Toledano, a Marxist intellectual and influential labor leader from the 1920s to the 1940s, also challenged the notion of total incorporation. For Lombardo Toledano, the root of problems in the Mexican countryside lay in unjust economic relations rather than in "backward" systems of belief. Lombardo Toledano was one of the strongest defenders of the idea that local cultures should be respected and preserved, actively promoting the rapid economic development of the countryside along with the defense of cultural pluralism (Hewitt 1985: 16). Although there was significant variation in the degree to which policymakers advocated the integration of indigenous peoples, Gamio and Vasconcelos were closest to advocating the total integration of the indigenous, while Sáenz best represented the model of cultural pluralism. The coexistence of these two competing and contradictory policy goals was one of the main dilemmas policymakers faced in the period immediately following the revolution through the administration of Lázaro Cárdenas (1934–40): the necessity of incorporating the indigenous into the national population and the desirability of promoting the preservation of distinctive Indian traits.

Indigenist Institutions

The first concentrated effort the state made to coordinate its activities in indigenous areas of the country was the creation of the Autonomous Department of Indian Affairs in 1936, proposed by Cárdenas's minister of education, Moisés Sáenz. The express purpose of the department was to coordinate the development efforts of all public agencies working in indigenous areas and to adapt them to the particular requirements of each group (Hewitt 1985: 15). These efforts culminated in the creation of the National Indigenist Institute (INI) in 1948. Sáenz based his philosophy not on the incorporation of the Indian, but on the integration of Mexico "through the building of a great nation [of pluralistic cultures] linked together in a just and efficacious economic system" (Sáenz, cited in Hewitt 1985: 16).

In 1948, under President Alemán (1946–52), the National Indigenist Institute was created "as a public, decentralized organism of the federal government in charge of designing and instituting government policy toward the indigenous peoples of Mexico" (INI 1994: 27).[7] The idea, dominant during the Cárdenas administration, of respectful, noncoercive integration, undergirded the institute's founding. INI's original mandate was to coordinate the activities of diverse government agencies and dependencies operating in indigenous areas; its chief function was to coordinate rather than to make and implement its own policies.[8] Due to the absence of government agencies in many indigenous areas, however, the INI gradually began to attend to indigenous needs—as they defined them—and to design and implement various educational, medical, agricultural, and general assistance programs.

The National Indigenist Institute's mission involved assisting indigenous peoples in "backward" areas of the country to integrate and acculturate into national life. Under President Alemán, Mexico embarked on an economic program of Import Substitution Industrialization (ISI), in which the state subsidized the development of infrastructure to allow industry to produce competitively for the domestic market—thus diminishing the country's external dependence. The INI would aid in the country's economic program by promoting development in rural, indigenous areas—which were some of the nation's poorest.

INI's administrative structure in rural areas followed a model developed by anthropologist Aguirre Beltrán in the 1950s. Aguirre Beltrán argued that Mexico's indigenous people lived mostly in what he would later call "regions of refuge"— isolated and backward regions of the country located near more technically so- phisticated and developed mestizo centers. Indians would only develop, he maintained, if the government actively promoted their integration through ac- culturation. To this end, Aguirre Beltrán established a program of indigenous acculturation that was divided into developmental stages and that included interdisciplinary teams, trained personnel, and the creation of Coordinating Centers (Centros Coordinadores Indigenistas, CCIs) to be located in the mes- tizo metropolis of each region (Gutiérrez 1999: 102).[9] The inaugural CCI (Tzotzil- Tzeltal) opened in 1951 in San Cristóbal, with Gonzalo Aguirre Beltrán at its head. Following Aguirre Beltrán's original idea, CCIs were intended

> to promote the coordinated action of the various organisms interested in diverse aspects of social betterment. Their [CCI] headquarters are always to be established in the most important city or village of the region. . . . The principal object of these Centers is to stimulate the integral development of indigenous communities, so that communities will be freed from the stagnation of tradition in order to join the concert of national life. (INI 1976: 41)[10]

Programs administered by the INI at its regional Coordinating Centers were designed for indigenous peoples, not by them—a characteristic of indigenist policy both before and after the revolution. It was during the administration of Presi- dent Luis Echeverría (1970–76), however, that Indian peoples began to appropriate institutional spaces from within the INI and build support for indigenous self- determination. Talk of self-determination and autonomy emerged, for the first time, at an INI-sponsored national congress at Pátzcuaro, Michoacán, in 1975.

The Pátzcuaro Congress and Formation of Consejos Supremos

From the start of his administration, Echeverría made the "Indian question" a priority, increasing the INI budget from 26 million pesos in 1970 to 450 million by 1976 (INI 1976: 12). Echeverría's populist policies, however, were not successful in curbing the tide of land invasions and the growth of independent peasant organizations that challenged CNC dominance. After a highly visible Indian congress held in San Cristóbal and organized by the diocese in 1974, the administration moved to respond to the growing cries of discontent that threatened to disrupt the fragile social balance in the countryside and completely spill outside corporatist control.

In October 1975, hundreds of indigenous peoples from around the country were invited to an Indian congress to be held in Pátzcuaro, Michoacán. The INI, the CNC, and the Ministry of Agrarian Reform organized sixty regional congresses in preparation for Pátzcuaro, using organizing strategies similar to the ones used by leaders of the 1974 Indian congress. At this congress, the creation of fifty-six Consejos Supremos de las Etnias (Supreme Councils of Ethnic Groups) was announced; they would be supervised by the newly created National Council of Indian Peoples (Consejo Nacional de Pueblos Indígenas, CNPI). Congress leaders organized the Consejos Supremos around pre-Columbian Indian authority figures, such as the mayordomo and the council of elders. Referring to these traditional structures, Medina argues that "all of this was completely new for indigenous communities. The very idea of Consejos Supremos was new" (Medina 1977: 23).[11] That indigenous peoples were also assigned to ethnic categories based strictly on linguistic identification further demonstrated the distance between leaders' notions and actual indigenous practices. For most indigenous peoples, the local community—not linguistic group—has been the primary reference point for collective identity. In highland Chiapas, for example, Tzotzils of San Juan Chamula have historically viewed neighboring Tzotzils from Zinacantán as rivals, even though both speak the same indigenous language and live side by side in contiguous municipalities (see map 3).

What were the state's motives in organizing the indigenous along ethnic lines? Hernández Castillo (2001c: 108) speculates that "rather than the demands that were presented during the 1974 Indian congress, what may have attracted the state's attention was the appeal that a discourse focused on 'indigenous rights' could have and the potential danger that such demands could be radicalized." Fear of the radicalization of ethnic demands made in 1974 was a

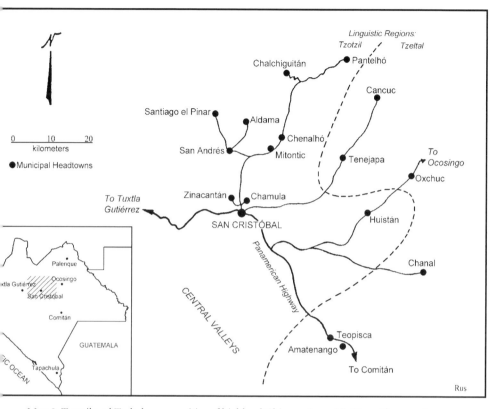

Map 3. Tzotzil and Tzeltal communities of highland Chiapas. From Mattiace, Shannan L., Rosalva Aída Hernández, and Jan Rus, eds., *Tierra, libertad y autonomía: impactos regionales del zapatismo en Chiapas* (México, D.F.: CIESAS, 2002). Original map in Spanish. Courtesy of Jan Rus.

strong motivating factor in the state's decision to convene its own congress in 1975. Barre suggests that the creation of the Consejos Supremos also responded to the government's need to assure an electoral mass of voters (Barre 1983: 66). Scholars concur that one of the state's primary motives for organizing the congress was to preempt growing independent peasant/Indian organization, which had initiated a discourse of ethnic and cultural demands (Medina 1977).

Despite its limitations, however, the 1975 congress produced some significant results. Among the most notable were demands that the constitution be modified to increase the possibilities of electing indigenous representatives to the national Congress, that Indian languages be declared official, that the state make a commitment to promoting and distributing Indian language materials, and that information be disseminated about the history of the country's ethnic groups and Indian traditions and artistry (*Acción Indigenista* 1975b). Other demands included the acceleration of paperwork concerning the resolution of agrarian demands and increased indigenous participation in federal programs such as CONASUPO (National Basic Food Company) and FONART (National Fund for the Arts) (*Acción Indigenista* 1975b; Medina 1977).

The congress and the CNPI structure also opened up opportunities for inter-ethnic cooperation among Mexico's fifty-six indigenous ethnicities. For many indigenous peoples, this was the first time they had extended contact with other Indians. Gregorio Morales, member of the first Mam Supreme Council from Chiapas, spoke of his experience at meetings of the National Council of Indian Peoples (CNPI), created at the 1975 congress at Pátzcuaro, and held in Mexico City:

> There in the capital I met other Supreme Councils; they told us there were around fifty-four different indigenous languages assembled there; imagine, some of them did not understand Spanish too well. I heard Chamulas speak their own language, and also the Mochó very near here at Motozintla, but I had no idea there were so many *idiomistas* [people who speak indigenous languages] in this country. I used to think that it was good that my children spoke only Spanish but there I saw that in other places they had not lost their language, even children spoke it, so I thought it was not good to lose our root.[12]

At the 1975 Pátzcuaro congress, indigenous organizations first articulated the demand for self-determination, which, despite the congress's official character, foreshadowed what would later become the principal demand of an independent Indian movement. The demand for self-determination appears in a summary document that discusses the role of the newly created National Council of Indian Peoples (CNPI), which was created to oversee the Supreme Councils: "This new organism [CNPI] would have as its main goal to increase and maintain the unity of indigenous peoples in order to satisfy their demands as well as allow for the self-determination of our communities" (INI 1978b: 363). Andrés Medina (1977) argues that this congress was the first political referent for Indian autonomy. He maintains that the congress was in part a response by the state to the intense activity of numerous Indian communities, who were fighting for land and promising a solution to old agrarian problems. Increasingly, he notes, these communities proposed solutions to the land problem that included national ethnic and cultural demands. At Pátzcuaro, however, Indians as a whole were careful not to appear separatist in any way, situating their demands within the national revolutionary tradition:

> In order to facilitate our incorporation into the objectives of the Mexican Revolution that will emancipate us, we demand of the society in which we live a respect of indigenous communities' self-determination. To us, self-determination means the conscious integration into the national community and a complete exercise of the democratic rights that we are privy to under the order of the Constitution of the Republic. It is not, by any means, a sign of privilege or isolation. (*Acción Indigenista* 1975a)[13]

Indians' insistence on situating themselves within the official party's national-popular project is not surprising, given the historical moment in which the congress was held and the sociopolitical context within which it occurred. In 1975 indigenous peoples were just beginning to organize independently from government-sanctioned peasant organizations. More vocal critics of indigenismo, however, also emerged at this time. One such group of critics was a group of anthropologists called the "Five Magnificent Ones."

The End of Integration: Toward a Participatory Indigenismo

From the early years of the Echeverría administration (1970–76), a young group of anthropologists at the National School of Anthropology and History (ENAH) were vocal critics of the state's decades-old policy of assimilation and integration of indigenous peoples.[14] These anthropologists took exception to the official view that Indian ethnic traits inhibited national development and progress. Rodolfo Stavenhagen and Guillermo Bonfil, for example, argued that the underdevelopment of Indian regions was due to economic subordination by mestizos, whose racism justified the extraction of wealth from Indian communities. Anthropologists such as Salomón Nahmad lambasted the Echeverría administration and its director, Aguirre Beltrán, for sustaining a policy of ethnocide, which, Nahmad believed, rested on the goal of ethnic and cultural homogeneity. Referring to the official position of the Echeverría administration, Nahmad claimed:

> There is opposition to the inclusion of groups who seek to participate in a society that is not homogeneous (pluri-cultural or multiethnic),

but apparently we want to make it homogeneous (mono-ethnic), and it is not so. We are a multicultural society, not uni-cultural, one in which we all have the same language, the same tradition, the same customs, the same habits. No, that kind of society does not exist. (Nahmad 1977: 14)

During the Echeverría regime, the integrationist and the multiculturalist camps engaged in a battle for the future of indigenist policy. A 1973 INI publication warned about the ideological dangers represented by the proposals of "a group of politico-social anthropologists and sociologists with anarchic tendencies who desire to turn Mexico into a multi-ethnic and multi-cultural nation; to do that they propose full respect for native cultures and the creation of an ethnic consciousness among the groups who practice it in order to transform them into small nations" (cited in Hernández Castillo 2001c: 104).

The López Portillo administration (1976–82) dealt with Nahmad's criticism by inviting anthropologists who had been highly critical of INI's integrationist position to join the INI, including Salomón Nahmad. These anthropologists' views dominated indigenist policy during López Portillo's *sexenio* (six-year term). Although the new administration inherited a policy of integration, a 1978 INI document outlining indigenist plans of action illustrates an early distancing from assimilationist and integrationist models: "The indigenista political project cannot be other than an option that the indigenous themselves choose: an expression of themselves and their organizations" (INI 1978a: x). Seemingly overnight, the INI shifted from an assimilationist posture to one emphasizing the participation of indigenous peoples:

> The preservation of ethnic identity must be an option freely chosen by indigenous communities. It is an indisputable right of these groups and an essential part of the personality of a pluralist nation such as ours. The participation of autochthonous peoples, beginning with this new policy initiative, will be a priority. In light of the oppressive conditions in which the indigenous live, the defense of their rights and access to resources designed to strengthen their economies will be emphasized. And, with that, we will give sustenance to their self-determination, which will be oriented to conserve and develop their ethnic identity. This ethnic identity invigorates and distinguishes Mexico from other nations of the world. (INI 1978a: xi)

The INI recommended the end of "compulsive methods that have homogenization and cultural mestizaje as their goal, as well as paternalistic methods that supplant the communities' own initiatives and inhibit the development of their creative potential" (INI 1978a: xxv). State officials now defined the nation as "ethnically and culturally plural" (INI 1978a: xxvi).[15] This did not mean, however, that the administration of López Portillo or the new national director of the INI, Ignacio Ovalle Fernández, were necessarily supportive of independent indigenous organization. While participatory indigenismo opened up greater opportunities for Indian participation than had previously existed, state officials closely monitored any independent organization.[16]

What were the main factors leading to the demise of assimilationism, the foundation of Mexican indigenismo from the revolution to the late 1970s? Although major policy shifts are the result of numerous factors, this one resulted from an unusual alliance between radical and moderate reformers within the López Portillo administration.[17] During the first two years of the sexenio, the view of hard-liners dominated policy making. Echeverría's nationalist populism had alienated business and large-scale farming sectors; in response, López Portillo immediately reassured them and attempted to restore investor confidence in the regime. Additionally, his support for capital-intensive, export-oriented agricultural development promised a way out of the current economic crisis. Even without these domestic pressures, an International Monetary Fund (IMF)-imposed adjustment package locked the administration into a plan of economic austerity. Under this plan, the administration was forced to keep inflation low by tightening money supply and by reducing social spending across the board. Yet, López Portillo kept most of Echeverría's team on board, a decision that suggested that he was waiting for a more opportune moment to institute governmental reform. That moment arrived halfway through his sexenio.

The institutional centerpiece of López Portillo's antipoverty policy was COPLAMAR (National Plan for Depressed Zones and Marginal Groups). Formed soon after he took office, the president asked Ignacio Ovalle to head the agency (Ovalle served simultaneously as the national INI director). Fox (1993) notes that for the first three years of the sexenio, the agency did little. But in 1979, COPLAMAR joined with CONASUPO to provide a "basic market basket" of subsidized food to the poorest of Mexicans, to be distributed by CONASUPO-COPLAMAR regional stores. In short, policymakers created a system of storage, transportation, and community participation networks to distribute food to rural communities. In contrast to the production-first programs applied in other areas, this initiative made a deliberate, "behind-the-scenes" decision at the highest levels to encourage peasant organization independent of the PRI. Fox (1993) argues that this policy situation was the result of an unusual alliance between radical and moderate reformist policymakers. According to Fox:

> Reformists clearly occupied a subordinate role within the ruling coalition, and they lacked the power to fundamentally change the allocation of land or production inputs. Both reformist and more orthodox policy currents did agree, however, that reforms undercutting the power of rural intermediaries, or caciques, would improve both peasants' living standards and the government's political image. (Fox 1993: 125)

One of the most innovative aspects of the CONASUPO-COPLAMAR program was that it encouraged community-based collective action. Program officials set up regional food councils to oversee and coordinate the distribution of subsidized food and encouraged the participation of organizations and community leaders not affiliated with the official party. Indeed, Fox (1993) noted that government officials based in Mexico City viewed community leaders not affiliated with the official party as more effective and efficient leaders because they enjoyed more respect in their communities. Because of overlapping interests and goals, as well as the fact that Ignacio Ovalle headed both agencies, COPLAMAR and INI officials enjoyed a close official relationship. In the jointly administered project, COPLAMAR used the INI as a consultant in the selection of warehouse sites for food storage.

The goal of involving communities and grassroots organizations in the CONASUPO-COPLAMAR project was consistent with the INI's turn toward participatory indigenismo. Still, the CONASUPO-COPLAMAR case study suggests that the move to involve communities occurred most often in the program implementation stage and not at the level of design. This joint effort was not a direct response to grassroots mobilization or to increased levels of social mobilization. Rather, incentives within the social policy arena changed, opening a window of opportunity for radical reformist policymakers interested in economic and social change (many of whom had also served in the Echeverría administration) to ally themselves with moderate reformers. These moderate reformers, in turn, believed the participation of grassroots leaders was important to ensure the program's success and their own.

For the INI, the policy turn toward participatory indigenismo resulted in internal restructuring. The INI created new departments to promote and support indigenous culture. Local community committees were created as consulting institutions for the INI, in which indigenous peoples could participate more actively in the development of broader programs and policies. New departments established in Mexico City such as the External Contact and Publishing Department and the Audio-visual Archive sought to "aid national society in recognizing itself in its cultural diversity" (INI 1982: 41). Additionally, INI officials founded the Department of Anthropological Research and Social Organization, whose aim was "to suggest ethno-development strategies that fit the particular characteristics of each ethnic group" (INI 1982: 88). Despite these internal changes and new policy direction, however, no Indians held middle- or high-level administrative positions within the CCI structure, or on the national level. Initiatives such as CONASUPO-COPLAMAR were notably top-down in their design. Despite the shift from integration to participatory indigenismo, Barre notes that "participative indigenismo, while departing from integrationist models, ultimately perpetuated the system through a political reordering of indigenous peoples" (Barre 1983: 72).

Although participatory indigenismo was limited, it did offer indigenous peoples new spaces for organization and appropriation within the state. Indigenous peoples used INI-sponsored programs. I examine two such programs here—one in Chiapas and one in Michoacán—as platforms for making demands that ultimately transcended program goals.

"Rescuing" Culture and "Inventing Tradition"

Part of INI's abandonment of the assimilation model and shift to participatory indigenismo in the mid-1970s included an initiative for cultural and language rescue. The INI now saw indigenous culture and language as valuable commodities that needed to be rescued from disuse and neglect. The INI included lesser-known indigenous peoples such as the Tojolabal and Mam peoples of eastern and southeastern Chiapas in these projects of cultural rescue. Carlos Saldívar, director of the Tojolabal CCI in Las Margaritas from 1993 to 1996, describes the origin of this program:

> [In the early 1980s] we worked in the National School [of Anthropology and History] on a project for the rescue of these groups. It was decided that it would be good to diVuse information about groups like the Seri, the Tojolabal, and the Mam who were less visible than the Tzeltal

or the Purépecha. We began a project focused on the cultural rescue of seven of these groups. One of them was the Tojolabals. . . . The idea was to rescue certain cultures that had not had much national visibility. We came to the region in a brigade with a photographer, a movie-maker, a sociologist, an anthropologist, and a musicologist. This group made a registry, so to speak, of the zone. They took pictures, made movies of the people, of how they lived and their costumes. We taped them, how they spoke and played music and their dependence on agricultural cycles.[18]

The INI also sponsored a cultural rescue movement called Danzas Mam (Mam dances) among the Mam people of southeastern Chiapas. Danzas Mam was originally an INI project formed with the support of the Mam Supreme Council in 1981. The project's main goal was to resurrect Mam traditions and customs no longer practiced in everyday life, to introduce these "traditions" to new generations, and to perform them during cultural activities organized by the state government. Danzas Mam is a peasant theater group that, apart from dancing to marimba music, represents everyday scenes of traditional Mam life and performs important religious celebrations. Older Mam participants perform dances such as the "End of the Harvest Feast," a story about a forlorn ear of corn that is sad because the Indians no longer honored it after they switched from corn to commercial coffee crops. Danzas Mam members also commonly perform dances celebrating the role of sheep in highland culture. Hernández Castillo (2001c) notes that the stories performed by older participants typically center on the importance of self-subsistence, nostalgic for times when "things from outside" were not essential to community sustenance. This vision of the past, she argues, is challenged by younger Danza participants who remind the audience that when "nothing was needed from outside," Mam had to go down periodically to Soconusco fincas (coastal coffee plantations) to work. The young people tell listeners about the suffering that their own parents endured at the fincas and about the ill treatment from overseers and the power of *enganchadores* (labor recruiters). Hernández notes that a large sector of the young people active in the Danzas have participated in peasant mobilizations in the 1990s, especially since the 1994 Zapatista rebellion.

Hernández argues that the impact of the Danzas Mam project on the communities has been mixed. It has not merely reproduced state discourse, but neither has it created a purely political space for raising members' consciousness.

In general, INI state and regional officials tend to fund community cultural projects that focus on the preservation of traditional handicrafts, traditional music, and dance. The communities, however, often appropriate these spaces to create their own cultural and political projects. In the case of the Danzas Mam project, Hernández concludes:

> What emerged as a space closely linked to the official culturalist perspective has acquired a dynamic of its own and has become in many cases a space for criticism and questioning of the state and the system in general. . . . Being Mam means not only speaking the language and celebrating the festivity of the little ear of corn but also working at the fincas and fighting for land. (Hernández Castillo 2001c: 153–54)

A similar phenomenon occurred during the 1970s with a peasant theater group sponsored by CONASUPO and run by the Chiapas state government during the populist administration of Governor Velasco Suárez (1970–76). This was a period of populist politics on the national level, and Echeverría administration officials mandated governmental agencies such as the INI and parastatals such as CONASUPO to seek grassroots support for their social development projects. The INI sent Mercedes Olivera, who was hired in Mexico City, to work in Chiapas in the early 1970s. Speaking of the INI's new goals, she says:

> We were supposed to coordinate all the work in indigenous areas, letting indigenous peoples know that our goal was no longer to make them into ladinos, but rather to strengthen their culture and develop the concept of autonomy so that they could strengthen themselves. Among the new things that we introduced was this idea of the theater. We had four or five theater groups at the time. We had Tzotzils, Tzeltals, Chols, and one Tojolabal group. It was a very enriching experience. The young people who participated came as promoters [*promotores*] to be trained. Of those promoters, we invited the ones with the most spark and initiative. They were really an excellent group of young men and women. They genuinely had a great capacity for leadership. . . . We worked very well together.[19]

Olivera was later let go by the INI, due to conflicts with the state director. "In 1974," she says, "they accused me of promoting Indian power. . . . In this moment the Black Power movement was strong in the United States, with all of its conflicts and confrontations. Well, I left the INI, and we continued with the project of the rural theater."[20] After leaving the INI, Olivera continued to organize the theater brigades through CONASUPO. In addition to writing and rehearsing the educational plays that were performed in rural communities throughout the state, the participants lived together in San Cristóbal in a kind of boarding school. As Olivera describes it:

> Among the compañeros, some of them had not finished the second year of primary school. At the same time that we worked with the theater, they finished primary school in an intensive correspondence class. This was very important for them. . . . They picked the themes [of the plays] and worked on the topics. They went to look for material and there were some excellent topics. For example, they took up the topic of creation from the perspective of the different ethnic groups. And they prepared a representation of the distinct cosmological conceptions the different groups possessed.[21]

The plays not only dealt with indigenous cosmology but also addressed repression against the indigenous by ladinos, the exploitation of overseers and *hacendados* (hacienda owners and bosses) on the fincas, the unequal exchange in regional markets, and the value of maintaining indigenous traditions. On this last point, Olivera describes a play that generated a heated discussion over the viability of maintaining local customs:

> We began to reflect on the question of whether it would be good if we broke with certain traditions. We discussed the problem of which traditions should be changed and which were better off left the same. We asked ourselves whether preserving our culture meant that we remained ignorant, that we never changed, or that we rejected development. What things did we need to change and what things did we need to maintain? It became clear that what we needed to maintain was our identity and not preserve culture for its own sake. Culture changes. . . . But we should conserve identities. Then, there was the idea that identities are preserved by maintaining indigenous governance structures and by making their own internal decisions, and so on. We discussed all this with our indigenous compañeros. Since then the seed of indigenous autonomy was sown, preserving identities while transforming culture.[22]

The CONASUPO theater brigades worked to foment the development of a radical political consciousness among the scores of young people who participated in them. Margarito Ruiz, the Tojolabal leader who had spearheaded the formation of the Gobierno Tojolabal, was a member of Olivera's brigades.

Local INI leaders in the Purépecha region of Michoacán were involved in cultural revival of a different sort in the early 1980s. Originally, a group of indigenous intellectuals and professionals who had been trained in the INI proposed the idea of reviving the Purépecha New Year celebration.[23] Eduardo Zárate, an anthropologist who has studied the celebration, describes the festival as a celebration of the end of one annual cycle and the beginning of the next. It typically includes music, dance, and games that are considered to be traditional. The climax of the celebration is the ceremony of the New Fire and the transfer of responsibilities for the hosting of the annual festival (Zárate 1993: 32). Because the responsibility of hosting the celebration rotates annually, the celebration takes on a different tone each year. And while INI teachers and other indigenous state officials originally sponsored the activity, a variety of local and regional organizations are now involved, such as the independent peasant organization Unión Campesina Emiliano Zapata (UCEZ), several political parties, and the Consejos Supremos Purépecha (one official and one independent).

Viewed singly, the New Year celebration does not communicate an overtly political message. Nor is its primary goal to foment greater sociopolitical organization among Purépecha communities. Yet, it has provided a forum for intercommunity collaboration and has facilitated regional political organization by uniting people from different communities in the region. Because the celebration is closely tied to other processes of ethnic revitalization in the region—such as the struggle for land, local political autonomy, municipal control, and control of cultural institutions and traditional ethnic spaces—it has also provided a link between symbols from Purépechan history and present political struggles. As Zárate notes, "The process of Phurhépecha ethnic reconstitution is not limited to the revitalization or invention of symbols. . . . Its principal preoccupation and demand is centered on the indigenous community as a particular form of territoriality" (Zárate 1993: 55).[24]

The Purépecha New Year celebration demonstrates the ways that the "past" can be used to fuel contemporary political struggles for land and resources. Zárate is not unaware, however, of its limitations:

> The past is present among the Phurhépecha. . . . But it is also true that the past has a constrictive aspect, that it is reproduced through symbols

that limit the possibility of giving meaning to the transformations that occur within society. Given the fact that the social world is in constant flux, one holds on to that which is most secure: primordial identities that are historically constructed.... The return to primordial identities continues to be the most viable option for many to order the perceived social chaos. (Zárate 1993: 53)

With cultural rescue and revitalization comes the temptation to romanticize and essentialize the past. The past becomes something that can be known and apprehended, unlike the present, which is contested and open to multiple interpretations. Among the Mam, it is the young people who are challenging this romanticized view of the past. For the Purépecha, the link between the New Year celebration and the struggle for land reform within the UCEZ keeps indigenous peoples connected to current political issues that link culture, politics, and material survival. Although the Mexican state attempted to excise any political content from educational and cultural policies designed for indigenous peoples, these policies did benefit indigenous activists in an important way: they provided a space from which to seek political autonomy and address ethnic/racial subordination. A number of indigenous peoples throughout the country challenged the state's definition of culture as shorn of political and material content. By the late 1980s, a strengthened Indian movement would challenge President Salinas's (1988–94) attempt to divorce cultural politics from economic and political policy.

Solidarity with the "Poorest of the Poor": "Modernizing" Mexico's Social Sector

When he assumed office in 1988, President Carlos Salinas de Gortari and his team promised to catapult Mexico into the league of first-world nations by working toward the modernization of social, economic, and political life. Budget and programming minister under his predecessor Miguel de la Madrid (1982–88), Salinas had been a key architect of the administration's strict austerity programs that ushered in neoliberal economic reforms after years of profligate spending and borrowing under Echeverría and López Portillo. Salinas, unlike many of the U.S.-trained economists, or technocrats, who increasingly began to populate the Office of Budget and Programming and other high-level governmental agencies after 1982, was a savvy politician. He understood that the austerity measures put in place by his administration would cause "short-term" dislocation and discontent among some sectors. He also understood the need to design a political strategy to shore up support for the regime during this difficult period of transition to a more "rational" and leaner state. Salinas's pet social program, the Programa Nacional de Solidaridad (PRONASOL, or Solidaridad), was the centerpiece of this strategy.

In one of his first acts after the inauguration on December 6, 1988, Salinas signed a presidential resolution that inaugurated the Solidaridad program.[25] Solidaridad was a targeted social spending program focused on three main populations: indigenous peoples, poor peasants, and the urban poor. Salinas administration officials organized the program around material (social services/infrastructure provision and poverty alleviation) and institutional goals (rearrangement of state-society relations and the coalition supporting the PRI). At the center of Solidaridad was the formation of local solidarity committees *(comités de solidaridad),* where participants would come together to discuss areas of need within their communities. These committees would design community projects that would be two-thirds funded by Solidaridad, with the remaining funding coming from the local level (often in the form of in-kind contributions, such as manual labor and materials). Institutionally, Solidaridad officials sought to replace sectoral-based organization, such as the CNC, by a territorial-based system, thus bypassing traditional caciques and mid- and low-level bureaucrats, whose rent-seeking activities often diverted federal government funds destined for poor people. Equally ambitiously, Solidaridad officials hoped that the emphasis on community participation would help change Mexican political culture from one based on dependence and government assistance to one based more on personal responsibility.

The results of this strategy were mixed, largely because the program had widely differing impacts depending on the region and locale. In some areas, caciques or state governors diverted program funds, fearing that the funds would get into the hands of opposition sympathizers (for example, in Tabasco). In other areas, especially where independent organization was already present, Solidaridad funds aided in encouraging popular participation outside traditional patron-client channels (for example, in Oaxaca and in parts of Chiapas). Although the program helped develop basic infrastructure, constructing hundreds of miles of new roads and installing electrical lines in many areas for the first time, it was tainted by accusations that it was used to buttress support for the PRI in areas where the party had been losing popular support (for example, in Michoacán, Durango, and Juchitán, Oaxaca). Evaluation was mixed as to the degree of institutional change that the program effected; evidence suggested that it was not successful in replacing sectoral by territorial organization.[26] There was extensive community participation in project selection and implementation in local Solidarity committees (which totaled 120,000 by mid-1993), but there was virtually no popular involvement in the design of Solidarity programs and the setting of state- or national-level funding priorities. Because program officials often linked local Solidarity committees directly to the national government, scholars argue that the program reinforced executive dominance (Bailey 1994; Dresser 1991).

During the first three years of the Salinas administration, INI's budget increased eighteenfold.[27] Solidarity projects targeting indigenous peoples emphasized health, education, housing, and employment levels (Warman n.d.). INI's national director, Arturo Warman, announced that the institute would be a member of the Solidaridad Commission, which set program priorities and evaluation standards and would support grassroots initiatives. The INI would turn over selective functions to indigenous organizations in coordination with federal, state, and municipal institutions. "INI activity," he asserted, "must be understood as that of promoter, coordinator, and collaborator" (Warman n.d.).

Although other programs directed at the indigenous population were part of the Solidaridad strategy, such as a program of credit supports for coffee production and Fondos de Solidaridad para la Promoción del Patrimonio Cultural de los Pueblos Indígenas, the largest Solidaridad outlays for indigenous peoples went into Regional Funds.[28] Moreover, INI's Regional Funds program was the one most likely to promote qualitative reform and the only one that actually attempted to transfer decision making in the area of resource allocation to autonomous regional councils of representative social and economic organizations. In contrast to most Solidarity programs in which the state created its own interlocutors, the Regional Funds project bolstered existing representative organizations (Fox 1994: 180).[29] In implementing the project, the INI drew on its recent history of participatory indigenismo, in which the institute gave priority to dealing with existing Indian organizations in the implementation of programs, rather than creating new ones (for example, as did CONASUPO-COPLAMAR). The Regional Funds project was launched within INI's Coordinating Centers (CCIs), whose mandate was to convene general assemblies to elect leadership councils. Solidarity officials mandated that the INI provide technical support but not intervene in the actual decision-making process (Fox 1994: 196).

In a 1992 internal program evaluation of the country's Regional Funds, the funds in Chiapas, Veracruz, and Oaxaca were considered to be "doing well," while those in the Huasteca, Chihuahua, and the Yucatán Peninsula were thought to be doing "poorly" (Fox 1994: 198). Fox (1994) argues that two main factors largely determined whether "virtuous circles" of pluralistic policy implementation emerged in local arenas. The first was the prior existence of consolidated and representative peasant and Indian organizations; the second was the willingness of INI directors to devolve effective power over resource allocation. In instances where these two factors held, the Regional Funds project led to the creation of unique instances of power sharing among indigenous organizations and, as Fox argues, within and across ethnic groups (Fox 1994: 216).

To take one particular example, the Regional Funds project directed by the CCI-Tojolabal in Las Margaritas did seem to strengthen independent popular organization. In May 1995, thirty-five organizations in the area participated in the program.[30] The Regional Funds project included official organizations such as the CNC and independent peasant organizations such as the CIOAC. According to midlevel INI officials at the CCI-Tojolabal Regional Fund, monies were not dispersed to organizations with less than fifty members or to those projects that involved fewer than three communities. One INI official in Las Margaritas compared the Regional Funds program to previous INI initiatives by saying that "previously we imposed our programs on the communities. But that is not the case with the Regional Funds. The people propose the projects they want. They give twenty percent of the funding and we give the other eighty percent."[31] The INI regional director of Las Margaritas from 1993 to 1995, Carlos Saldívar Alvarado, also suggested that the Regional Funds program marked a departure from previous INI programs:

> Previously, the communities did not perhaps participate as much in the management of resources, but beginning with the creation of these committees [Solidaridad committees], it began to happen. Now, the communities and the organizations, whatever the type, whatever the color, participate. . . . The organizations act in accord with their particular needs; they themselves decide how to fulfill these needs. Our assistance is more logistical, administrative, bureaucratic. . . . I believe that the social meaning of this participation is the program's most important aspect. This is the part I know most about. The purpose is not to give "a man a fish, but teach him how to catch fish." And I feel that I have created a highly visible and advertised fund [Regional Fund] and I am very pleased with the support that we have given them.[32]

My observations suggest that the Regional Funds program in Las Margaritas met the two conditions Fox argued were necessary for the creation of "virtuous circles" of pluralistic policy implementation. Since the 1970s, Las Margaritas has had a history of active independent peasant organization (for example, Unión de Uniones Ejidales y Grupos Campesinos Solidarios de Chiapas [UU], the CIOAC, and the Unión de Ejidos de la Selva [Union of Ejidos in the Rain Forest]). Even Margarito Ruiz, one of the INI's sharpest critics, conceded that Chiapas Regional Funds project included the representation of numerous independent organizations:

> The situation in Chiapas is exceptional, since the majority of the so-called "independent" and "political" organizations are in the Regional Funds. This has been achieved because of the maturity of the Chiapas indigenous movement, and a certain separation between INI's political clientele and the governor's clientele, which have set up parallel indigenismos. As a result, the independent indigenous organizations have an important presence in the Regional Funds, while the other organizations work with the municipalities and the state government's indigenous offices, so they do not compete for the same spaces. At this moment the organizations and 123 communities that are members of the Frente Independiente de Pueblos Indios in Chiapas [FIPI] are incorporated in the Regional Funds. . . . When indigenous organizations are able to effectively take the Regional Funds into their own hands, they really can become an important space for participation and decision making, and can facilitate the creation of a phase of "transition"—not transfer—from indigenismo to postindigenismo. (Ruiz, cited in Fox 1994: 213)

Thus, the organizational structure of the Regional Funds was built with the active participation of community representatives who had previously established records and relationships of trust with their communities. This positive rapport between organization leaders and INI officials greatly improved the chances of program success. Conversations I had with INI personnel in Las Margaritas suggested that recent INI regional directors had been relatively proactive and not beholden to caciques and powerful landowners in the region. In 1990, in fact, the state governor, Patrocinio González Garrido, forced the INI regional director in Las Margaritas to resign. The governor accused the director of helping leaders of the Unión de Ejidos de la Selva get Solidarity funding to purchase a coffee-processing plant from the Mexican Institute of Coffee (INMECAFE) (Harvey 1994: 19).

In Chiapas as a whole, Solidaridad spending grew by 130 percent in 1989–90, 50 percent in 1990–91, 20 percent in 1991–92, and a further 1 percent in 1992–93 (Harvey 1994: 17). Nationally the state ranked first in the number of local solidarity committees (boasting 8,824, or roughly 8 percent of the national total) (Harvey 1994: 17). Yet while the Regional Funds program may have enlarged spaces for independent organization in Las Margaritas, other reforms enacted during the Salinas administration were a direct attack on rural producers, both indigenous and mestizo.

The dismantling of INMECAFE price-and-credit supports in 1989 and the 1992 changes to Article 27 were the two reforms most negatively affecting Chiapan peasants. According to data gathered by an independent coffee-producer organization, the amount of credit that coffee growers received from Solidaridad in 1993 was 13 percent less than the total received in 1988, when INMECAFE was still operating (Harvey 1994: 17). In October 1989, the federal government announced that it would modify its intervention in the coffee sector by limiting its involvement to research and technical assistance. That is, it would end its role in the harvesting, financing, and commercialization of coffee during a period of three cycles (Hernández Navarro 1992: 78). Since Chiapas is Mexico's top coffee-producing state, declining prices for coffee had a serious impact on thousands of rural producers. Data from the national level indicate that productivity and total output in the sector fell by approximately 35 percent between 1989 and 1993; small producers suffered a 70-percent drop in income (Harvey 1994: 111).

In 1992, Congress approved constitutional changes to Article 27, permitting ejido land to be sold on private markets. Since the promulgation of the 1917 Constitution, the law prohibited the sale of ejidal land, which had been granted by the state to agrarian communities and ejidos. Salinas's reforms definitively ended land distribution, but, perhaps more importantly, they ended peasants' hopes of resolving land disputes that had been pending for years and, in some cases, for decades.

Despite good intentions of individual INI officials, such as Carlos Saldívar of the CCI-Tojolabal in Las Margaritas, paternalistic patterns of personal and institutional behavior persist within the institute. INI directors typically establish relationships with leaders of organizations and use their discretionary power to allocate funding for specific programs. Within the Regional Funds project, for example, INI directors signed disbursement checks for each approved project. In the CCI-Tojolabal, no indigenous person has ever occupied a high-level administrative position. At this CCI, not unlike its counterparts around the country, Indians tend to occupy service and support positions, such as night watchmen, drivers, and building custodians.

Yet, despite INI's serious limitations in promoting greater autonomous participation of indigenous peoples, in states like Chiapas, many landowners and politicians believe that the institute instigates radical social reform. Luis Hernández Navarro describes the tense relationship between the INI and Chiapas state government officials:

> For at least the past twelve years, the federal government has promoted policies through its development agencies (especially INI, though not exclusively), which aim to mitigate the most pernicious effects of Chiapas' social disparities. These policies have consistently run into resistance from the executives of the state government, as well as from some opponents within the federal bureaucracy who distrust autonomous producer organizations. This conflict has at times reached grotesque proportions, as it did when the state government jailed three officials of INI in March 1992 for the crime of having supported independent campesino organizations. For better or for worse, despite resistance from state officials, federal officials from INI and other agencies have played an important role in the organization of campesino groups. (Hernández Navarro 1994: 55)

The arrest in March 1992 of three top functionaries of the INI in Chiapas foreshadowed the accusation made by some state political officials and local landowners in January 1994 that the institute abetted the EZLN rebellion through their work in municipalities with strong Zapatista support. Although these examples are extreme, the INI occupies an awkward position within the federal state apparatus. Although a substantial number of INI regional directors have worked extensively in indigenous regions and have been sensitive to the demands of indigenous communities, they tread lightly when it comes to criticizing national policy.

A good example of the tension between the INI and other national-level government agencies occurred during the height of the brief public debate over the proposed constitutional changes to Article 27. Someone leaked an INI document to the press that was critical of the administration's proposals to amend Article 27. At the time, the INI's national director, Arturo Warman, was the only major official to highlight the potentially negative impact of ejido privatization. Soon after the report leaked, Warman gave public support to the constitutional changes (Fox 1994: 213). In rural areas the INI represents all the power and authority of the state, yet many politicians accuse it of being too sympathetic to grassroots indigenous organizations. Mistrust of the institute has resulted in low budgets and low prestige within the federal state apparatus as a whole. Except for the Echeverría years and Solidarity funding under the Salinas administration, INI budgets have been abysmally low compared to funding for other social-service agencies.

This pattern of low funding and prestige did not change under President Zedillo (1994–2000). In fact, in May 1996, Zedillo publicly announced that the INI would be converted into a National Indigenous Commission (Comisión Nacional Indigenista) and that its functions would be transferred to state governments. This decision (which was never implemented) was not made in consultation with indigenous peoples but was a unilateral one—a pattern throughout the post-1917 period.

The Future of Indigenismo

When examining indigenist policy making in Mexico, what general patterns emerge? First, one of indigenismo's enduring characteristics has been its top-down quality. Quite simply stated, indigenist policies are policies made for indigenous peoples by a white/mestizo elite. Despite the changes in policy focus over the years, indigenismo continued to reflect this exclusive quality. Second, though the INI often represented more progressive positions on the "Indian question" than the president in turn, its cultural and educational policies have not included a political or economic dimension. Culture has, more often than not, been defined as tradition—shorn of any political or economic reference points. Even when INI functionaries, such as Aguirre Beltrán, regional director of the Tzotzil-Tzeltal Coordinating Center in San Cristóbal, Chiapas, highlighted the economic exploitation Indians experienced at the hands of landowners, the institute never seriously challenged the link between economic and cultural exploitation. It was simply too risky.

On occasion, however, indigenous peoples themselves appropriated INI-sponsored programs and used them toward their own ends. Participants in Danzas Mam, the CONASUPO theater project, and the revival of the Purépecha

New Year combined community rituals and celebrations with land "recoveries" and denunciations of exploitative landlords. For these participants, Indian "culture" was not separate from demands for land/territory or from economic and political rights. Autonomy was to become a key dimension of Indian politics, as two different models of self-determination emerged from within the Indian movement after 1994.

AFTER JANUARY 1, 1994: INDIGENISMO

In the fall and spring of 1995, the Mexican Congress organized a series of state- and local-level meetings throughout the country on the topic of Indian rights. The project was called the Consulta Nacional sobre Derechos y Participación Indígenas (National Consultation on Indian Rights and Participation). Thirty-three forums were held in every state of the nation (plus two in the Federal District). It was no coincidence that this national *consulta* occurred when it did, coinciding simultaneously with the negotiations between the national government and the EZLN on Indian culture and rights. Although the sponsors of the consulta may have hoped to upstage the Zapatistas and their supporters, the conclusions culled from these forums affirmed, rather than contradicted, the demands expressed in the San Andrés Accords signed subsequently on February 16, 1996, between the government and the EZLN. I was curious whether the peace negotiations between the EZLN and the government had changed the government's staging of official indigenist events, and I thought that a good place to find out would be the Chiapas state consulta, which took place on February 28, 1996, in San Cristóbal.

After we had downed our first and second cups of weak coffee from the obligatory white styrofoam cups and the ten-o'-clock hour had long since passed, it looked like the inauguration of the Chiapas Consultation on Indian Rights and Participation was about to begin. So far, all the pieces of official indigenismo were in place and those on stage looked the part—most wearing an odd mixture of traditional and modern garb. PRI politicians in polyester pants and wool "Chamula" vests draped over their business shirts got ready to give their opening speeches; mestiza women, dressed as *indígenas* with too much jewelry and makeup, served third and fourth cups of coffee to all on the makeshift stage; and folkloric music played from the marimba.[1] The staging of Indian politics had begun, and everyone knew their roles.

Among those on stage were Carlos Tello from the National Indigenous

Institute in Mexico City; Tzeltal Indian Jacinto Arias, head of the Chiapas State Office for the Attention of Indigenous Peoples (a state-level INI of sorts); the interim governor of Chiapas, Julio César Ruiz Ferro; and the municipal president of San Cristóbal. According to government sources, six hundred people were in attendance, ten "ethnicities" were represented (Tojolabal, Tzotzil, Tzeltal, Chamula, Mam, Chontal, Náhuatl, Zoque, Ch'ol, and mestizo), 149 papers were presented, and 667 different demands were made that day in San Cristóbal (Memoria: Informe de resultados 18).[2] Representing the federal government, Tello called for a new relationship between the state and Indian peoples. "We must overcome the idea that cultural differences make for differences among Mexicans," Tello insisted, "The Indian question is a political one, a question of human rights and of natural resources" (field notes). Yet, what was occurring behind him belied his words. The "cultural" was being performed on stage, complete with traditional music, mestiza cum indigenous women served coffee (illustrating the confluence of ethnic and gender discrimination), and mestizo men played at being Indian peasants. The municipal president of San Cristóbal (not known for his subtlety or for his commitment to democratic principles) highlighted for the public the difference between pluralism, represented by the forum and all present, and the armed route, the route that the EZLN had taken.

The agenda for the one-day meeting was extensive. What took the Zapatistas and the government months to discuss, the organizers of this consulta planned to conclude in a few hours. After the inaugural ceremony, participants divided themselves into six working groups: traditions and customs in the juridical and political organization of Indian communities, Indian culture, participation and political representation, customary (or consuetudinary) law and the exercise of justice, development and social well-being, and, finally, land and patrimony.

I attended the third working group on participation and political representation, along with about sixty others representing a diverse group of social and political organizations from around the state. There was a candidate representing the Partido Popular Socialista (PPS) from Mazapa de Madero (on the south-central border with Guatemala), a few Mexican academics, a member of the National Peasant Confederation (CNC) (who argued that the state of Chiapas had been robbed of its resources by the national government since 1824—the year Chiapas became part of Mexico), and members of an independent indigenous organic coffee cooperative, ISMAM, from the southern region of the state. There were bilingual teachers present, as well as representatives from civil society who demanded constitutional reforms to create indigenous electoral districts for state- and federal-level elections. Several participants demanded that municipal government be strengthened. One indigenous PRIista spoke in favor of sports as a mechanism to avoid vice. Several indigenous women from Pantelhó called for more indigenous women's participation in decision making at all levels. The same CNC representative who had spoken earlier about the federal government's exploitation of Chiapas praised Governor Absalón Castellanos (well known for his polarizing policies and for escalating the level of violence in Chiapas during his tenure in office, 1980–88), thanking him for visiting his village years ago and putting it on the map. Finally, a representative from the Multi-Ethnic Autonomous Regions (RAP) submitted a written proposal on political autonomy.

Despite the official tone and sponsorship of the forum, demands for autonomy were made and discussed in the afternoon *mesas* (roundtables) as well as during the plenary session. Participants juxtaposed autonomy against liberalism, defined autonomy as renovated federalism and as a mechanism for improving indigenous representation on federal, state, and municipal levels, and claimed that autonomy was a way to ensure respect and acknowledgment of Indian traditions and customs (*"usos y costumbres"*).

After breaking for a lunch that was provided by the sponsors (surely not an insignificant factor in drawing participants), a plenary session was held. At this session, representatives from each working group summarized their findings. The demands that were presented during this session were uncannily similar in tone and in content to the San Andrés Accords. Participants from several different groups called for greater juridical flexibility in recognizing Indian law to elect officials, for greater indigenous control of natural resources found on Indian land, and for the restitution of Article 27 to its original language. One proposal that I found particularly compelling was the demand that Indians own and operate national archeological sites and that indigenous peoples receive free admission to these sites.

The reports delivered were read aloud, but no time was allotted to discuss them or their feasibility. Immediately after the last summary was read, Ruiz Ferro, interim government, congratulated, not the participants, but himself and other governmental officials present: "Only a few years ago this type of event would have been unthinkable." Jacinto Arias, the token Indian representative, added a few words of Indian cosmology to the mix: "We said our words, the words that our hearts speak. We came together as brothers." (To protect himself from any accusation of being exclusionary, Arias also acknowledged the presence of "our mestizo comrades.") While not addressing directly any of the proposals or demands made that day, those on stage did speak out clearly against the "division of the national and state territory." In other words, there would be no political autonomy—at least not if it involved territory.

As I sat in the audience listening, I was not hopeful that any of the concrete demands made would be implemented. Political culture in Mexico, shaped largely by the PRI, rewarded flowery language and elevated ideas but was short on implementation. And even when legislation was passed, implementing legislation often was not written, making it impossible to begin enforcing the law. This was the case with the 1992 amendments to Article 4. The amended Article 4 recognized Mexico as a pluri-cultural nation and explicitly prohibited discrimination based on race. Yet, since no implementing legislation was written, the changes have had little impact.

I tried to think positively about something as I sat there. Was the INI's time running out, despite the familiar language and the pomp and circumstance? During the eighteen months I spent in Chiapas in 1995–96, it seemed to me and to many others that the INI's time was up. There was a lot of hope among those of us in Chiapas who witnessed the talks between the government and the EZLN that indigenismo would give way to an Indian-designed and implemented set of policy initiatives.

Had indigenismo changed after January 1, 1994? What did indigenismo after January 1, 1994, look like? In some ways it looked the same as indigenismo had always looked: it was paternalistic, folkloric, and staged. But I had to believe that it was not the same tired story. Despite the scripted nature of this event, its limited scope and time frame, new demands were made: for regional autonomy and indigenous electoral districts, for control over resources, and for women's rights. Despite the government's attempt to maintain the status quo, Indian politics in Mexico had indeed changed after January 1, 1994. If nothing else, the new demands being voiced did not fit as comfortably into the indigenist framework. Now, even the PRIista Indians were speaking a new language.

CHAPTER FOUR

TIERRA, LIBERTAD, Y AUTONOMÍA
Indian Autonomy and the EZLN Uprising

On April 11, 1998, forces totaling approximately one thousand men from the federal and Chiapas state judicial police, the offices of migration, and the Mexican army were sent in to dismantle the autonomous municipality of Ricardo Flores Magón (officially part of the municipality of Ocosingo). Less than one month later, on May 1, 1998, troops razed Tierra y Libertad, an autonomous municipality formerly known as Amparo Agua Tinta (see map 4, no. 31).[1] Ricardo Flores Magón and Tierra y Libertad are only two of a handful of autonomous municipalities razed by federal and state officials during the first six months of 1998. What was so threatening about Indian autonomy to warrant such a violent response from the Mexican government? And what exactly does it mean for a community or a region to declare itself "autonomous"?

Since the Zapatista uprising, the word "autonomy" has become a watchword for indigenous peoples across the country, including the National Indigenous Congress (CNI), formed in 1996. It is not, however, easy to define. Indian demands for autonomy are diverse and varied, due in part to their local character. Indian autonomy projects in Chiapas include, for example, the uniting of various municipalities to form regional governments that replace officially sanctioned municipal governments. (This practice has occurred mainly in EZLN-controlled areas of Chiapas.) Autonomy projects often include greater control over natural resources within indigenous regions. Autonomy is also defined as the exercise of Indian law in communities, that is, "usos y costumbres" ("traditions and customs"), in effect demanding that the state acknowledge a dual system of law. Today, in Chiapas, both the EZLN and unarmed indigenous civilian organizations are participating in a broad movement for autonomy on both regional and the community levels.

Demands for Indian autonomy in Chiapas today include a wide range of political, economic, social, and cultural rights. In the context created by the EZLN uprising, the Indian movement has made autonomy a central focus of its efforts to redefine the relationship between the state and indigenous peoples.

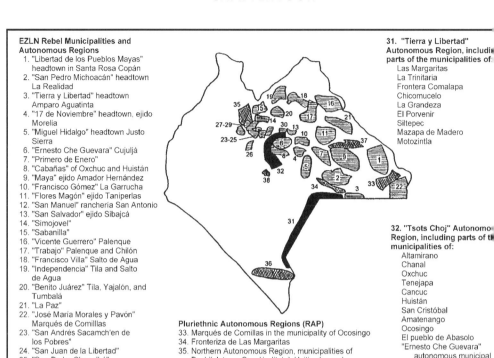

EZLN Rebel Municipalities and
Autonomous Regions
 1. "Libertad de los Pueblos Mayas"
    headtown in Santa Rosa Copán
 2. "San Pedro Michoacán" headtown
    La Realidad
 3. "Tierra y Libertad" headtown
    Amparo Aguatinta
 4. "17 de Noviembre" headtown, ejido
    Morelia
 5. "Miguel Hidalgo" headtown Justo
    Sierra
 6. "Ernesto Che Guevara" Cujuljá
 7. "Primero de Enero"
 8. "Cabañas" of Oxchuc and Huistán
 9. "Maya" ejido Amador Hernández
10. "Francisco Gómez" La Garrucha
11. "Flores Magón" ejido Taniperlas
12. "San Manuel" ranchería San Antonio
13. "San Salvador" ejido Sibajcá
14. "Simojovel"
15. "Sabanilla"
16. "Vicente Guerrero" Palenque
17. "Trabajo" Palenque and Chilón
18. "Francisco Villa" Salto de Agua
19. "Independencia" Tila and Salto
    de Agua
20. "Benito Juárez" Tila, Yajalón, and
    Tumbalá
21. "La Paz"
22. "José María Morales y Pavón"
    Marqués de Comilllas
23. "San Andrés Sacamch'en de
    los Pobres"
24. "San Juan de la Libertad"
25. "San Pedro Chenalhó"
26. "Zinacantán"
27. "Santa Catarina" Pantelhó and Sitalá
28. "Bochil"
29. "Magdalena de la Paz"
30. "San Juan K'ankujk'"

Pluriethnic Autonomous Regions (RAP)
33. Marqués de Comillas in the municipality of Ocosingo
34. Fronteriza de Las Margaritas
35. Northern Autonomous Region, municipalities of
    Bochil, Ixtapa, Soyaló, Jitotol, Huitiupán, and
    Simojovel
36. Soconusco Region, municipalities of Tapachula
    Huixtla, Tuzantán, Cacahuatán, and Unión Juárez
37. "Selva Las Tasas" Region
38. "Nicolás Ruiz" Autonomous Council

31. "Tierra y Libertad"
Autonomous Region, includi
parts of the municipalities of:
    Las Margaritas
    La Trinitaria
    Frontera Comalapa
    Chicomucelo
    La Grandeza
    El Porvenir
    Siltepec
    Mazapa de Madero
    Motozintla

32. "Tsots Choj" Autonomo
Region, including parts of t
municipalities of:
    Altamirano
    Chanal
    Oxchuc
    Tenejapa
    Cancuc
    Huistán
    San Cristóbal
    Amatenango
    Ocosingo
    El pueblo de Abasolo
    "Ernesto Che Guevara"
    autonomous municipal

SOURCE: CIEPAC, A.C

Map 4. Autonomous municipalities and regions of Chiapas, 1998. Courtesy of Centro de Investigaciones Económicas y Políticas de Acción Comunitaria (CIEPAC), based in San Cristóbal de las Casas, Chiapas.

Anthropologist and vocal advocate of Indian autonomy Héctor Díaz-Polanco speaks of the crucial impulse the Zapatista uprising gave the "autonomists":

What we have, then, if we could divide the entire long period into two parts: we could say that in the first phase, until 1994, the autonomist current within the national Indian movement is a minority, a relatively small group with certain prestige, with a certain amount of influence within the Indian movement but without being able to take control of the central direction of the movement as a whole. What the Zapatista uprising does in 1994 is give the movement a new direction. Beginning at this moment, autonomy becomes hegemonic within the more organized sectors of the movement and this manifests itself in the negotiation

process, in round one [Indian Rights and Culture] at San Andrés.
(Interview, May 21, 1996)[2]

The National Assembly of Indigenous Peoples in Support of Autonomy
(ANIPA) itself grew out of the dynamic generated in the wake of the Zapatista
rebellion. In the last months of 1994 and early 1995 the idea of forming a group of
Indian autonomy supporters emerged from within the national Indian movement.
After the two initial forums in the spring of 1995, the assembly met in late May
1995 in Yaqui Indian territory in Sonora. Subsequent assemblies were held in Oaxaca
in August, in Chiapas in December, and in Guerrero in April 1996. These assemblies served to organize many local and regional Indian organizations
around support for autonomy; the EZLN invited a substantial number of ANIPA
conference participants as advisors or guests in the official peace negotiations.[3]

The struggle for autonomy in Mexico has a long history. To be sure, ethno-
peasant and peasant organizations demanding increased autonomy vis-à-vis
the Mexican state before 1994 did not couch their demands within the frame of
Indian politics, as Indian organizations did after 1994. However, years of struggle
in support of autonomy on the part of peasant and ethno-peasant organizations set the stage for these later demands. Although indigenous peoples have
greatly expanded the use and meaning of "autonomy" since the Zapatista uprising, the term was not an unfamiliar one within the context of popular social
and political struggles in Mexico before 1994.

Historical Precedents

During the 1980s, popular groups became increasingly organized as coordinating
agencies, rather than as centralized, hierarchical organizations. As the state withdrew
from key socioeconomic sectors after 1982 and the power of client-based, state-
sponsored confederations waned, actors assumed greater responsibility for
organizing themselves. In the years preceding January 1, 1994, politicians
commonly heard demands for autonomy by popular organizations desiring
some degree of independence from the state. In fact, since the late 1970s,
autonomy has been a central demand among popular groups that have organized
outside official corporatist channels. In a nation with such a powerful state, it
should not be surprising that so many independent organizations in Mexico
have stressed autonomy from the state. The official party was extremely adept
at co-opting opposition leaders.[4]

Demands by popular organizations for some degree of independence from state control has been closely associated with calls for decentralization. Not a new theme in Mexican political circles, decentralization has been a central topic of discussion and legislation since the start of Miguel de la Madrid's administration in 1982, when the Mexican government embarked on a systematic program of decentralization. However, while the state made some substantial changes, such as shifting governmental agencies to the provinces, reworking the equations that distribute tax revenues to state governments, and shifting the locus of primary control over municipalities from the federal to the state level, municipal governments still only receive about 5 percent of total government outlays.[5]

Important antecedents to the autonomy demands that emerged from within the national Indian movement in the 1990s are found in the experiences of peasant organizations that attempted to augment their political and economic autonomy from the government. Fox and Gordillo argue that during the Echeverría administration (1970–76) state intervention in the countryside through governmental agencies increasingly resulted in the displacement of the CNC from decision making (Fox and Gordillo 1989: 141). Concomitantly, during this decade there was a gradual increase in the number of rural organizations that demanded greater autonomy. In 1975, for example, second-tier organizations, such as *uniones de ejidos,* were created to encourage two or more local producer groups (for example, ejidos, indigenous agrarian communities, or private-production societies and cooperatives) to join together. Rural Collective Interest Associations (ARICs) were also developed as third-tier organizations that united two or more second-level groups (Fox and Gordillo 1989: 142). Beginning with the administration of López Portillo (1976–82), there was a shift in state discourse from a focus on land reform to one focused on the productive process. The state targeted its resources at increasing agricultural productivity, for example, by providing credit and fertilizer. As the opportunity structure for collective action changed, many peasant organizations and new producer associations began to shift their attention to the appropriation of the productive process. Julio Moguel notes that from the mid-1980s, "the appropriation of the productive process was considered, from a perspective of autonomy, a concept that implied 'the smallest possible intervention of the state' (beginning by transferring a good deal of state functions to agricultural productive organizations)" (Moguel 1992: 16).

The political actors behind the creation of uniones de ejidos and ARICs designed them not as hierarchical corporatist models, but as autonomous networks. One of the most important examples of these networks is the National Union of Autonomous Regional Peasant Organizations (UNORCA) that was created in 1988 in an attempt to seek unity among distinct regional forces and "to act on the national level as a factor of convergence" (Hernández Navarro 1992: 238). Soon after the highly contested 1988 presidential elections in which Carlos Salinas de Gortari was declared the victor in the face of massive public outcry and accusations of fraud, Salinas called for a new pact between peasants and the state. On January 6, 1989, the national leader of the CNC, Maximiliano Silerio Esparza, announced the formation of a Permanent Agrarian Congress (CAP), which, according to Luis Hernández, "represented the end of the state monopoly of official peasant organizations, particularly the CNC, in their almost exclusive role of interlocutor with the State" (Hernández Navarro 1992: 239). The initial participants in CAP represented a diverse mix of official and independent peasant organizations, among them CNC, CCI (Independent Peasant Confederation), CAM (Mexican Agrarian Council), UGOCM (General Union of Workers and Peasants), UNORCA (National Union of Autonomous Regional Peasant Organizations), and CIOAC (Independent Central of Agricultural Workers and Peasants).

Why did Salinas seem so intent on supporting the efforts of autonomy by independent and semi-independent peasant organizations? Hernández Navarro argues that "for the Salinas government the agreements were, besides an instrument to apply his new politics to the rural sector, a mechanism to reassert his presence among the most productively organized peasant sectors in a moment in which many of them had shown sympathy for Cardenismo" (Hernández Navarro 1992: 244).[6] If peasant sectors agreed to take over responsibilities that the formerly interventionist state had performed, neoliberal technocrats such as Salinas and his team were more than willing to accommodate them. To be sure, the state had to ensure that this autonomy did not increase the costs of containing and controlling the sector as a whole and that it did not spill over into demands for political autonomy. However, under certain conditions, peasant autonomy fit well within the neoliberal state's goals to reduce its overall size and activity, especially in social spheres.

While Salinas used CAP as a way of controlling independent peasant organizations by offering them concessions and a privileged relationship with the state, monies from the National Solidarity Program (PRONASOL) also catered to these new, more autonomous channels of peasant organization. During the first year of PRONASOL's operation (1989), funds went directly to the municipal level, either to municipal governments or to local solidarity committees, thereby bypassing state governments and regional bosses. Later, the state channeled monies for project implementation through state-level Convenios Unicos de Desarrollo (CUDs), which attenuated much of the program's decentralization effect and gave governors enormous power (Hernández Navarro 1992: 246).

Although demands for autonomy within peasant organizations centered around the right to make decisions about means and ends internally, by the 1990s Indian activists in Mexico—buttressed by international legislation protecting Indian rights—began to talk about "Indian autonomy." Indigenous peoples in the Americas became the focus of a great deal of attention after 1992 with the upsurge of indigenous activism that emerged around the Quincentenary of the "discovery" of America. Rigoberta Menchú, a Maya woman from Guatemala, was awarded the Nobel Peace Prize in 1992, and soon after the United Nations declared an international decade of indigenous peoples. Indian peoples through-out the Americas, including Mexico, began to look to international organiza-tions and legislation in an effort to pressure their national governments to pass legislation protecting Indian rights. The most progressive legislation in the world at this time was the International Labor Organization's Convention 169.

International Visibility for Indian Rights

The Mexican Senate's ratification of Convention 169, the International Labor Organization's legislation on Indian rights and the protection of Indian work-ers in September 1990, provided an important spark for national-level indig-enous organization in Mexico. When the ILO approved the legislation in Geneva in 1989, it replaced the previous legislation in force since 1957 (Convention 107). The integrationist and protectionist language used in Convention 107 was re-placed by language that acknowledges the importance of indigenous peoples' participation in decisions that affect them as well as Indians' right to set their own development priorities. Another important shift from Convention 107 to 169 was the latter's use of the term "peoples," which replaced "populations." The authors of Convention 169 point out, however, that the use of the term "peoples" "shall not be construed as having any implications as regards the rights which may attach to the term under international law" (C169 Indigenous and Tribal Peoples Convention 1989). In general terms, and compared to previ-ous legislation, Convention 169 represents a clear and detailed outline of specific economic, cultural, social, and political rights for indigenous peoples and of state responsibilities toward them. To date, Convention 169 is the most pro-gressive legislation on Indian rights in the world and its importance to indig-enous organization in the Americas cannot be overstated (see Assies, van der

Haar, and Hoekema 2000: chap. 1; Dandler 1999; Hannum 1990: 77).

During the drafting of Convention 169, indigenous organizations fought hard in favor of wording that *required* indigenous peoples' consent concerning policies that affected them and that gave indigenous peoples control over natural resources on their land. These provisions were not included in the final document, but Convention 169 does emphasize states' responsibility to consult with indigenous peoples and to involve them in decision-making processes (Schulting 1997: 110, cited in Van Cott 2000a: 262).

Like all international legislation, Convention 169 functions mainly as a series of recommendations, despite the fact that countries recognize it as legally binding (so long as it does not contradict existing national law). After Norway, Mexico was the second country in the world to ratify it. With the ratification of Convention 169, the Salinas administration sought to co-opt the increasingly vocal Indian opposition and growing activism in the preparations leading up to the 1992 Quincentenary of Columbus's "discovery of America" (see Díaz-Polanco 1997: 130–32).

Although Convention 169 had few immediate, practical consequences for the relationship between the Mexican state and indigenous peoples, it gave the Indian movement a legal referent of enormous strategic value (Hernández Navarro 1997: 32). In addition, its ratification gave the national Indian movement a political and legal platform on which it could make demands to reform the Mexican constitution.[7] The promulgation of strong international legislation protecting Indian rights also boosted national-level indigenous organization. After the ILO approved the legislation in Geneva in 1989, the Inter-American Indigenist Institute, which is housed in Mexico City, invited prominent indigenous activists, such as Araceli Burguete and Margarito Ruiz (Independent Front of Indian Peoples, FIPI), to a roundtable to discuss the implications of the legislation in Mexico. According to Burguete, at this roundtable she and Ruiz "suddenly understood that what we were talking about was a question of international law. From that point on, we took note that there was much work to be done in the area of Indian rights."[8]

After this roundtable, Burguete and Ruiz—along with other Indian leaders such as Carlos Beas Torres (Union of Indigenous Communities of the Northern Zone of the Isthmus, UCIZONI) and Antonio Hernández Cruz (CIOAC)—formed the Regional Council of Indian Peoples in the Mexico City metropolitan area. During the early 1990s, this regional council became the base on which a national *consulta* (survey or poll) was organized to work toward the constitutional recognition of Indian rights. At the same time, activists in Mexico and throughout the Americas met to prepare for the countercelebrations that would accompany the Quincentenary. Beas, Ruiz, Burguete, and others from UCIZONI planned the first Human Rights Encounter of Indigenous Peoples, which was held in Matías Romero, Oaxaca, in 1990.[9] From 1989 to 1993, activists within the Indian movement organized hundreds of workshops on Indian rights, which they gave to organizations around the country.[10] The activists used illustrations and stick figures didactically to explain Convention 169. The idea was to teach the general notion of Indian rights, such as those found in Convention 169.[11]

With the ratification of Convention 169, the Mexican government assumed the responsibility of modifying national legislation and state policy accordingly (Hindley 1996: 232). Anticipating this, in April 1989, the Salinas administration formed the National Commission of Justice for Indian Peoples (CNJPI), which served as a consultative organ of the INI (Ewen 1994). Even before Convention 169 was ratified, the commission had begun a process of consultation and survey polling to create a database for subsequent legislative changes. According to José del Val, INI's director of research and cultural promotion, the CNJPI and INI officials held 136 meetings with different indigenous and nonindigenous groups, opinion leaders, jurists, anthropologists, as well as official unions, municipal presidents, federal deputies, and state governors in different parts of the country to gather information for future legislative changes (cited in Hindley 1996: 233).

Yet Indian groups quickly charged the CNJPI and the INI with excluding them from the decision-making process. They complained that when their opinions were sought out, they were advised of meeting times at the last minute and in an ad hoc fashion. In addition, Indians were only one of several groups polled, and no Indians were members of the commission (Díaz-Polanco 1997: 130; Hindley 1996: 233). Despite such criticism from Indian leaders and organizations, administration officials pushed the reform process forward. On December 7, 1990, President Salinas presented Congress with his proposed reforms to Article 4. A new first paragraph was added:

> The Mexican Nation has a multicultural composition, originally based on its indigenous peoples. The law will protect and promote the development of their languages, cultures, traditions, customs, resources, and specific forms of social organization and will guarantee their members effective access to the jurisdiction of the State. In the agrarian judgments and procedures in which they are part, their juridical practices and customs will be taken into account in the terms established by the law.[12]

Significantly, with this reform the government abandoned assimilation and acknowledged the plural composition of the Mexican nation. Native peoples are also referred to as "peoples," a term that has more authority in international law, for example, than "groups."[13] Any collective rights to be exercised by the indigenous as peoples, however, were severely diluted by the location of Article 4 within the framework of the constitution, which is situated in chapter 1 of the first section, entitled "Of Individual Guarantees."[14] Hindley argues that both the position of the reform within the constitution and the context of the existing paragraphs of Article 4 "effectively sever any connection between indigenous peoples and sovereignty, which might arise from their association with the Nation" (Hindley 1996: 235; see Díaz-Polanco 1997: 131). Additionally, because the government anticipated and pushed through the reforms to Article 4 so quickly, national Indian movement leaders had little opportunity to elaborate and gain support for their own proposal. Instead of presenting a counterproposal, Indian leaders were limited to critiquing the shortcomings of the government's reforms.[15]

During the same time the Salinas administration was proposing reforms to Article 4, activists were preparing countercelebrations of Columbus's "discovery" of America. In Mexico, a grassroots campaign of "500 years of Indian, Black, and Popular Resistance" began in 1989 and increased in intensity until the Quincentenary year of 1992. Activists participated in numerous continent-wide meetings and congresses—the first of which was held in Bogotá, Colombia, on October 12, 1989—that served to systematize analysis and to articulate a unified platform on Indian rights. In the second congress held in Guatemala in 1991, a decision was made to incorporate Latin American black and popular sectors; originally, the campaign consisted exclusively of indigenous activists.[16] One of the most significant results of the organization that took place in preparation for the Quincentenary was the coordination among popular groups and expansion of possibilities for united action (see Gabriel 1994).

Convention 169 gave Indian activists a leg to stand on as they pressured the Mexican state to recognize native peoples as peoples, with rights accorded them in international law. Indian activists' demands for autonomy in the 1990s went beyond demands for land reform. They demanded territory and self-rule.

Models of Autonomy: Regional, Communal, and Municipal

The current debate on Indian autonomy in Mexico has three tiers. The first consists of intracommunity debates. These debates have taken place among indigenous men and women, among Protestants and Catholics, and among members of different political parties within indigenous communities. The second level of discussion has occurred between Indians and non-Indians over the viability of creating autonomous governments within the Mexican federalist system. Will autonomous regions be multi-ethnic or monoethnic? Will they include mestizos? Will individual rights be respected alongside collective rights, or will one set of rights take preference over another? These discussions have occurred both in the press and in forums and conferences where Indian and non-Indian academics and activists have participated.[17] A third level of discussion has taken place between national government representatives and the Indian movement, represented most broadly by the National Indigenous Congress. On this level, the debate has revolved around the kind of autonomy projects each side supports; the three principal autonomy projects currently circulating are regional, municipal, and communal-based projects.

In the forums and congresses leading up to the signing of the San Andrés accords, two principal autonomy projects were on the political agenda: one model for regional and one for communal autonomy.[18] The first is the RAP project, which has been most closely identified with the National Indigenous Assembly in Support of Autonomy, although ANIPA has incorporated all three levels of autonomy in its legislative proposal. The second proposes communal autonomy, which the Mixe people of Oaxaca have most strongly advocated. The Mixe do not reject municipal and regional autonomy proposals, but simply assert that the level of communal autonomy best represents their situation. Although there has been tension between the two camps since 1994, open conflict between the regional and communal autonomy proponents has not been the rule; both ANIPA and CNI documents support protective legislation for all three levels of autonomy. During the first round of peace negotiations in Chiapas, however, EZLN advisors engaged in heated debate concerning the extent to which they could push the government to accept a regional autonomy proposal. Finally, the majority of advisors decided that in the present context (January 1996) of military encroachment and hostility, the EZLN needed to move quickly to forge a consensus on an autonomy agreement the government would sign. Although the government was willing to agree in principle to some degree of communal and municipal autonomy, advisors from both sides abandoned the regional proposal.[19]

Despite their differences, both autonomy proposals insist on the possibility of political representation for Indian peoples without the participation of political parties. Many indigenous peoples have spoken out about the division that partisan political conflict has caused in communities.[20] Both proposals support the notion of independent candidacies so as to broaden the political playing field. Both regional and communal autonomy proponents link autonomy to effective political representation. They have proposed the creation of one proportionally elected national district *(circunscripción)* from which an indigenous representative would be elected (there are currently five such districts from which two hundred deputies are elected [forty per district]).[21] For indigenous autonomy proponents, political autonomy does not mean exclusion from national political representation.

Proponents of both proposals have consistently reiterated that autonomy does not denote separatism and that it is not to be confused with the sovereignty of the Mexican nation-state. In the first days of the uprising, the president and other high-ranking officials accused the Zapatistas of being foreigners and of threatening the nation-state. The EZLN quickly responded that they were simply asking that the promises of the constitution and the Mexican Revolution be fulfilled for all Mexicans. In the first peace negotiations held in the cathedral of San Cristóbal in February 1994, the Zapatistas presented a Mexican flag to the president's chief negotiator, Manuel Camacho. The Zapatistas told Camacho that they had come to the negotiation table to see if indigenous peoples and the poor of Mexico could live better under that flag.[22]

Although some right-of-center Mexican intellectuals continue to insist that Indian autonomy proposals are separatist and encourage the isolation of indigenous peoples, Indians have responded by claiming that the autonomy proposals are intended to help democratize the country and not to create Indian enclaves.[23] For example, Héctor Aguilar Camín, renowned public intellectual and novelist, has insisted that "the indigenous peoples and individuals who have had less bad fortune than most in this country are those who have developed an increased level of contact, mixing, and integration with the basic currents of national life. I believe that the best opportunities for indigenous peoples lie in contact, not in isolation" (cited in Correa and Corro 1996: 23). In a public debate with Aguilar Camin on the pages of the Mexico City daily *La Jornada* in October 1996, Mixe leader Regino Montes (founder of SER) argued, "The demand for autonomy should not be viewed as an attempt at isolation from the rest of the country." He insisted, "We understand the recognition of our autonomy as something that will benefit and strengthen not only indigenous peoples but will consolidate the unity of the entire nation."

Both autonomy projects challenge the pact that links mestizo identity to the Mexican nation, and they both support the creation of a new democratic national project and constitution. RAP proponents claim, "The RAP and a regime of autonomy strengthens national unity and integration. It favors harmonious coexistence among the many sociocultural groups and would strengthen democratic life." For their part, the *comunalistas* state that "state recognition of our autonomy will benefit and strengthen not only indigenous people but will consolidate the unity of the entire nation" (organization documents). Although both proposals reject mestizo identity as a foundation for the modern Mexican state, they differ on how to construct a more plural, multicultural Mexican nation.

Autonomous Multi-ethnic Regions (RAP)

The centerpiece of the RAP project is the addition of another level of government between the state and municipality: the regional government. This regional government would have partial jurisdiction in political, administrative, economic, social, cultural, educational, judicial, resource-management, and environmental spheres. Its representatives would negotiate with state and municipal governments concerning areas of overlapping jurisdiction. The National Indigenous Assembly in Support of Autonomy has been identified with the RAP project since it was formed in early 1994, but it has modified its position after each successive assembly held. For example, in May 1995, the Second Assembly took place in Yaqui-Mayo territory in Sonora. The experience of listening to Indians who have lived in monoethnic autonomous regions for decades forced ANIPA leaders to accept the possibility of monoethnic regions and not just the multi-ethnic ones originally proposed. After assemblies in Oaxaca in August 1995 and Chiapas in December 1995, ANIPA accepted a gradualist formulation of its objective by admitting the coexistence of communal and municipal autonomy in areas where communities were not ready to join larger, regional associations.

RAP political documents attribute the marginalization and poverty of indigenous peoples to unequal and subordinate relations between Indians and non-Indians. They point to the social and political exclusion that they have suffered since the conquest to explain the inequality that exists, rather than to sociocultural or ethnic characteristics. They insist on the fact that isolation is not the cause of the poverty and marginalization in which they live, but rather these result from the lack of access to political power:

> These same peoples [indigenous] have been subject to the most

severe and inhuman conditions of marginalization and poverty. For example, in municipalities with an indigenous majority, the level of illiteracy is 43 percent, more than three times the national average; 58 percent of children under five years old do not attend school and close to a third of the population between six and fourteen years of age cannot read or write. . . . The causes of this marginalization and poverty cannot be attributed to sociocultural or ethnic characteristics of indigenous peoples, but rather to the unequal and subordinate relations that have been imposed on them, to the social and political exclusion that they have suffered during three centuries of colonial regime and that they continue to suffer since Mexico became an independent country. (ANIPA 1996)

RAP proponents have stated that "it is necessary to rethink the project of the homogenous state" while reiterating that their project is not a separatist one. "The regime of autonomy proposes to strengthen unity and national integration, favoring the increase of harmony among all the sociocultural components of the Mexican nation and providing the impetus for democratic life" (ANIPA 1996). Supporters of the RAP project assert that it is possible to enjoy the constitutional liberties guaranteed by the liberal state while simultaneously "conquering spaces to reproduce difference." Because racial and cultural discrimination have been so pervasive in Mexican society, Indian leaders have insisted that the resulting inequalities cannot be addressed on the basis of equal rights for all Mexicans under the constitution. Indians are now demanding rights based on the very ethnic and racial differences mestizos have used against them. At the National Indian Forum held in San Cristóbal in January 1996, one Indian noted that "with the term 'Indian' they oppressed us, with the term 'Indian' we will be liberated. We want to be recognized as Otomí, Purépecha, and Maya."

The notion of autonomy, especially as expressed by proponents of the RAP project, highlights the profoundly political nature of space. In autonomous regions, leaders would draw new political boundaries to enhance the possibilities of electing indigenous representatives to local, state, and national congresses. RAP supporters recognize political representation as being partially constituted by spatial boundaries, and Indian leaders have linked spatial boundaries and political power to demands concerning larger national issues such as federalism and democracy. In the final document emerging from ANIPA's fifth meeting held in San Cristóbal in December 1995 one of the principal reasons cited for the "miserable and oppressive situation of indigenous peoples in Mexico today" is the extreme centralism

Figure 4. The regional market at Las Margaritas has served to bring Tojolabals from different ejidos together on a regular basis. Courtesy of National Indigenous Institute, Mexico City.

of the current Mexican political system (ANIPA 1996). ANIPA participants argue that the government cannot recognize genuine de jure autonomy without a profound restructuring of political and economic power in Mexico.

RAP documents and conversations with RAP proponents suggest that the RAP proposal does not attempt to substitute a new nationalism for the current one; rather, it proposes a restructuring of the Mexican state. As Díaz-Polanco states, "The regional autonomy project seeks to transform the present system of political organization and the actual state regime (centralized, exclusive, authoritarian, homogenizing) and replace it with a state of autonomies that make a respect for plurality possible and opens the doors for the participation of Indian peoples" (Díaz-Polanco 1996). Because Indians have practiced autonomy largely due to state neglect and abandonment, during the Dialogue of San Andrés PRI government officials reacted strongly against the RAP proposal—fearful that strong, autonomous regions would reduce their electoral support as well as wrest control of natural resources from the state.

On October 12, 1994, the CEOIC, an organization formed immediately after the uprising that united 280 peasant and Indian organizations in support of a peaceful resolution of the conflict, declared seven autonomous RAPs in the

Figure 5. Having swept the church, Tojolabal region, Altamirano municipality. Photo courtesy of the photographer, Gemma van der Haar.

state of Chiapas. In the days and weeks following the CEOIC's declaration, activists organized a series of regional forums throughout Chiapas to discuss the details of how these regions would function in practice. For these activists, the Tojolabal experiment with regional government—the "Gobierno Tojolabal"—served as a model. Although this model may be transferable to other regions of Chiapas and Mexico, the continuing strength of local, ejido identities, as well as intracommunity divisions and tensions among Tojolabals, point to the potential difficulties that could arise.

Autonomy among the Tojolabals

That the Tojolabal experiment with regional autonomy should have become a model in Chiapas and nationally is not without irony. The emergence of regional government in the Tojolabal region over the last generation was possible in large part because the community structures common to other indigenous regions of Mexico were destroyed in the nineteenth century by mestizo landowners. As a result, a strong local, community identity has not been as prevalent in the Tojolabal region as it has been in other indigenous regions throughout Mexico. Moreover, the Tojolabal custom of making pilgrimages, or *romerías,* to neighboring Tzeltal and Chuj-Maya holy places has facilitated greater openness toward other Indian ethnic groups than that seen in the highlands of Chiapas, for example.[24] Although romerías are infrequent today among Tojolabal communities, they previously served as privileged spaces for inter-communal contact and communication (Ruz 1994: 47). Ruz notes that romerías were one of the four most common mechanisms or rituals of interethnic coop-eration in the Tojolabal community, the others being loans, the barter of goods, and the Sunday market in the regional center (Ruz 1993: 305) (see figure 4).[25]

Migration from areas of traditional Tojolabal settlement to the Lacandon rain forest beginning in the 1950s and accelerating through the 1980s enhanced the possibilities for interethnic organization. Community structures were reformed and rebuilt in the Lacandon jungle, where Indian peoples from Chiapas and—to a lesser degree from throughout Mexico—attempted to create a new life for themselves and their families. The coffee cooperatives, ejido unions, and church-based organizations that formed in the jungle tended to be based on common goals rather than on discrete community identities.[26] This trend to more inclusive, regional forms of "ethnic" organization accelerated in the 1990s with the growing presence and strength of the EZLN. The widespread break-up of Tojolabal com-munities in the nineteenth century, then, and the extensive migration to the Lacandon jungle in the second half of twentieth that made the Tojolabals distinc-tive from Chiapas's other Mayas historically—particularly the highland peoples—actually prepared them to be trailblazers in the regional forms of organization and development that are now being thrust on indigenous groups throughout the state as their community-based social organizations fall into crisis.

Powerful forces work at cross-purposes to split and diffuse the consolidation of regional identity and regional autonomy processes. Among the Tojolabal, the ejido continues to be a principal reference point; community and regional identities and loyalties coexist in tension. Araceli Burguete, an activist closely associated with the Tojolabal experiment with regional government, speaks about this tension:

> In our view, the ejido has been a disarticulating experience with re-spect to identity. [The idea of regional identity] was something that we tried to forge among the Tojolabals and that we could not because it would have meant dividing the ejido borders. We felt that we had to divide the ejidal borders and return to the idea of a Tojolabal territory. That is, the municipal borders of Las Margaritas, Comitán, Altamirano,

do not matter. We are Tojolabal people. And the compañeros [Tojolabals] said no, so-and-so is from Bajucú [an ejido in the Cañada Tojolabal], so-and-so is from 20 de noviembre [an ejido], so-and-so is from Justo Sierra [ejido], so-and-so is from Gavino [ejido Gavino Vásquez], and so on. Their identity was based on the ejido, and we did not want to reinforce ejidal identity. For us, ejidal identity constituted an obstacle to conceptualizing a Tojolabal identity. Also in this period [late 1980s], the idea of a Maya-Tojolabal identity began to mature. We understood this as we developed a closer relationship with the Guatemalans, including visits and caravans between the Guatemalan Maya and Tojolabal regions. For us, the concept of Maya-Tojolabal was a concept that unified all Tojolabals with all Mayas: Tzotzils, Tzeltals, and so on. It signifies that the Mayas are one people, and at the same time multiethnic. . . . We always saw Tojolabals as a large region in which the municipalities were an obstacle: an obstacle to unity. (Interview, April 9, 1996)

Conflicts within individual communities may also work against the formation of regional unification and identification. Since the 1980s, for example, affiliation with Protestant religious groups has risen among the Tojolabal population; by 1990, one-fifth of the population of Las Margaritas identified themselves as Protestant. Growing political divisions among Tojolabals challenge the notion of a unified Tojolabal ethnic community.

José Antonio Vásquez, regional leader of CIOAC-Comitán and Tojolabal from Bajucú, Las Margaritas speaks of the gap between autonomy practiced at the regional level and that practiced at local levels. Among the Tojolabals, he says, "people are autonomous, but in their own way, from their own community, as they see it" (interview, November 22, 1995). While Tojolabal leaders from CIOAC-Comitán have been at the forefront of the autonomy movement in Chiapas and on the national level, Vásquez admits that he does not clearly understand the details of the RAP project:

> When at times I have spoken to the people about the RAP project, it is not clear to me yet what it actually consists of. Or maybe I am seeing it like the people do because I am judging it with them from their perspective. . . . Words on paper are one thing. The law is one thing but the trick is how it is practiced. That is how I see it. I am in agreement with autonomy. Maybe it just needs to be explained to the people better.[27]

Similarly, local CIOAC leaders of the ejido union Pueblos Tojolabales told me that they could not comment on the RAP that had been declared in the region where they live and work because "we don't know anything about it" (interview, December 18, 1995). Yet, when I asked them more specific questions about the election of authorities, internal forms of justice, and community organization, I noted that the daily practice of autonomy is operative in Tojolabal communities. One local Tojolabal leader spoke of the fact that most problems are resolved within the community in negotiation with local authorities: "Now, if the problem is very grave we work it out within the CIOAC. We see how it can be arranged there and smooth things out. As a community and as an organization we see how things can be worked out. Our problems are resolved within the community or the organization [CIOAC]" (interview, December 18, 1995). Comments made by local ejido union leaders suggest that members of the PRI-affiliated union in the region, Lucha Campesina, often present complaints at the state prosecutor's office in Las Margaritas, whereas CIOAC-affiliated union members tend to work problems out within communities or within regional structures, such as the CIOAC. Opposition political activists make demands for autonomy more frequently than activists affiliated with the official party. According to local leaders from the ejido union Tierra y Libertad (also affiliated with CIOAC) in the Lacandon jungle region of Las Margaritas, autonomy means that the people have decision-making capacity to name their authorities: "For example, in the community and the municipality, the people have the right to name their own authorities. . . . All the work that is being done in the community here makes it easier for the people to understand what autonomy is because they are now beginning; it is already working" (interview, January 2, 1996).

While RAP proponents aim to strengthen the Tojolabals' sense of regional identity, for this to succeed considerable work must still be done to build up regional and pan-ethnic organizations. This is because, in practice, most Tojolabals, despite their regional affiliations, continue to identify strongly with local spaces as well. Accordingly, within the Indian movement, demands that transcend specific locales and territories—for cultural revival, national bilingual education, and protection from racial discrimination—are typically juxtaposed, and even subordinated, to demands for land. Given that this connection to the land has been a source of indigenous peoples' continuity, a key question for the Indian movement is thus how to strengthen regional and pan-ethnic identities precisely at the moment when the tie to land is becoming increasingly tenuous.

RAP proponents have attempted to transcend local identities by deliberately designing their project to be multi-ethnic, again taken from the Tojolabal experience of living side by side with Tzeltals in Altamirano and mestizos in the municipalities of La Independencia and La Trinitaria. As Araceli Burguete put it, "Our experience is that it was possible to live together with autonomous governments that were governments for all people because we had come from an experience of political formation where Tzotzils, Tzeltals, Tojolabals, and mestizos all shared one region" (interview, April 9, 1996). Again, the Tojolabals' rich history of regional organization and identity coexists with loyalties to ejidos and individual ejido communities. These ejidal loyalties are especially strong in regions of older settlements, like the Cañada Tojolabal for instance, while multi-ethnic organization has been easier in the Lacandon jungle, where the Tojolabal residents are people who have left their communities of origin to create new ones.

In the months following the Zapatista uprising, the attention of Mexico's politicians and the public at large focused briefly on Indian rights. Indian leaders in Chiapas, in turn, hoping to take advantage of what they understood might be a limited window of opportunity, rushed to ensure legal protection for some form of autonomy. As Antonio Hernández Cruz remembers, even though there had been little practical, grassroots preparation for the RAPs in Chiapas "we had to declare the RAPs where the conditions were present . . . [and] where they are not . . . say that we are in the process of forming them."[28] This pressure, in part, explains the CEOIC's declaration of seven RAPs in Chiapas on October 12, 1994. While understandable on a strategic level, however, the follow-up and operationalization of the RAP has been very difficult because they were in a sense designed "from above" by leaders—both Indian and mestizo. This is not to say that autonomy does not exist as a daily practice: the long history of electing local leaders and exercising local forms of justice and community decision-making illustrates that the practice of autonomy is widespread in Chiapas. What it does mean, however, is that much political work remains to be done to consolidate the practice of regional organization among Tojolabals and other indigenous peoples in the state.

Communal Autonomy Project

According to proponents of the community-based (comunalista) autonomy project—the most vocal of whom are Mixes, Zapotecs, and Mixtecs from northern and central Oaxaca—indigenous resistance is located first and foremost at the community level. Jaime Martínez Luna, Zapotec anthropologist and comunalista, describes the central importance of the community in maintaining the history and traditions of indigenous peoples:

> The community has been responsible for the fact that we have not forgotten our customs, fiestas, and ways of thinking. By necessity, perhaps, our villages have taught us to fulfill community responsibilities [*cargos*], *tequio* [communal work], and participation in the communal assembly. Our elders have transmitted, from generation to generation, the limits of our territory, histories about land, the mountains, hills, and the caves. (Martínez Luna 1993: 159)

For Martínez Luna, community identity is the result "of the dynamic between our ancestral and present organization, which rests on communal work: work to make decisions (assembly), work for coordination (cargo), work for construction (tequio), and work to enjoy (fiesta)" (Martínez Luna 1993: 160). Martínez Luna and other comunalista supporters clearly distinguish their definition of community identity from those who have viewed indigenous communities as insulated "closed corporate communities" (Wolf 1957). Martínez Luna makes this point when he insists that "the community is not a symbol of harmony, nor is the community the perfect expression of the cosmic. On the contrary, the community confronts enemies daily; communality is created in the tearing down and building up of consensus, of work, and of communal power" (Martínez Luna 1993: 162).[29]

Comunalista activists do not preclude the possibility of broader regional organization and coordination among communities, although they tend to focus their energy on strengthening communal institutions and practices. Martínez Luna, for example, views regional organization and coordination as appropriate for the resolution of particular, concrete projects requiring larger coordination: "Regional organization is the result of a particular conjuncture or, conversely, an answer to very specific demands" (Martínez Luna 1993: 167). Comunalistas, however, are concerned that regional coordination may create propitious conditions for the creation of regional bosses and insist that "we must never lose, or risk losing, the material and political bases of the community" (Martínez Luna 1993: 166). For comunalistas, regional associations are most successful when they are built from the community level. Comunalista proponent Regino Montes has argued that the guarantee of communal rights actually promotes the exercise of Indians' individual rights because membership and participation in a local community reduces high levels of uncertainty and vulnerability: "We are peoples and, therefore, require the recognition of our collective rights in order to enjoy the exercise of our individual rights" (Regino n.d.: 134).

The caution exercised by Oaxacan comunalista advocates regarding the creation of regional bossism has deep historic roots. Although in Chiapas indigenous struggles have been targeted primarily against the exploitation and repression of mestizo cacique/landowners, in Oaxaca, indigenous struggles against neighboring Indian caciques have been the norm (see Stephen 2002). Yet, despite the fact that the community continues to be the primary space of identification and sociocultural reproduction in Oaxaca (as well as in the majority of Mexico's indigenous areas), since the late 1970s sixteen indigenous communities in the Mixe area of northern Oaxaca have formed a loosely associated region. The Mixe people live and work in their individual communities, but the area functions as a region for the commercialization of agricultural products, the provision of transportation, and the coordination of activities that supersede the community level. In part, this regional identification has been possible due to particular historical circumstances, specifically the formation of an ethnically Mixe district in the eastern part of the Sierra Juárez during the Cárdenas administration. This special district was created in 1938 and forms part of Oaxaca's governing structure today (Stephen 1996: 11).[30]

For the Mixes of eastern Oaxaca, the exercise of autonomy is practiced from below, that is, from the community level. They worry that a regional structuring of autonomy could create new bosses and reduce the freedom of individual ethnic groups. They tend to favor monoethnic over multi-ethnic autonomy because of long-standing conflicts they have had with other Indian peoples in the region, especially the Zapotecs. After the Mexican Revolution, the Mixe fought for the creation of an ethnically distinct district that was established in 1938. This region was formed in part as an attempt to redress the historic economic and political domination of the Mixe by the Zapotec people (Stephen 1996). Whereas in Chiapas mestizos have historically governed municipalities in majority Indian districts, Oaxaca's 435 municipalities (more than one-third of Mexico's total number of municipalities) have been governed by Indians. This is not to suggest that Indian municipal leaders in Oaxaca have been less corrupt and heavy-handed than Chiapan mestizo functionaries. Nevertheless, the municipality in Oaxaca (which in many cases is coterminous with the community) enjoys greater legitimacy than its counterpart in Chiapas and in other largely indigenous states of Mexico. In Oaxaca, independent Indian leaders have attempted to recapture municipal power, whereas in other states Indian organizations have fought to bypass municipal authorities who have been their natural enemies by establishing direct contact with the national government (Victoria 1996: 40).

One communal autonomy proposal issued from the best-known organization supporting communal autonomy in Mexico, the Oaxaca-based Servicios del Pueblo Mixe (SER), recognizes the merits of the RAPs proposed by ANIPA, but notes that "there is not, today, a clear consciousness in our region concerning the convenience of installing a RAP and is therefore not in our present interests." Rather, for the Mixe people, "the communal level of autonomy is the most adequate form to preserve the aforementioned values of the community" (Servicios del Pueblo Mixe 1996). Similar to the RAP project, communal autonomy proposals condition the exercise of individual rights on the recognition of collective rights. According to the SER proposal, the Mexican state needs to take affirmative action "not to create inequalities among Mexicans but to redress those inequalities that already exist."

The Mixe people of western Oaxaca are not the only example of ethnic resistance and communal autonomy in the state. The Zapotec people of Juchitán have a long history of obstinate self-determination. From the colonial period, Juchitán has emerged as a site of ethnic resistance rooted in illicit commerce, in defense of communal lands and salt flats, and in opposition to colonial and mestizo Tehuantepec (the capital of the Isthmus region) (Campbell 1994: 242). Juchitecos, in contrast to other Indian groups in Mexico, have historically cultivated a positive sense of being Zapotec. Howard Campbell notes that during the nineteenth and twentieth centuries, conflicts hardened between residents of Juchitán and authorities of Tehuantepec, Oaxaca City (the state capital), and Mexico City (the national capital). Juchitecos turned in on themselves and developed a fierce localism, regional identity, and love for the Zapotec language and customs (Campbell 1994: 243; Díaz-Polanco 1997: 134–39; Rubin 1996, 1998). During a period of political opening under the progressive administration of Luis Echeverría (1970–76), the Coalition of Peasants and Students of the Isthmus (COCEI) was born. Unlike previous ethnic organizations active within the Juchitán community, COCEI espoused class politics and a politicized cultural identity. The COCEI used ethnic identity to win a class battle with upperclass Zapotecs who claimed that they were the "legitimate" representatives of Zapotec culture, as opposed to peasant and working-class Indians. As Stephen points out, the COCEI used a class-based ethnic identity to fight a very specific class battle within Juchitán (Stephen 1996: 27).

In the 1980s, the COCEI was the first leftist opposition group in the country to be recognized by PRI political leaders in municipal elections. During the two-and-a-half-year term of the "people's government," the COCEI embarked on an ambitious cultural program centered on the Zapotec language, attempted to regain land lost by peasants to large landholders, and developed public works projects that would benefit the city's poor majority (Rubin 1996). In 1986, it took part in municipal elections and joined a coalition municipal government. In 1989 it won the elections and governed jointly (but in a majority role) with the PRI. The COCEI won again in 1992 and governed the city until 1995. Unfortunately, attempts at applying the Zapotec experience to other Indian areas in Mexico have not been very fruitful. It is a movement whose experiences are largely based on the particular history of Zapotec Indians from one city. Zapotecs from Juchitán have been reticent to include even Zapotec neighbors in their project (Stephen 1996).

The regional and communal autonomy projects are closely linked to particular geographic spaces and historical experience. Chiapan Indian leaders have been instrumental in the leadership of ANIPA; the RAP project originated in Chiapas under the guidance of Tojolabal leaders Margarito Ruiz and Antonio Hernández. The SER proposal is the product of Mixe experience in a largely monoethnic region where infighting among Indian peoples has occurred for generations. Indian struggles in Chiapas have been directed primarily against an exploitative ladino oligarchy; in Oaxaca conflicts are typically waged against hostile Indian neighbors. Because of the widespread system of debt-servitude and sharecropping that often forced Indians from different ethnic groups to mix together and opened up the possibility for regional association and organization, Chiapan Indian peoples have cooperated across ethnic groups to a degree unimaginable in Oaxaca. The early loss of land in Chiapas during the colonial period and the historic control of Indian areas by ladino municipalities contrasts sharply with the situation in Oaxaca where Indians have been more successful in maintaining control of their land and govern themselves in small communities. The colonization of eastern Chiapas since the 1940s also has facilitated the possibility of interethnic cooperation in the state. The presence of progressive Catholic clergy and leftist organizers working in Chiapas since the 1970s has also been a significant factor in stimulating interethnic alliances. Stephen (2002) notes that state repression in Chiapas has been more generalized than in Oaxaca. Ironically perhaps, harsh state repression provided Chiapan Indians with a common enemy and facilitated multi-ethnic organizing strategies.

The principal point of contention between the comunalista and the RAP camps is the emphasis each places on the level at which indigenous autonomy is exercised. RAP proponents want to see legislation guaranteeing the exercise of regional governments, which, they argue, simultaneously protects communal and municipal autonomy. Comunalistas worry about the creation of regional *cacicazgos* (rule by political bosses, or caciques) and additional bureaucracies that would take attention away from the much-needed task of strengthening community-level autonomy efforts.

Although the comunalista and regional autonomy proponents have their differences, they agree on many issues. Comunalistas and RAP supporters agree on such fundamentals as the protection of Indian rights, including autonomy, the enforcement of Convention 169, and an end to indigenismo. The comunalistas correctly point out that any lasting autonomy project must have a strong foundation of community support because the community continues to be a point of reference for many Indians. If future legislative reforms protecting Indian autonomy are to have any meaning, Indians must be creative in developing viable and diverse community development projects on this level. Nevertheless, I echo the concerns of authors who worry that the community level is too vulnerable to sustain the current attacks on it by migratory pressures, state agricultural policy reforms, and increasing militarization. As Vera notes, "While it is indispensable that the values of self-government on the community level are practiced . . . and that we find and recover these experiences that can serve as a reference point to develop proposals, it is nevertheless illusory that self-government on its own can be sufficient" (Vera 1995: 38).

In the final analysis, comunalista and RAP supporters agree that any regime of autonomy must involve some combination of these two projects. Despite differences between the two views, activists from both camps concur that legal or juridical autonomy proposals must be backed up by grassroots experiences of autonomy. Both camps also agree that without some legal guarantee that the state will respect the exercise of indigenous autonomy, abuses by the state and local caciques will continue to impede the exercise of autonomous practices on community, municipal, and regional levels. Both camps also face the dilemma of radicalizing the terms of the debate—such as asserting that their projects fall outside the purview of the nation-state or harshly critiquing racism within the left—and losing their popular allies, which they badly need to gain the smallest victories.

Indians today seek independence from the state, and they desire to be self-governing on the communal, municipal, and regional levels. Yet, they also seek state recognition of this autonomy. Are these two goals irreconcilable? In the Mexican context, Indian activists demand that the state recognize their right to autonomy, but they also insist that the state fulfill its general responsibility to indigenous people as citizens (education, health care, and housing) as well as meet their particular needs as Indians (bilingual education, state respect for the use of indigenous languages, and cultural preservation).[31] How do Indian autonomy projects envision the relationship between the state and autonomous communities, municipalities, and regions? Does autonomy mean independence from the state, and, if so, to what extent? What responsibility would the state have under a regime of autonomy? These questions are important ones that autonomy proponents have not fully addressed to date. Likewise, responsibilities that correspond to the state under the autonomy proposals have not been concretely defined; even the accords reached in San Andrés are imprecise on this note.

THE VOICE OF THE
SOUTHERN BORDER: XEVFS

El Camerón's voice kept tuning in and out as we bumped along the back roads from Comitán to Las Margaritas.[1] It had just starting raining again and the dusty potholes had turned to small ponds that we mostly avoided. El Camerón kept up a steady commentary as he swayed sharply from right to left with the direction of the steering wheel. The subject of conversation that day was the takeover of a National Indigenous Institute (INI)-run radio station—XEVFS, Voz de la Frontera Sur—that had occurred a few days before. (See figure 6.)

On April 29, 1996, a Tojolabal by the name of Esteben Cruz and the New Tojolabal Alliance (NAT) entered XEVFS and announced its takeover. XEVFS broadcast over a large region that stretched across the municipalities of Las Margaritas, La Independencia, Comitán, and even as far as Motozintla in southern Chiapas. The station began broadcasting in 1986 in an attempt to promote indigenous culture, which for INI officials meant programming focused on dance, music, and language. Cruz and the New Tojolabal Alliance believed that the San Andrés Accords signed two months before (on February 16) gave indigenous peoples like the Tojolabal the right to control their own means of communication. They viewed the National Indigenous Institute as an obstacle in exercising this right. Instead of waiting for the federal and state governments to implement the accords (which they believed was unlikely, anyway), they decided to act.

This was not the first time the INI had lost control of XEVFS. On January 1, 1994, as part of its brief occupation of the municipal capital, Las Margaritas, the EZLN took INI officials hostage for several hours while it broadcast its first communiqué from the station. After the EZLN left, the INI regained control, which it had maintained—somewhat unsteadily—until that April. Those responsible for the second takeover were not the Zapatistas, however, but the FZLN—Frente Zapatista de Liberación Nacional—the civil wing of the Zapatistas. Only a few weeks before he led the takeover of XEVFS, Cruz became the leader of a new organization in Las Margaritas, the New Tojolabal Alliance

Figure 6. For twenty years, the National Indigenous Institute has owned and managed XEVFS "Voz de la Frontera Sur" in Las Margaritas, Chiapas. Courtesy of National Indigenous Institute, Mexico City.

(NAT). Based in Las Margaritas, NAT was an FZLN affiliate.

Cruz followed the signing of the San Andrés accords closely and had read the fine print granting indigenous peoples the right to control "their own means of communication (radio, television, telephone, written press, fax, CB radio, computers, and satellite access)" (Point 8 of the San Andrés Accords). In the early morning hours of April 29, Cruz and his followers entered the offices of the station's director, Carlos Romo, and announced the takeover. INI officials responded quickly by promising to enter into discussions with NAT and other local Indian organizations about the eventual transfer of XEVFS.[2] In truth, the INI had little room to maneuver. Since the late 1970s it had emphasized the participation and involvement of Indian organizations in the planning and administration of its programs. Although indigenous involvement in INI-sponsored programs was more limited in practice than official rhetoric suggested, events after 1994 forced the INI's hand.

On one of my frequent visits to the CIOAC-Comitán headquarters in early May, El Camerón told me about the takeover and invited me to accompany him to a negotiation meeting on the station's transfer. Cruz had invited leaders of social organizations active in the region to participate in talks with INI officials from Mexico City, Tuxtla Gutiérrez, San Cristóbal, and Las Margaritas. I was not surprised to hear about the recent events: the political and social situation in the region had been touch-and-go since the uprising. I was very interested in observing how local and regional organizations were interpreting the San Andrés Accords on the ground. I also knew Carlos Romo, the station's manager, and had visited XEVFS before. So, I accepted El Camerón's invitation without hesitation and hopped into his Volkswagen bug, eager to hear his viewpoint on the takeover and what it meant.

We arrived just in time to hear the director of the Tzotzil-Tzeltal CCI in San Cristóbal, José Patrocinio Ramos, make some introductory comments, which turned out to be a historical overview of the INI's work in Mexico's indigenous regions. (Even in a moment of local political crisis, no state official could give up an opportunity to grandstand!) Ramos spoke of assimilation as an outdated policy that had given way to "participatory" indigenismo: Indians were not to be subjects of indigenist policy but actors involved in making decisions that affected them.[3]

At this first meeting, it looked as if INI would hand over control of XEVFS and that the "appropriation of the means of communication" would be expeditious. INI officials proposed the formation of three main councils to oversee the transfer: a plural council of consultation, centers of radio production, and community correspondents.[4] However, ten days later, on May 18, 1996, the direction of the negotiations shifted dramatically. To begin with, INI officials made it clear that the "appropriation" process would be slow and gradual. The process would begin with the substantial participation of INI representatives, who would gradually withdraw as local organizations assumed increased responsibilities. In addition, the technical council would consist of the director, his personnel, and a state INI representative. In short, the INI would continue to control the technical aspects of the radio, while Indian organizations would participate in the new council of consultation (or participatory councils as they were later called).

Since recent INI policies and programs supported plurality and "participatory" indigenismo, officials returned again and again to this issue in the meetings that were held to discuss the transfer, even while they were openly skeptical about whether the social organizations would promote pluralism within the participatory council. There was an implicit threat in the concerns expressed by officials that if the participatory council were not sufficiently plural, the INI would not transfer the radio station. The meetings eventually reached an impasse, due in no small part to each group's different understanding of the main issue. For the INI, the question was primarily a legal one. XEVFS and radio stations like it across the country were the property of the INI, which held a license from the state for airwave use. However, INI officials also knew that they could continue to exercise power within XEVFS if they played their cards right.[5] The Indian organizations present were also interested in the question of ownership, but they made it clear that they first must be convinced that the INI was committed to transferring the station. The organizations seemed skeptical of the INI's intentions, repeatedly accusing INI officials of seeing them as "inept, incapable, and incompetent."

There was little agreement among the many local and regional social organizations participating in the talks about what to do with XEVFS. This was not an ideologically homogeneous group: both official and independent organizations participated in the discussions. No consensus existed among this diverse group about what "Indian" cultural programming might mean. Who were "the indigenous peoples" referred to in the San Andrés Accords who would control the radio stations?

My friends from the CIOAC-Comitán did not seem too interested in the outcome of the talks, mainly because their work focused on land reform and credits to work the land. Cruz and NAT wanted to use the radio station to promote the EZLN, which my friends were not crazy about either. (The CIOAC-Comitán split into pro-EZLN and independent factions soon after the uprising.) I myself was not sure about what the CIOAC-Comitán representatives hoped to gain from their participation in the talks.

My confusion was heightened on a return trip to Comitán after another round of negotiations, when, out of the blue, El Camerón asked me whether I would be interested in taking over the radio station. "*¿Perdón?*" I stuttered, hoping I had not heard correctly. El Camerón continued on without missing a beat, "Lorena [my middle name, which I used while living in Chiapas], you should stay here and be the director of the station. *¿Por qué no?*" I laughed and assumed the invitation was part of the persistent flirtation between us. Yet, after El Camerón left me at the bus stop in Comitán and I was on my way back to San Cristóbal, I found myself puzzling over our conversation. I asked myself, "How could El Camerón even joke about something so serious? I'm writing a dissertation about ethnic organization. Am I, *acaso,* making too much of ethnic ties and of race? Did it matter as much to them as I thought?"

My mind then turned to something that had occurred months before at a RAP (Multi-ethnic Autonomous Regions) conference held in San Cristóbal in

December 1995. As part of the preparations to begin work on one of the mesas on the inaugural morning of the conference, a rapporteur had to be chosen. Several of the *compañeros* nominated me for the job. I slid down into my seat as I heard my name being floated. Finally, a friend who served as an independent consultant for the RAPs stood up. She suggested that the compañeros reconsider their choice and choose someone more representative of the group. I was momentarily relieved, but the feeling of discomfort persisted. "Why aren't these guys more sensitive to their image as an *Indian* organization?" I wondered. "Don't they see how bad it looks to have a gringa participating directly in these deliberations?" "Aren't they fighting to rid themselves of gringo and mestizo control over their organizations?"

As I reflect on these experiences, I wonder if the organizations I worked with had brought so many accumulated demands to the table that the specifically ethnic or racial dimension was sometimes overshadowed. The CIOAC's demand for credit and land reform, for example, was tied to a demand for political autonomy, which in turn was tied to a sense of collective discrimination and group identity. Yet, that same discrimination had produced a racial hierarchy in which gringas were admired for their *ojos claros* (light-colored eyes) and white skin. Indian men, particularly those who had spent time living in the mestizo world, perceived their status as being boosted if they caught the attention of a gringa. I wanted to resist this, and for that reason avoided seeking these men out. Yet, the gender dynamics of doing fieldwork in Mexico played a significant role in my getting interviews and in the relationships I developed with my informants.

XEVFS was never transferred to social organizations in Las Margaritas during that spring of 1996. It continues, instead, to form part of an INI-run network of radio stations. There are twenty-four stations in all (seven more than in 1994) operating throughout the country that "encompass 954 municipalities, have 22 million listeners, and transmit in 31 Indian languages and Spanish" (INI). The INI defends its continued management of these stations by claiming that 85 percent of station employees are Indian and that indigenous peoples run the stations (Vértiz 2001). The questions that framed the takeover of 1996 continue to be relevant ones: How do indigenous organizations define Indian culture and envision the uses to which a radio station should be put? How are indigenous peoples to get training on their own terms when the INI continues to control the ownership and management of the stations? Indigenismo in Mexico—despite growing cries since 1994 that it be dismantled—is not dead yet.

CHAPTER FIVE

THE DIALOGUE OF SAN ANDRÉS AND MEXICO'S TRANSITION TO DEMOCRACY

On October 17, 1995, guests and advisors of the EZLN and the Mexican government sat down in six working groups to discuss "Indian Rights and Culture," the first of four broad themes as part of the official dialogue process.[1] The first working group, which would discuss issues of community and autonomy, was based at San Andrés Sacamch'en, a small, Tzotzil community approximately forty kilometers northwest of San Cristóbal (see map 3 in chapter 3).[2] The remaining five working groups were based at the Casa de la Cultura in downtown San Cristóbal.[3] For the EZLN delegation, it was a triumphant return to the city it had held briefly in the early hours of January 1, 1994. It was no coincidence that San Cristóbal was one of four cities occupied by the EZLN that day. The state's second largest city, San Cristóbal is widely regarded as a bastion of political and religious conservatism. Until the late 1950s, Indians were not allowed to walk on the sidewalks and well into the early 1970s Indian products were sold to intermediaries, or coyotes, who would meet Indians on the outskirts of town to buy their products for resale in the central market. It is difficult to exaggerate the impact that the EZLN occupation had on the city's "native" *(coleto)* population.[4] Given San Cristóbal's history of exploitative relations between Indians and non-Indians, the EZLN's occupation of the city—even if only for a few hours on January 1, 1994—fulfilled the coletos' worst fears. The EZLN's presence in San Cristóbal also posed the possibility that the historic domination of the mestizo population over the Indians had reached its limit (Viqueira 1995: 227–28).

The San Andrés Dialogue on Indian rights and culture resulted in the only accords reached to date between the EZLN and the Mexican government. This dialogue is important for our purposes because the issue of Indian autonomy figured prominently: the EZLN and the government had very different ideas about its scope. Whereas the government defined Indian autonomy as a kind

of decentralization of resources to municipal governments (that is, administrative autonomy), the EZLN understood autonomy to mean territorial rights,
control over natural resources, and recognition of local political practices (that
is, politico-economic). Ultimately, the Mexican debate over Indian autonomy
figured as part of the country's transition to democracy.

Mesa Uno: Indian Rights and Culture

The phase of official talks between the EZLN and the government called the
"San Andrés Dialogue" lasted more than a year. To get the EZLN, the government, and their respective guests and advisors together on three separate occa-
sions between October 1995 and February 1996 was the result of a process that
began in April (1995) at San Miguel, a small Zapatista settlement in the Lacandon
jungle. At San Miguel, representatives from both sides, along with representatives from two mediating bodies, the CONAI and the COCOPA, agreed on
four general themes that would form part of the official dialogue process, as
well as on the rules that would govern it.[5]

The first topic that representatives slated for discussion was "Indian Culture and Rights." The rules structuring the dialogue stipulated that each side
could invite as many advisors and guests as they wished. The EZLN took full
advantage of this, inviting almost three hundred individuals and organizations
on the center, center-left, and left of the political spectrum. Those invited included
members of indigenous, peasant, and women's organizations throughout
Mexico, environmental activists, as well as many of the country's most distinguished
social scientists, intellectuals, and political activists. After the EZLN made public
their list of guests and advisors, the pickings were slim; the government moved
slowly to fill its advisory and guest slots—ultimately drawing on the National
Indigenist Institute (INI) to fill these positions.[6]

Finally, on October 17, 1995, more than two hundred guests *(invitados)* and
advisors to both sides sat down to six working groups.[7] The first group discussed themes related to community, autonomy, and Indian rights. The second
group examined guarantees of justice for indigenous peoples. The third working group looked at questions of political representation and participation. The
fourth concerned itself with diagnosing the current situation of indigenous
women, as well as with women's rights and culture. The fifth and sixth groups
examined access to the means of communication and the promotion and
development of indigenous cultures, respectively.

Many of those invited by the EZLN did not have extensive experience speaking

Figure 7. Mexican army tanks outside San Andrés Larraínzar during the peace negotiations. Photo by Shannan Mattiace.

in public. For many it was the first time they had publicly voiced their demands. The governmental delegation was forced to sit down and listen to Indian people in their own voices—not through INI mediators or representatives named by the government.

According to the agreed-on rules, guests from both sides would be permitted to speak freely about the topic of their specific working group. The point of this first phase was to air ideas that later would become the basis for consensus. Surprisingly, in all six working groups, guests invited by both the EZLN and the government engaged in a remarkably open and frank interchange, in which common ideas were shared and a fair amount of consensus was achieved. Andrés Aubry, an anthropologist who served as advisor to the EZLN, described the atmosphere in his working group as charged with emotion on both sides. One governmental representative, Aubry notes, was so profoundly moved by the dialogue that he claimed he had never before understood Mexico's "pluri-cultural matrix" until San Andrés (interview, July 3, 2000). The enthusiasm and emotion that accompanied the first phase, however, did not last.

Consistently throughout the course of the dialogue, after every successful encounter between the government and the EZLN, a destabilizing event occurred that put the future of the dialogue at risk. Two days after the first phase of talks ended in October, the government's arrest of EZLN comandante Germán (Fernando Yáñez) provided the trigger. When the two delegations and their advisors and guests sat down to the second phase of talks in November 1995, the atmosphere was tense. In contrast to the cooperation and good will manifest by both sides during the first phase, the second session was—in the words of one advisor—"ríspida" [harsh] (interview, July 4, 2000). To begin with, the government arrived with very few invited guests. In a surprising move, the government uninvited its "experts" on indigenous affairs from the National Indigenous Institute (INI) after the first phase ended. Critics claimed that the government became disenchanted with its INI because they had "gone native," openly supporting many of the demands expressed by EZLN's invited guests.[8]

In an effort to buttress the dialogue process, and to strengthen its position within it, the EZLN issued an open invitation to Mexican "civil society" to participate in the National Indian Forum to be held January 3–8, 1996, in San Cristóbal. One of the strategies the EZLN employed to keep pressure on the government during the dialogue process was to use popular mobilization—congresses, marches, and peaceful demonstrations—to demonstrate the support that it had from "civil society." "Civil society" consisted of the EZLN's indigenous bases of support located throughout the state (primarily in the highland region and in the Lacandon jungle), members of independent peasant and Indian organizations, nongovernmental organizations (NGOs), and international and national citizens who supported the EZLN cause. Both Mexican and international "civil society" has been crucial in providing support for the EZLN. They organized solidarity movements in Mexico, the United States, and Europe, put pressure on the Mexican government to seek a peaceful solution to the conflict, and worked diligently to keep the Zapatistas in the news as much as possible.

After the initial fighting between EZLN troops and the Mexican government in January 1994, the EZLN called on "civil society" to take up its struggle for "democracy, justice, and peace with dignity." In the Fourth Declaration of the Lacandon jungle issued in February 1996—the same week as the San Andrés Accords were signed—the EZLN further elaborated on what it meant by "civil society" (see Ross 2000: 154–56). In that declaration, the EZLN contrasted "civil society" to those who participated in political parties and "power politics." It called on the latter to renounce their organizations and join "civil society" in the formation of the Zapatista Front of National Liberation (FZLN). During the first days of January 1996, "civil society" came out in full force to participate in the National Indian Forum.

Figure 8. Hundreds of volunteers from civil society made the San Andrés Dialogue possible. In the foreground, citizens form a human chain *(cinturón de seguridad)* to protect the EZLN during the talks in 1995 and early 1996. Photo by Shannan Mattiace.

The National Indian Forum

The forum was convoked, organized, and presided over by the Zapatista commanders (CCRI) and was moderated by EZLN advisors. The COCOPA and the CONAI helped facilitate security arrangements and logistical details. The six working tables that formed the basis for discussion at the forum paralleled those at San Andrés. More than five hundred Indians from throughout Mexico and North America, students, human rights activists, representatives from Zapatista solidarity committees from around the world, nongovernmental organizations such as Global Exchange and SIPAZ (International Service for Peace), scholars, and independent observers participated in this historic forum. The large national and international turnout made it difficult, if not impossible, for the government to reduce the scope of the conflict to Chiapas.

Given its broad representation of indigenous organizations and Mexican "civil society," the National Indian Forum provided momentum and strength to the Zapatista delegation going into the final negotiations at San Andrés. The concluding document read by the EZLN at the end of the forum encapsulated the consensus that was achieved across the six working groups. With respect to community and autonomy, forum participants stated Indians' right to self-determination within the context of autonomy exercised at the communal, municipal, and regional levels, all the while being careful to ensure that Indian autonomy would not threaten the integrity of the Mexican nation. Autonomy could not be fully exercised, participants argued, without access to territory and natural resources. At the center of debate was the restitution of Article 27 (reformed in 1992), which would return ejido land to its previous inalienable status, prohibiting its purchase or sale. Participants also demanded that national agrarian legislation should incorporate the norms of the International Labor Organization's (ILO) Convention 169. Indians' access to justice within the present juridical system (including the right to legal counsel, the right to give testimony in Indian languages, and the use of anthropologists as sources of "expert" opinion in specific cases) was also the subject of much discussion and debate. Forum participants demanded that the state recognize Indian law; they also raised the possibility of juridical pluralism on the constitutional level. In the working table on political participation, Indians demanded full participation in federal and state-level legislatures, redistricting for federal and local deputies, and the creation of a new method for incorporating indigenous peoples into the Senate. Participants spoke of the need for Indians to have access to the means of communication, such as their own radio and television stations for the promotion and diffusion of Indian culture, as well as the need to protect the thousands of migrant Indians living outside their communities of origin. The forum's concluding paper highlighted a series of demands that combine the protection for individual rights guaranteed in the constitution with demands for the protection of collective rights. Forum participants argued that these collective rights, including the right to autonomy, territory, and language, cannot be protected individually but involve Indian peoples as a collectivity.

The relationship between individual and collective rights was at the center of discussion in working group four: indigenous women's rights and culture. Indigenous women at the forum expressed concern over specific "traditions and customs," such as forced marriage, that threaten women's individual rights. Although indigenous women were careful not to undermine the project of protecting Indian law more broadly, they were vocal in expressing their criticism, which was based on their experience of living in indigenous communities.

The San Andrés Accords, signed in February 1996, echo, to an astonishing degree, the conclusions reached at the National Indian Forum. The accords are historic in that governmental representatives admitted, right from the start, the importance of reforming the relationship between indigenous peoples and the state. For years, the assumption behind indigenist policies was that the "Indian problem" was the result of socioeconomic marginalization, or poverty. The San Andrés Accords provide the foundation for arguing that the marginalization of indigenous communities and regions is not just a question of socioeconomic underdevelopment, but is tied to social and cultural discrimination.[9]

At San Andrés, both parties recognized Indians' right to self-determination within the context of autonomy. At the National Indian Forum, regional autonomy was mentioned specifically as an option and model for indigenous peoples. The San Andrés Accords do not mention it; rather, they focus on communal and municipal autonomy. The government forcefully resisted talk of regional autonomy, possibly because they viewed the region as stronger than the community and thus more difficult to control.[10] The government also refused to negotiate the restitution of Article 27, which had made ejido land inalienable. With respect to Indians' access to the Mexican juridical system, the accords state the necessity of affording Indians access to justice within the context of positive law. There is much talk in the accords of recognizing and respecting Indians' "usos y costumbres" in the election of local officials. There is no mention, however, of juridical pluralism; rather, the language of the accords is that of adjusting positive law(s) to accommodate local "usos y costumbres." The language of the San Andrés Accords, to a degree much greater than that used in forum documents, emphasizes Mexicans' equality before the law, reiterating that no special privileges for Indians should be created. The accords also insist that Indian autonomy—at both the communal and municipal levels—poses no risk to Mexican sovereignty.

In general, the EZLN and its advisors considered the accords to be a significant step toward the final goal of a peace settlement between the two parties. At the same time, they were careful to point out that the accords were limited, particularly with respect to land and territorial rights (Article 27). There was also substantial disagreement over the use of the word "people," or *pueblo* in Spanish.[11] For the EZLN, "pueblo" signified "people," with all of the corresponding legal rights assigned in international law to peoples. The government, by contrast, tended to define "pueblo" as community or town, without giving it the significance or weight that "people" has in international law. No consensus was reached on this point.

The relationship between individual and collective rights was also a sticking point. The government, while it professed respect for the use of Indian "traditions and customs" on the local level, was not willing to countenance recognizing Indian law as a body of law on par with national, positive law. The EZLN and its advisors, by contrast, pushed for some recognition of juridical pluralism. Also unresolved was the subject of economic sustainability and its link to the survival of Indian cultures. How were Indians to have access to territory and natural resources (guaranteed in the accords) within the context of the state's current macroeconomic model, which drains resources away from the countryside to the cities? These and other related questions were left pending for another table of discussion, specifically that of "Social Welfare and Development" ("Bienestar y Desarrollo"), which would come later in the dialogue process. It seemed unlikely, however, that the government would be able to substantially alter the current trends in rural (under)development, because Mexico had locked in a "neoliberal" macroeconomic project with the signing of NAFTA in 1993. Since then, the state has had limited negotiating power in terms of macroeconomic policy, which affects price supports, social policies, and subsidies to rural producers.

After the accords were signed, the government and the EZLN charged the COCOPA to draw up a document based on the signed accords that would be presented to Congress for approval.[12] In addition to those provisions described above, the COCOPA's proposal included wording related to the protection of indigenous women's rights, particularly with respect to the exercise of "traditions and customs" on local levels. In order to legislate on the basis of the proposal, the COCOPA recommended reforms to Articles 4, 18, 53, 73, 115, and 116, among others.[13]

In the meantime, the EZLN and its advisors began work on the second theme for discussion: "Democracy and Justice." Advisors and guests from both sides met for a first session in March 1996. Tensions were high from the start. The EZLN claimed that there was no dialogue, but, rather, a monologue; the government had brought only a handful of advisors. Tensions increased dramatically at the end of March when state security police evicted peasants from land they had occupied for more than a year on farms located in the municipalities of Nicolás Ruiz and Pichucalco, in the northern region of the state. At least six peasants and two police officers died during the evictions.

Why would the governor of Chiapas, Julio César Ruiz Ferro, and his secretary general, Eraclio Zepeda (who was charged with oversight of the state's security forces), choose this particular moment during the dialogue to evict these peasants, who had occupied the land for more than a year? It is difficult to specify the nuances of the relationship between federal and state governmental officials during the dialogue, but in general Chiapas state officials perceived the federal government's negotiation with the Zapatistas as inimical to their interests. When the federal government appeared united in their goals and on how to achieve them, state-level officials moved cautiously. When the federal government hesitated or appeared divided, Chiapas state officials tended to act aggressively against the EZLN and its forces. In March, right before the forcible eviction of peasants in Nicolás Ruiz and Pichucalco, lawyers consulted by Zedillo administration officials publicly warned that if the accords were implemented, Mexico was in danger of balkanization. After this declaration, Chiapas state government officials made moves that further jeopardized the dialogue process.[14]

Tensions increased further on May 2, when a federal district judge in Tuxtla Gutiérrez sentenced two individuals, presumed Zapatistas Javier Elorriaga and Sebastián Entzin, to thirteen and six years of prison respectively. Elorriaga and Entzin were charged with terrorism, rebellion, and conspiracy. The judge based Elorriaga's thirteen-year sentence on the latter's presumed role as an ideologue behind the EZLN's public relations and "propaganda" campaign. The judge also accused Elorriaga of authoring the EZLN's first communiqués after the uprising began (Balboa 1996). Elorriaga's case captured national and international attention. He was a journalist who had been working for a video company and as a correspondent for foreign television stations when army soldiers captured him on February 9, 1995, in Las Margaritas. Named along with other known and presumed members of the EZLN, subcomandante Marcos, Fernando Yáñez (Gérman), Jorge Santiago, and Silvia Fernández (Sofía), Zedillo ordered their capture in the military operation of February 9, 1995. Throughout the sixteen months he was held in the state penitentiary, Cerro Hueco, Elorriaga maintained that he was not a member of the EZLN, but, rather, had served as a messenger for president-elect Ernesto Zedillo and subcomandante Marcos, delivering a series of letters the two leaders exchanged in the fall of 1994. The day after the judge handed down Elorriaga and Entzin's sentences, Heberto Castillo, member of the COCOPA and senator for the Partido de la Revolución Democrática (PRD), resigned from the COCOPA in protest. Leaders of popular organizations in Chiapas and the PRD's congressional delegation accused the federal government of declaring war on the EZLN, jeopardizing the dialogue process, and executive interference in juridical affairs. On June 6, 1996, a judge in Tuxtla Gutiérrez revoked the sentence, freeing both Elorriaga and Entzin.

Although the freeing of Elorriaga and Entzin lifted tensions momentarily, it only postponed the eventual suspension of talks, which the EZLN officially announced in early September. The reasons it gave were several, chief among them the lack of progress in implementing the San Andrés Accords. Also at issue was the functioning of the Comisión de Seguimiento y Verificación (Commission of Follow-up and Verification), which was to monitor the implementation of accords signed during the dialogue process. The EZLN accused the government of being uninterested in participating in the stated commission, refusing, for example, to send representatives. The government, not surprisingly, denied these accusations, claiming that the EZLN had unilaterally suspended the dialogue, and expressed its willingness to continue.[15] All efforts by third parties to restart the talks were unsuccessful. Meanwhile, the COCOPA occupied itself with the legislative initiative based on the San Andrés Accords that they planned to present to Congress after getting approval from the executive branch and from the EZLN. That approval proved ultimately to be elusive.

On December 8, 1996, President Zedillo asked for fifteen days to "make observations with respect to the initiative" (referring to the COCOPA's proposal). At the end of December, the president announced that after consultation with constitutional law scholars, he had found that significant parts of the COCOPA's proposal were unconstitutional—particularly those referring to autonomy. The EZLN responded by reiterating its refusal to renegotiate the San Andrés Accords and accused the government of reneging on its promise to accept the COCOPA's legislative initiative without making additional changes. The COCOPA found itself between a recalcitrant executive who insisted on the unconstitutionality of their proposal (which made it impossible to get the two-thirds vote necessary in Congress to make constitutional changes) and the EZLN, who accused the COCOPA of being a pawn for the government. Juan Guerra, rotating president of the COCOPA, said that in the final analysis neither side was satisfied with the role they had played as interlocutor: "The EZLN has good reason to see us as a vehicle that contributed to raising expectations to which the government would not respond, and because of that it considers us traitorous—the EZLN considers us accomplices. We resent that because we tried very hard, [to represent] the best interests of society and in achieving peace for the country" (cited in Correa 1997: 35).

From the start, the dialogue process was fraught with tension. To begin with, the EZLN never trusted the governmental interlocutors and came to the negotiating table with the memory of decades of broken promises. The governmental officials representing the Zedillo administration at San Andrés, even

Figure 9. Military checkpoint. Courtesy of the National Indigenous Institute, Mexico City.

despite their efforts to hide it, often responded to the EZLN and their representatives with arrogance and thinly veiled racism, refusing to engage the issues and enter into conversation with the delegation and their supporters. Even if we assume that federal government officials were willing to make good on their promises to end the conflict, there was no guarantee that Chiapas state government officials would comply. The EZLN's experience with politics in Chiapas had been one beset with alternating repression and neglect. By 1996, Chiapas had five governors in the space of as many years. Perhaps most significantly, the two sides had very different ideas about what constituted democracy and how best to establish a democratic regime in Mexico.

San Andrés and Mexico's Democratic Transition

In August 1995, the EZLN hosted an international consulta, in which it asked "civil society" about the future direction of the EZLN: Should it become a political party? Join a coalition of forces on the left? Lay down its arms and become an independent civil organization? The majority of the people who participated in the poll opined that the EZLN should not become a political party, but rather an unarmed civil organization that would continue to struggle independently for its demands. The consulta tapped a groundswell of support from sectors of Mexican (and international) society, thoroughly disillusioned with political parties and partisanship. The EZLN itself was highly suspicious of electoral democracy and political parties. In October 1995, for example, the EZLN called on its supporters to boycott local elections in Chiapas, which shifted the balance of power away from the PRD and toward the PRI, which emerged victorious after the EZLN's boycott.[16]

By the end of September 1995, the EZLN responded to the results of the consulta by calling for the creation of the FZLN—The Zapatista Front of National Liberation. The FZLN would be the unarmed civilian wing of the Zapatistas. It would not be a political party—it disavowed any claim to power for its own sake—but a grassroots social movement. For Javier Elorriaga, the FZLN's national coordinator, democracy could only be forged from the grassroots, circumventing political parties and political society.

By the summer and fall of 1996, however, the public's attention began to wane. The conflict was more than two years old, accords on Indian Culture and Rights had been passed, and—perhaps most importantly—Congress had finally begun to debate an electoral reform law, which was passed in the fall of 1996. Among other things, this legislation made the National Electoral Institute (IFE) independent from the PRI, which was key to that party's defeat in the presidential election held in July 2000. By the fall of 1996, the public's attention shifted away from the EZLN and toward the realm of institutions and formal politics.

From the EZLN's first public pronouncements, the demand for democracy figured prominently as one of three central demands (the other two were justice and peace). Observers debated what exactly the EZLN meant by "democracy." After initially declaring war on the Mexican government, honoring a cease-fire twelve days after the fighting began, and subsequently turning over the political struggle to civil society, the EZLN only gradually revealed its ideas about the kind of democracy it envisioned for Mexico. The EZLN's ideas about democracy became clearer when it called for the formation of the FZLN in September 1995, although the EZLN was deliberate about not issuing directives to local FZLN groups, or comités. Local FZLN groups would be organized loosely into progressively larger networks stretching across Mexico. Its leadership style was to rule by obeying *("mandar obedeciendo")*. This was a grassroots view of democracy, a view that scorned electoral democracy for being top-down and unrepresentative.[17]

In the scholarly work on transitions from authoritarian to democratic rule, scholars have debated the relative importance of political elites and grassroots social actors in these transitions. Some scholars have argued that democratic transitions occur most often through elite pacts, in which all key political actors sit down together to hammer out the rules of the postauthoritarian regime (Burton, Gunther, and Higley 1991; Di Palma 1990; Karl and Schmitter 1991; O'Donnell 1989); others have emphasized the importance of civil society in pressuring elites to liberalize closed political systems (Cardoso 1986).[18]

The link between a strong civil society and democracy has been commented on widely in the literature on democratic transitions and democracy. Military governments in Argentina and Brazil stepped down in the face of massive public protest. In Eastern Europe in 1989, large public protests put communist governments under tremendous strain—eventually toppling them. If a strong civil society can be influential in pressuring authoritarian governments to step down, its role is just as crucial in the consolidation phase.[19] Yet, as Linz and Stepan (1996: 7) point out, it is not uncommon for tension to occur between civil and political society during the democratic consolidation phase. The organizational style of civil society, they suggest, does not easily accommodate qualities necessary for democracy's consolidation: institutional rationalization, the presence of intermediaries between citizens and the state, and compromise. The EZLN, feeding on the public's cynicism after seventy-one years of one-party rule on the national level that ended with Vicente Fox's election in July 2000, has focused exclusively on the importance of civil society in Mexico's transition—often pitting it against political parties and institutional politics. Within the dichotomy it set up between civil and political society, the EZLN situated indigenous peoples squarely within civil society.

The EZLN and National Indigenous Congress (CNI) have pushed for official recognition of indigenous decision making on the local level as an alternative to electoral democracy. The recognition of Indian "traditions and customs" would not displace electoral politics in regions where indigenous peoples chose to elect officials using political party slates and a system of "one person, one vote." But it would send a clear signal that multiple systems for decision making exist in Mexico. This position has caused heated debate in Mexico since the signing of the San Andrés Accords. Many complex and difficult questions have emerged: Is electoral democracy incompatible with Indian tradition? Will the recognition of Indian "traditions and customs" further democracy in Mexico? Can two legal systems coexist?[20]

Juridical Pluralism and Indian "Tradition"

Indian "traditions" are not timeless customs set in stone and outside history. Indian tradition is shifting and ever-adapting to changing conditions. Indian communities have had to adapt and change in order to survive. Thus, while observers—and some Indians themselves—may refer to Indian "tradition" as timeless and free of contamination from outside influences, it is, like tradition in every human community, a constant reworking of old and new. Electoral laws in the United States, for example, represent the accumulation of local tradition and history just as Indian decision-making procedures on the local level do.

The optimism generated by the 2000 presidential elections caused some observers to emphasize the benefits of electoral democracy as the exclusive vehicle for democratic change in Mexico. Political "progress" has been associated with the individual vote and "backwardness" with Indian "traditions and customs."[21] It is true that in practice the Indian plebiscite—in which community members line up behind their favorite candidate—is problematic in communities marked by violence and cacicazgo; intimidation can prevent people from participating freely. Nevertheless, within the context of elections, intimidation also occurs—illustrated by cases in which communities and municipalities received fewer government services because they did not vote for the party in power. A truly democratic political culture would be one in which both the Indian plebiscite and elections expressed the popular will. The community assembly, with its long, drawn-out discussions in view of constructing a consensus, can be exclusive and hierarchical. Nevertheless, in some areas of Mexico, these assemblies have played a crucial role in maintaining community cohesion in the face of multiple pressures (Hernández Castillo 2001b; Leyva 2001). Among the Mixe people of Oaxaca, David Recondo (1999) has documented a fascinating case in which communities have combined the individual, secret vote for state and federal elections and decision making by community assembly for local, municipal elections.

For Mexico's indigenous people, the political alternatives do not have to be categorical: either a return to the past or a wholesale acceptance of a homogeneous and standardized version of the current electoral system. Recondo (1999: 97) speaks, for example, about the possibility of combining elections and community practices, which would imply "the construction of an articulated set of diverse electoral systems in which several communities or groups could associate in independent formations or in alliance with a national political party without that implying direct interference with community practices to name authorities, with community solidarity, and with the construction of consensus." These types of experiments, however, turn out to be more complex than having a single electoral system. Recognizing the multicultural composition of the nation, if it is to have any teeth, means the construction of spaces that go beyond simply signing accords or emitting laws.

As I finish writing this book in 2002, the debate over constitutional reform and Indian rights continues. President Vicente Fox sent the COCOPA's proposal for constitutional reforms—based on the San Andrés Accords—to the Senate on December 5, 2000, four days after assuming power. (During the campaign Fox assured voters that he would resolve the Zapatista conflict in "fifteen minutes.") During the spring of 2001, the Senate significantly reworked the COCOPA's proposal. Among other changes, the Senate version limited Indian autonomy to the municipal level, recognizing Indians' right to elect municipal officials according to their "traditions and customs." Although the COCOPA proposal recognized municipal autonomy, it opened the door to the possibility of regional autonomy as well, something the Senate version does not contemplate. The language used in the Senate version reiterates state prerogatives in the areas of resource use and management and emphasizes the importance of national unity. In the Senate version, Indians are subjects of "public interest," for example; in the COCOPA proposal, they are subjects of "public law."[22] Both versions of the reform proposal disallow any form of Indian autonomy that violates individual human rights laid out in the Mexican constitution. Additionally, in both proposals the Mexican state continues to be the sole owner of all subsoil rights.

Members of the COCOPA, who represent Mexico's four largest political parties (PRI, PAN, PRD, and PT), publicly repudiated the Senate version, as did the EZLN and the CNI. Sponsored by Senators Diego Fernández de Cevallos (PAN), Manuel Bartlett (PRI), and Jesús Ortega (PRD), the reform proposal passed unanimously in the Senate on April 25, 2001. Three days later, the House of Representatives approved it—without changes—by a 386 to 60 margin. Because the proposal was not legislation per se but constitutional reform, a simple majority of state congresses was required to ratify it. During the summer of 2001, nineteen (of thirty-two) state congresses voted in favor of the proposal and nine voted against it.[23] On August 14, 2001, the constitutional reforms on Indian rights and culture became law. In the weeks and months following the promulgation of the reforms, scores of indigenous municipalities throughout the country registered their opposition by submitting "constitutional controversies" to the Supreme Court. Constitutional controversies are brought forth by governmental officials (for example, municipal presidents, state governors, and congressional legislators) and presented to the Supreme Court when some violation of power among levels/branches of government is perceived to have occurred.[24] By June 2002, indigenous municipalities in twenty-one states (for example, Puebla, Veracruz, Oaxaca, Chiapas, Tabasco, and Guerrero, among others) had submitted more than three hundred such controversies.[25] These controversies address the content of the constitutional reforms on Indian rights and culture as well as the procedure followed in ratifying them.

Those controversies dealing with the content of the reforms are based on the claim that many of the "rights" granted to Indian peoples are constitutional rights Indian peoples already possess. For example, the reforms explicitly permit indigenous communities within a municipality to cooperate and coordinate their actions for the good of the municipality, according to the law. Lawyers submitting this particular controversy claim that this right is already articulated in the Mexican constitution (Los Pueblos Indígenas: 8). Other controversies deal with procedural issues regarding the way that the reforms were ratified, both on the national and on the state level. First, the indigenous municipalities submitting the controversies claim that there was no consultation with Indian peoples during the process of drafting these reforms, which, according to ILO Convention 169, is required. Other controversies address the procedures followed by state legislatures in ratifying the reforms. In addition to the fact that there was little or no consultation with indigenous communities, the controversies allege that some state congresses did not follow their own legislative procedures in ratifying the reforms. Finally, complaints were submitted regarding the final vote tally made by the Permanent Commission of Congress. All of the controversies submitted demand that the Supreme Court declare the reforms invalid and that Congress resubmit and vote on the Cocopa proposal, which was, in fact, resubmitted by 156 Federal Deputies (from all political parties except the PAN) in February 2002 (Reyes 2002).

Given the current correlation of political forces, it seems unlikely that the COCOPA proposal will be discussed on the floor of Congress. However, even in the unlikely event that Congress approved the COCOPA proposal, that is no guarantee that implementing legislation would be written. (Recall that no implementing legislation was ever written for Article 4 after it was amended in 1992.) In the meantime, on the margins of legality, Indian communities have continued to carve out their own regional and communal spaces of autonomy.

Indian peoples throughout the Americas have exercised de facto autonomy in the absence of legal or official acknowledgment of indigenous peoples' right to autonomy in political, economic, social, and cultural matters. Yet, in some countries, such as Panama, Nicaragua, and Colombia, ethnic autonomy regimes have been established that guarantee, at least in theory, de jure autonomy for indigenous peoples.

WOMEN'S RIGHTS AND
INDIAN LAW

Since childhood we have been taught to obey, not to complain, to be silent, to endure, not to talk, not to participate. But now we do not want to stay behind; we do not want to be trampled upon. We demand to be respected as Indians and as women and that our rights be taken into consideration. We want our customs to be respected, those that the community finds [to be] good for all, women, men and children. We also want to participate in making laws that take us and our people into account and that respect our rights.

—*Participant in a seminar on women's rights
and Indian customs and traditions held
in San Cristóbal de Las Casas, May 1994*[1]

During the spring of 2001, debate raged in the Mexican press concerning the relative merits of the Indian rights' legislation proposed by Congress. The National Indigenous Congress (CNI) and the EZLN came out strongly against the proposed legislation, calling for a bill that was anchored securely in the San Andrés Accords. In March, as a delegation from the EZLN left Chiapas in a convoy destined for Mexico City, social and political commentators debated the legislation and the larger issue of Indian rights. As I followed these debates in the Mexican press, I was struck by the fact that several highly respected academics commenting on the legislation opposed it because—among other reasons—they claimed that it legalized the abuse of indigenous women by allowing communities to sanction "bad" Indian traditions. It was interesting to me that these academics were raising a question that indigenous women themselves had been discussing intensely and publicly since the Zapatista uprising: How does one distinguish between "good" indigenous traditions that the state should sanction and "bad" traditions that the state should abrogate?

In an article written during the height of public debate on an Indian rights' reform proposal before Congress, one author congratulated the many indigenous women who, in the peace negotiations between the federal government and the EZLN at San Andrés Larráinzar, insisted that Indian laws conform to international human rights standards. The author then went on to question the basis on which indigenous women would distinguish between "good" traditions—traditions consistent with human rights standards—and "bad" traditions: "If women recognize that there are good and bad traditions, are they not acknowledging that it isn't respect for tradition that should be at the center of the debate but, rather, that which is ethically above these traditions?" (Viqueira 2001: 32). That which is above Indian law, Viqueira suggests, is the liberal, democratic tradition, which holds up human rights as a universal standard.

Carlos Elizondo, economist and former director of CIDE, a prestigious think tank and research university in Mexico City, was more blunt. In an article entitled, "Are There Superior Cultures?" appearing in *Reforma,* a leading Mexico City daily, Elizondo answered the question posed by the article's title with a resounding yes. "From a moral vantage point, a culture that respects the right of women to study and work must be defended, without ambiguities, as superior to a culture that does not." Cultures that protect women's rights, Elizondo noted, tend to hold individual values as superior to communal values. Elizondo illustrated this general point by pointing to indigenous Mexico: "Only then [when a society prioritizes individual rights] can we avoid situations in which a Huichol [Indian] girl is raped by her stepfather as his 'right' or when supposed witches are burned by their communities."[2]

Since 1994, Indian women, and not liberal male commentators in Mexico City, have raised the issue of Indian tradition and women's rights in countless forums, community meetings, and workshops throughout Chiapas and Mexico. Working tables on women's rights were included in the numerous congresses convened by the EZLN, and women organized parallel conferences at national-level ANIPA (National Assembly in Support of Autonomy) meetings held since 1994 throughout the country.[3] I attended several ANIPA gatherings in 1995 and 1996 and saw these women in action. Whereas the men often talked about autonomy in vague terms, referring, for example, to the International Labor Organization's Convention 169 without explaining to those present exactly what it was, female leaders made posters with easy-to-understand drawings and stick figures to educate participants about the Indian rights enshrined in international law. I suspected that the male leaders of these congresses did not use any of these pedagogical tools because they were afraid of looking childish and insulting their members. The women, in contrast, sallied forth unabashed and with missionary zeal.

One of the most striking differences between the EZLN and other revolutionary movements/armies was its early and emphatic proclamation of women's rights. On the day the EZLN took over four municipal capitals in central and eastern Chiapas—January 1, 1994—it promulgated the Revolutionary Women's Law. The law consisted of ten basic rights, including women's "right to participate in the revolutionary struggle in a way determined by their desire and capacity . . . the right to work and receive a just salary . . . the right to decide the number of children they will have and care for . . . and the right to participate in the affairs of the community and hold positions of authority if they are freely and democratically elected."[4]

Two women played a crucial role in getting the Revolutionary Women's Law drafted and approved. These two women were comandante Ramona and major Ana María. Both Tzotzils, they quickly became international figures after January 1. In a 1994 interview with Ramona and Ana María, the women praised the gender equality practiced within the EZLN, saying, "In the EZLN, everything is shared. There are no differences; one day it's the men's turn to make the meal, on the following day the women's turn, and so on. If there are clothes to wash, the men can do it." They readily admitted, however, that within the Indian communities where they live and work, much remains to be done and gender equality is far from being realized.

One of the most prominent themes that reappeared in the many working tables and forums on women's rights was the relationship between indigenous law ("usos y costumbres") and women's rights. Women pointed out the many abuses against women that have occurred and continue to occur in the name of Indian law: bride kidnappings, in which a woman is literally snatched away by a man desiring to be her husband without having her consent to marry; land apportionment that excludes women; and the absence of female voices in community assemblies where decisions are made that affect the entire community. In these congresses, indigenous women discussed the tension between being committed to their men and the struggle to secure legislation on Indian rights and their objections about those "traditions" that violated women's human rights.

In a May 1994 workshop, entitled "The Rights of Women in our Customs and Traditions" and held in San Cristóbal, the Indian women present spoke of community traditions that preclude women from inheriting land rights. Women can

Figure 10. Zapatista women come to San Cristóbal to celebrate International Women's Day on March 8, 1996. Photo courtesy of the photographer, Ricardo Carvajal.

inherit land in some Indian communities, but in many others, women are excluded systematically. As the women reflected on the amendments to Article 4 of the Mexican constitution, they examined how these changes would affect women:[5]

> If the authorities of the community state that land cannot be inherited [by women] this Article Four is going to support them and women will remain without land. And if we are widows or have many children, we are going to be left without land. Traditions of land apportioning have to be changed; they must be fair for women and men. We want women to be taken into account regarding land problems (credits, agrarian apportioning, family inheritance). (Rojas 1995)

The tension between women's loyalty to broader political goals and their commitment to protecting their own rights as women is one that has arisen not only in Chiapas, but in revolutionary movements around the globe (see West 1997). This dilemma is particularly complicated for indigenous women, who are the targets of both gender and racial discrimination. Within the CNI,

Figure 11. International Women's Day was the setting for this march and demonstration of Zapatista women in front of San Cristóbal's cathedral on March 8, 1996. Photo courtesy of the photographer, Ricardo Carvajal.

indigenous women forged a consensus to support the CNI's official position upholding Indian communities' right to practice Indian law while insisting all the while that laws that infringe on women's individual rights would not be tolerated.

Scholars like Viqueira and Elizondo were latecomers in championing women's rights, arguing that Indian law was so deeply flawed that no modern, liberal state could consider legislation that protects it. For Viqueira and Elizondo, modernity requires adherence to a set of uniform laws, under which all Mexican citizens—including Indian citizens—would live. Modernity meant respect for women's individual rights, while it also meant that there would be no legislation protecting communal rights.

At least one more layer of complexity exists in this debate. What would happen if national laws came into conflict with international laws protecting Indian rights? Convention 169 of the International Labor Organization clearly states that Indian peoples—defined communally—have the collective right to protect the resources necessary to their material and cultural reproduction. Mexico is a signatory to Convention 169 (it was one of the first countries in the world to sign the convention into law in 1990). Is respect for international law a sign of modernity?

The interview with Ramona and Ana María cited above took place the night before International Women's Day, March 8. A parade and demonstration in San Cristóbal was planned, and Ramona and Ana María would be attending. Ana María told reporters that the EZLN had celebrated International Women's Day religiously since its inception. In Zapatista territory, she told the reporter, parties will be thrown, and the men will be responsible for preparing the food. That does not mean, however, that the food will be good, she added, with a wry smile.

CONCLUSION

ETHNIC AUTONOMY REGIMES
IN LATIN AMERICA

Examination of ethnic autonomy in the Mexican case illustrates that several levels of de facto ethnic autonomy coexist: regional, community, and municipal. In the area of de jure autonomy, indigenous organizations in Mexico failed in their attempts to get Congress to codify an ethnic autonomy regime that recognizes indigenous politico-territorial structures in which their own authorities have autonomous powers of self-government, administration of justice, and control over state resources. When we broaden the view to include Latin America, the picture becomes complex.[1] The shape and form that autonomy takes depends largely on specific historical and political contexts, the number and geographic location of indigenous peoples, the relative weakness of the state, and the correlation of political forces, among other factors. One characteristic common to autonomy advocates throughout the continent, however, is their commitment to national unity. Demands for political secession are glaring in their absence. On the contrary, indigenous leaders have argued that autonomy would facilitate the political, social, and cultural participation of indigenous peoples in national life. Included among the types of autonomy typically demanded throughout the region are: linguistic; educational (education that promotes cultural diversity and pluralism); territory; some degree of control over natural resources within an autonomous territory; and some level of political autonomy (recognition of local or regional authorities and "traditions and customs" in election of these authorities) (Stavenhagen 1999: 11–16).

Throughout Latin America, indigenous peoples have exercised de facto autonomy for centuries and continue to do so. In several Latin American countries, constitutionally codified ethnically defined autonomy regimes also allow for the exercise of de jure autonomy.[2] Currently, Panama and Colombia have the strongest constitutionally codified regimes. Nicaragua codified regional ethnic autonomy in 1987, which, while strong in theory, has been weakened in practice due to a lack of funds, internal conflicts among indigenous peoples, and changes in governmental administrations (Díaz-Polanco 1997; Hale 1991, 1994b). Van Cott (2001), in an examination of both successful and unsuccessful attempts to construct ethnic autonomy regimes in the region, argues that indigenous peoples' organizations were successful "when they could raise their autonomy claims in a forum that was part of a larger regime bargain, allowing them to insert their claims in a discussion of fundamental regime issues" (Van Cott 2001: 32).[3] Panama was the first country in Latin America to establish an ethnic autonomy regime, as well as the first, in 1972, to constitutionally recognize Indian rights (Clavero 1994). Negotiations between the Kuna people and the Panamanian government began as early as the 1920s in the context of armed conflict.

Among the five indigenous peoples of Panama, the Kuna have organized most successfully to defend their territory and culture from governmental incursion. (Kuna territory primarily consists of San Blas, an archipelago of islands on the Caribbean coast.)[4] In 1925, the Kuna people staged an uprising and declared the formation of a self-governing Kuna Republic. The government granted them partial autonomy in 1925, which guaranteed the Kuna people citizenship rights and the right to "maintain order among themselves" without the interference of police (Howe 1998: 280–89, cited in Van Cott 2001: 35). The issue of land rights, however, remained unsettled, and the government immediately undermined the partial autonomy achieved in 1925 by initiating a low-intensity war against rebel villages. Negotiations resumed in 1930 and continued until 1938 when San Blas was recognized as an autonomous *comarca* (reserve) (Howe 1998: 280–89, cited in Van Cott 2001: 36).

Today, the Colombian constitution (1991) is the most advanced in the continent in its recognition of Indian rights. In contrast to the Panamanian case in which Indian autonomy was achieved within the context of armed struggle and negotiations to end that struggle, in Colombia, an ethnic autonomy regime was forged within the context of constitutional reform (Van Cott 2000a).[5] Throughout the nineteenth and twentieth centuries, indigenous peoples in Colombia managed to hold onto more of their land *(resguardos)* than their counterparts in the rest of the continent.[6] While Colombian indigenous peoples may be stronger vis-à-vis the federal government than other indigenous peoples in the region, the codification of an ethnic autonomy regime in that country was not solely the result of indigenous mobilization and organization. Van Cott (2000a) argues that the Colombian indigenous movement rode a wave of acute political crisis that peaked in the early 1990s when Colombian citizens demanded a new political pact with their leaders;

at this point in Colombia, citizens' faith in government was at a nadir.

Recognition of Indian autonomy in the 1991 constitution was achieved through alliances between indigenous organizations and political elites, who were eager to extend the reach of the state into remote, rural regions. Although Colombia's indigenous population is tiny, comprising only 2.7 percent of the population, its territorial reach is significant. Before the 1991 reforms, about 84 percent of the indigenous population lived on reserves totaling 27.8 million hectares, comprising 24 percent of the total national territory (Van Cott 2000a: 45). Yet, territorial questions alone cannot explain how political elites came to accept the idea of enshrining administrative-territorial units and group-specific rights in the constitution. Van Cott (2000a) argues, not without irony, that it was precisely Indians' marginalization and subordination that led to elites' embrace of Indian rights and autonomy.[7] The logic of Colombia's political elites went like this: if Indian rights could be protected in the new constitution, it would send a powerful signal to other social actors that the changes proposed by the political class were real (Van Cott 2000a).

Van Cott sums up the process of constitutional reform in Colombia by saying that "the constituent assembly provided a fortuitous 'political opportunity' for the already organized and mobilized indigenous movement to frame its particular grievances in more universalist terms" (Van Cott 2000a: 76). According to Van Cott, the three indigenous delegates' key achievement in the constituent assembly was the institutionalization of the presence of Indians as a group with special rights in Colombian society.[8] Indigenous peoples are mentioned no fewer than twenty times throughout the new constitution (Sánchez, Roldán, and Sánchez 1993: 23, 66, cited in Van Cott 2000a: 85). For the first time in Colombian history, the constitution now recognizes the collective and inalienable nature of the country's existing resguardos. As Van Cott argues, the recognition of the territoriality of indigenous communities (their preconstitutional jurisdictional and autonomy rights over their traditional lands, as opposed to property rights), together with a share of state resource transfers, provides the material basis for the exercise of the Indians' right to difference under the constitution (Van Cott 2000a: 85). In addition to allowing Indians to exercise customary legal practices within indigenous territories, as well as the exercise of self-government rights by indigenous cabildos or other native forms of self-government, Article 171 created a national two-seat senatorial district for Indians (Van Cott 2000a: 85). Provisions in Article 329 allow for the consolidation of reserves into indigenous territorial entities (ETIs), which created the possibility of forming vast autonomous regions in some areas.[9]

In Colombia and throughout the continent, legal reforms have been indispensable in strengthening indigenous peoples' claims to a larger share of resources and greater participation in political institutions on the national, state, regional, and local levels. Even after a long struggle to gain legal recognition and autonomy, however, there is no guarantee that the reforms will be implemented. A case in point is Nicaragua, where, on September 2, 1987, the Autonomy Statute was passed by the Sandinista legislature, which established two multi-ethnic Atlantic coast autonomous regions (Díaz-Polanco 1997: 119–25; Van Cott 2001: 37). This statute included guarantees of equal citizenship for Atlantic coast indigenous peoples, as well as protection of their special rights. Under the agreement, the state recognized communal forms of landownership and indigenous peoples' right to "provide themselves with their own forms of social organization and to administer their local affairs according to their traditions" (cited in Díaz-Polanco 1997: 122). Implementation of this statute, however, proved to be even more difficult than the long process of establishing such an accord.

Historically, the Miskito Indians on the Atlantic coast of Nicaragua had established closer relationships to Anglos that colonized the area than to mestizos in the center and Pacific coast of the country. In fact, during the entire nineteenth century, the British exercised de facto sovereignty over the area under the Mosquitia Protectorate (1824–60) and the Mosquitia Reserve (1860–94) (Díaz-Polanco 1997: 119). Even while the Miskito were citizens of the Nicaraguan state, their daily lives revolved around relationships with British colonists, North American company managers, and traders and missionaries of the Moravian church (Díaz-Polanco 1997: 119; Hale 1991: 24). Miskito relations with the central government had long been fraught with tension. In the 1980s, the Miskito fought against the Sandinistas (FSLN) in defense of ethnic autonomy and Miskito rights, continuing a long tradition of resisting the central government. According to Hale (1991), Miskito "ethnic militancy" revolved around demands for land, control of natural resources, self-government, and respect for Miskito culture. The FSLN grossly misunderstood Miskito resistance to the state and, given the region's historic ties to Anglo culture, accused the ethnic militants of being CIA dupes (Hale 1991, 1994b).

Talks between the Sandinista government and Miskito leadership began in 1984, but it was not until three years later that an agreement on ethnic autonomy was reached. In the meantime, Sandinista government officials posted to the region worked through less militant Miskito organizations, attempting to "buy off" ethnic militants by increasing the government's presence in the areas of health, education, food distribution, and funds for community development on the Atlantic coast. According to Hale, the accord that was finally reached in 1987 was the result of compromise on both sides. By 1987, a number of Miskito people came to the conclusion that continuing the armed conflict was not tenable. At the same time, the Sandinista leadership realized that if it wanted to resolve the conflict, it needed to open up a space for (limited) political autonomy among the Miskito people. Implementation of the statute has been disappointing; from the start, the autonomous government structures set up to represent Miskito people were dramatically underfunded. Problems of representation and accusations of fund mismanagement by autonomous government officials were also widely reported (Hale 1991: 27).

In Mexico, in the wake of the EZLN uprising, many indigenous and popular organizations throughout the country demanded the convening of a constitutional convention, or assembly, to rewrite the Mexican constitution. In addition to the inclusion of indigenous rights and ethnic autonomy, popular demands were aired, for example, restoring Article 27 to its original (1917) status and decentralizing power to municipal governments. Those demanding a new constitution argued that the Mexican state was in acute crisis and that the only way to restore citizens' faith in the political system was to wipe the slate clean. Indeed, in 1994 it seemed as if the Mexican political system—based on one-party rule—was disintegrating. The assassinations of two major political figures that year—the PRI's presidential candidate, Luis Donaldo Colosio, in March and secretary-general of the PRI, José Francisco Ruiz Massieu, in September—rocked the country. When the Mexican peso lost half its value overnight in December 1994, leaving many middle-class Mexicans with dollar-held debt and the poor with greatly reduced buying power, the public's anger peaked. Yet, for the most part, this anger remained diffuse and never coalesced into a national movement behind concrete goals. By the fall of 1996, electoral reform in Congress proceeded apace and the public's interest in the EZLN began to wane.

If we examine Mexico within Van Cott's (2001) framework of ethnic autonomy regimes in Latin America, Mexico, unlike the Panamanian and Nicaraguan cases, failed to establish an ethnic autonomy regime as it negotiated the end to armed conflict. Van Cott (2001) explains this failure by two factors: (1) access to decision-making spheres was closed to indigenous participants and (2) indigenous peoples had no influential ally to back their claims vis-à-vis the central government.[10] An additional factor to consider is the relative strength of the Mexican state, which is much stronger than the Panamanian state of the 1930s or the Nicaraguan state under Sandinista leadership in the 1980s. State incentives to establish an ethnic autonomy regime in Mexico, therefore, are potentially weaker.[11]

If we compare and contrast ethnic autonomy regimes in Latin America, the Guatemalan case emerges as most similar to the Mexican. In both cases, negotiations over indigenous rights occurred within the context of negotiations to end armed conflict. Although constitutional changes were made in both Mexico and Guatemala (both countries officially declared their commitment to multiculturalism and limited self-rule), in neither case were ethnic autonomy regimes established. In Guatemala, the negotiations that ended a thirty-six-year civil war generated a separate accord on Identity and the Rights of Indigenous Peoples, signed on March 31, 1995, by the government, the military, and Guatemalan National Revolutionary Unity (the main umbrella organization of guerrillas [URNG]) high command. The accord emphasized cultural rights (that is, recognition of Guatemala's multicultural composition, the legitimacy of using indigenous languages in official and public spaces, recognition and protection of Maya spirituality, and commitment to education reform), recognition of communal lands and the reform of the legal system, as well as indigenous political participation (see Warren 1998: 52–68). Maya movement leaders, while recognizing the accord's achievements, criticized its failure to frontally address the question of collective rights. Warren notes, "Major issues such as the recognition of regional autonomy, historic land rights, and the officialization of Maya leadership norms were deemed irreconcilable and dropped" (Warren 1998: 56).

Van Cott (2001) argues that during the peace negotiations in both Mexico and Guatemala, access to decision-making spheres was closed to indigenous leaders. In Guatemala, Mayanist movement leaders were not directly involved in the peace negotiations. Only later, when civil society organizations pressured governmental and guerrilla leaders to substantively include indigenous voices in the process, did Mayanists serve as members of advisory committees. Despite the limitations of the process and the accord itself, however, Mayanist leaders publicly hailed it as a breakthrough for the movement (Warren 1998: 56). Through their collaboration with the government in joint commissions to implement the accord, Mayanist leaders hoped to reintroduce the issue of autonomy lost in the accord process, specifically through the design and development of decentralization projects, which would allow decision-making powers to devolve regionally and locally (Warren 1998: 63). In the Mexican case, the ethnic autonomy proposal developed by indigenous organizations and the EZLN in the context of peace negotiations was not brought before Congress; instead, nonindigenous political elites developed their own proposal behind closed doors.

Van Cott highlights a second variable to explain the failure of countries to establish an ethnic autonomy regime in the context of negotiations to end armed conflict: the absence of an influential ally that actively supports the establishment of such a regime. In the Panamanian and the Nicaraguan cases, the United States supported the Kuna and the Miskito movements for ethnic autonomy (Van Cott 2001). In both cases, the United States used its support for the Kuna and Miskito demands to further U.S. foreign-policy goals in the region (Hale 1994b; Howe 1998). During the negotiations over Indian rights and autonomy between the Mexican government and the EZLN in 1995 and 1996, the U.S. government did not bring similar pressure to bear on the Mexican government. If anything, an ethnic autonomy regime in Mexico would have weakened the position of U.S. business, interested in extracting the valuable natural resources on indigenous land. Unlike the situation in Panama in the 1930s or Nicaragua in the 1980s, the United States viewed the central Mexican government as friendly to U.S. interests; this coincidence of interests between the U.S. and Mexican governments has accelerated under the North American Free Trade Agreement (NAFTA).

De Facto Autonomy on the Margins

Since Vicente Fox assumed power on December 1, 2000, the attacks on autonomous Zapatista municipalities have stopped and thousands of Mexican federal soldiers have returned to their barracks in Chiapas. Official peace talks between the two sides have not yet resumed, however, and a comprehensive peace agreement between the EZLN and the federal government appears more distant today than it did in December 2000. Now, after the initial excitement of the EZLN uprising has long died down, Indian communities are left to reorganize themselves. The challenges involved in this reorganization are formidable.

Returning to the Tojolabal case, although regional identity and organization among the Tojolabals have a long, rich history, and are still pushed along today by strong forces, there are also countervailing forces that threaten to split and divide them. At the same time, many Tojolabals—especially those in areas of traditional settlement—continue to identify with their local ejido community. In some cases, this "new" identification is now several decades old. In the Cañada Tojolabal, for example, most of the ejidos were created by the agrarian reform's division of large estates in the late 1930s and early 1940s. Similarly, contemporary intracommunal conflict, typically revolving around religious and political party affiliations, also threatens to pull the larger Tojolabal society apart. In short, forces provoking increasing fragmentation also exist and are perhaps growing stronger.

While the tension between regional and local (community) organization poses a potential challenge to the consolidation of regional autonomy among the Tojolabals, intracommunity conflict poses another, arguably graver one. Five principal cleavages dividing communities today are religion, political party affiliation, support for the EZLN, continuing land conflicts, and the drawing of municipal boundaries. Scholars disagree about the extent to which these conflicts are new. Some observers argue that Indians make use of these affiliations, such as religious and political party affiliation, for example, to distinguish themselves from those with whom they have been at odds for years. Others, taking a more romantic view of indigenous communities, claim that outsiders have fomented divisions by introducing "foreign" structures to the community, such as political parties and Protestantism.[12]

Today, it is not uncommon for Tojolabal communities to house liberationist Catholics, traditional Catholics, mainline Protestant, and evangelical Protestant groups. The mere existence of several distinct religious groups within a single community does not provoke conflict. However, as stable authority structures within the communities have broken down during the past twenty-five years, Indians have employed religious conversion and withdrawal of support for village fiestas and rituals as a means of challenging community traditions in general.[13]

A second significant cleavage dividing communities has been political party affiliation. In general, political party affiliation does not necessarily reflect ideological difference. Large subsections of communities—indeed, entire communities—have shifted their affiliation literally overnight if they perceive some advantage in doing so. There are four active political parties in Las Margaritas. The parties garnering the most support in the region since 1994 are the Partido de la Revolución Institucional (PRI) and the Partido de la Revolución Democrática (PRD). The Partido Acción Nacional (PAN) has a small presence, as does the Partido del Trabajo (PT). Relations between the PRD and the EZLN have been strained since the EZLN's boycott of local elections in October 1995. Postelectoral conflicts subsequently altered the results in these and other municipalities, however, as more than one-third of the municipal offices in the state changed hands during the 1995–98 period.

Since 1994, communities have also divided over their support for the EZLN.

Some Tojolabal communities are widely known as Zapatista. Others are clearly identified as anti-Zapatista, such as Bajucú. In many other communities, however, pro- and anti-Zapatista forces are more evenly divided. In some cases, this division has resulted in the formation of autonomous municipalities that coexist uneasily with "official" municipalities in the same space. In these areas, pro-Zapatista sympathizers refuse to recognize the constitutionally legitimate municipality and they replace it with a parallel government. The largest and most fully developed of such autonomous municipalities in the Tojolabal region was Tierra y Libertad (based in Amparo Aguatinta), an autonomous municipality encompassing eleven "official" municipalities in the selva-fronteriza area of the state.[14] On May 1, 1998, Tierra y Libertad was destroyed by government troops. During the police raid, buildings and houses were destroyed, including the offices of the autonomous municipality, and leaders were arrested.

The question of how municipal boundaries should be drawn has lately become another source of division between EZLN supporters and opponents.[15] When the state congress of Chiapas responded to widespread calls for more responsive local government by approving a remunicipalization of the state in July 1999, it was careful to be sure that the 7 new municipalities it created (in addition to the 111 "official" ones that already existed) were drawn so as to undermine the claims of local EZLN supporters for territories in which they could exercise control.[16] Complicating the issue is that in addition to pro- and anti-Zapatista positions on remunicipalization, there are some communities that have advanced proposals for remunicipalization based on their historic boundaries with neighboring municipalities. Sometimes these boundaries overlap with the state's plan for remunicipalization, sometimes with the EZLN's autonomous municipalities, and sometimes with neither. San Pedro Chenalhó, a municipality in the central highlands that is composed of three historic Tzotzil communities (Magdalenas, Santa Martha, and San Pedro), is a good example of the tension that exists in communities with divided interests (Burguete 1998). Since the 1930s, the municipal seat has been San Pedro Chenalhó, despite the fact that Santa Martha had previously governed itself. Since 1994, the Zapatistas have formed two autonomous municipalities in this region (Polhó and Magdalena de la Paz), honoring the insistence of the people of Magdalenas that they have their own municipality. Similarly, the government proposed the creation of a new municipality called Aldama, which is based in Magdalena de la Paz. Although both the EZLN and the government's proposals accommodate the demands of the residents of Magdalenas, both ignore the demands of those living in Santa Martha, whose insistence on a separate municipality have fallen on deaf ears. In the case of Chenalhó, then, there are at least three different interest groups within a single municipality, vying for distinct plans on how to redraw local boundaries.

The political landscape in Chiapas changed dramatically in August 2000 with the historic election of Pablo Salazar Mendiguchía as governor-elect, the first time a non-PRI candidate had been elected to run the state. The Alliance for Chiapas, Salazar's coalition composed of eight political parties, won 52 percent of the vote against the PRI's 46 percent.[17] Although abstentionism was high (50 percent), Salazar Mendiguchía's election generated widespread hope among the citizenry that peace would finally come to the state after more than six years of low-intensity war and social conflict. The very day he took office as governor (December 8, 2000), Salazar Mendiguchía canceled the Remunicipalization Commission and to date, all remunicipalization plans remain suspended (Burguete 2002a). Many of Salazar's supporters (including most social organizations and the EZLN) viewed the former state government's plan as counterinsurgent. The EZLN did not participate in the consultation process on the new municipalities and viewed the plan as a way of distracting attention from implementing other, more important, aspects of the San Andrés Accords. According to Burguete, who has published extensively on this issue, the Chiapas state government did not use remunicipalization as an instrument for dialogue, but rather to weaken the EZLN (Burguete 2002a: 6).

Hopes were high that Salazar's government would move quickly to dismantle old indigenist institutions and replace them with a much more effective, Indian-run Secretaría de Atención a los Pueblos Indígenas (SEAPI), but little has occurred in the year and a half that he has been in office.[18] The SEAPI, for example, continues to be grossly underfunded (Morquecho 2002). On the national level, the debate over Indian rights and autonomy appears to be at an impasse, while the philosophical debate over multiculturalism and identity politics continues. Any Indian rights legislation must recognize that Indians and non-Indians are different from one another, not because of anything "essential" or primordial, but because of different social, political, and economic histories. These histories developed in relation to one another—there is no "pure" Indian or Hispanic culture or history—but they have not been equal.

Today in Las Margaritas, and in Chiapas more broadly, the initial excitement generated by the EZLN has died down. After spending countless hours attending congresses and conventions on Indian culture and rights from 1994 through the signing of the unimplemented San Andrés Accords, a kind of collective exhaustion has set in. Hope for an alliance between EZLN forces and independent social and political organizations active within the state has diminished, due to internal bickering, fatigue after more than five years of low-intensity war, and constant government pressure on communities to disassociate themselves from the EZLN. Meanwhile, many of the thousands of foreign observers who came to Chiapas during the first years after the EZLN erupted onto the Mexican and international political scene have now gone home. Finally, as in the beginning, communities have been left to develop new models for political reorganization on their own. The cleavages presently dividing them will not go away, nor is it likely that traditional mechanisms of self-government and dispute resolution can be reinstated. In light of these circumstances, the most pressing challenge for indigenous people in Chiapas today is to open the spaces among and within communities for an open discussion on how to reorganize themselves.

The end of the national-popular project in Mexico highlights the problem of representation—of mestizos speaking for indigenous peoples and of some indigenous peoples speaking for all Indians. Under the corporatist political system of the 1930s to the 1970s, the PRI state/party spoke for Indian peoples and tolerated little competition. Since neoliberalism replaced corporatism after 1982, multiple voices claiming to speak for Indian peoples have filled the vacuum left by the state's exit. As indigenous peoples mobilize around ethnic identity to resist indigenismo and discrimination, they—like any collectivity—struggle with questions of representation. It is tempting for leaders to utilize the rhetoric of ethnic essentialism (that is, that there is something inherent, almost biological, that unites all indigenous peoples) as a way of mobilizing support for their cause. This strategy is common in contemporary Indian politics in Mexico. The third meeting of the National Indigenous Congress (CNI) held in Nurío, Michoacán, on March 2–4, 2001, closed with the following declaration in favor of Indian communal rights:

> In their name and with their Word, their true Word, planted from ancient times in the depth of our brown heart, with dignity and respect we say that we are a people. We are a people because we carry in our blood, in our flesh and in our skin all of history, all the hope, the wisdom, the culture, language and identity, the roots and branches of wisdom, the flower and the seed that our fathers and mothers commended to us.

We want to plant that seed in our minds and hearts so that we will never forget or lose it. We are not individuals dispersed throughout the world, but a living harmony of colors and voices, a constant beating of desires and thoughts that are born, that grow, and that become fertile lovingly in one heart and with one will, woven with hope. (Congreso Nacional Indígena 2001)

In the above declaration, Indian identity is linked not to a historical experience of discrimination, a voluntary commitment to support a particular cause, or a connection to the land, but directly to blood. It is in the blood and in one's *"carne"* (flesh) and *"piel"* (skin) where culture, hope, language, identity, roots, and wisdom are said to reside. Observers have used these types of declarations to discredit Indian organizations, accusing them of reverse racism. Scholars have widely discussed this apparent paradox in identity politics: the essentialization of some aspect of subaltern identity, which is the very thing the movement is struggling against (Comaroff and Comaroff 1992; Hale 1997). As the Comaroffs argue:

Any activity aimed at the reversal of "ascribed" inequalities may reinforce the primacy of ethnicity as a principle of social differentiation; the very fact that such activity is conducted by and for groupings marked by their cultural identities confirms the perception that these identities do provide the only available basis of collective self-definition and action. Thus while ethnicity is the product of specific historical processes, it tends to take on the "natural" appearance of an autonomous force, a "principle" capable of determining the course of social life. (Comaroff and Comaroff 1992: 60)

Observers of Indian politics should be critical of this kind of ahistorical essentialism. It may be poetic, but as a political strategy it has serious limitations, not the least of which is blinding indigenous peoples to the necessary work that needs to be done to democratize indigenous communities and organizations. Yet, this discourse must be situated within its specific political and cultural context—that of widespread official and quotidian discrimination against indigenous peoples.[19]

As indigenous peoples become increasingly mobile and their local communities more complex, the foundation on which to forge a national Indian movement and identity shifts. The center of indigenous life has historically been the local community. Some activists within the national Indian movement—such as regional autonomy proponents—argue that this focus on local experience impedes broader identifications that would help forge a broader, pan-ethnic identity. Warren discusses a similar tension among the Maya peoples of Guatemala. Community identities, or what she calls "experience-based memories," are being replaced by ethnic nationalist explanations in building a wider ethnic revitalization. She argues that the most difficult dilemma currently facing Indian movement in Guatemala is the successful invention of a pan-community Mayan identity, since virtually all Mayas identify with their home communities as their primary ethnic unit or more diffusely with their language groups. For these ethnic nationalists, wider identifications are crucial if Mayas are to avoid modern forms of the divide-and-conquer strategy historically used by dominant groups (Warren 1992: 211). The Tojolabal case discussed in this book illustrates some of the challenges involved in regional organization and identification. While local communities are no longer as unified as they once were, regional organizations lack the cohesiveness that communities formerly provided. Nationally based Tojolabal leaders may have little difficulty expanding their "imagined" community, but those living and working full time in the area have had a harder time creating and sustaining regional identities and communities. Today, Indians in increasing numbers migrate to cities, speak Spanish, and travel abroad to work and to live. Subsistence farming is, indeed, a thing of the past. The communities that are left by migrants—and returned to—are more diverse today than they were twenty-five years ago. Communities are divided around political party and religious affiliations, making the question of representation and consensus building—the foundation of local decision making in indigenous communities—more challenging than ever before.

Final Remarks

I took the title of this book from a statement made by Victor Hugo Cárdenas, Aymara intellectual and vice president of Bolivia from 1993 to 1997. During the 1980s as leader of the Kataristas, an ethno-peasant movement promoting the idea of a multi-ethnic state, Cárdenas urged fellow Kataristas to see reality with "two eyes," that of the exploited peasantry, together with the entire exploited class, and that of the oppressed Aymaras, together with all the other oppressed peoples (or "nations") in the country (cited in Albó 1994: 55). Although the language today is passé, Cárdenas sought to harmonize class-based organization with the incipient Indian rights discourse and organization emerging in Bolivia during this period. During the 1970s and 1980s in Chiapas, peasant organization also provided a foundation for ethno-peasant and Indian rights organizations, particularly among the Tojolabal-Maya people. For the national Indian movement in Mexico, the Indian rights movement drew on the leadership of those active within independent peasant organizations. This experience provided an important material base for the Indian movement. With its focus on access to land, credit, and a just price for agricultural products, indigenous peasants tied the reproduction of Indian culture to concrete material demands. To be sure, the relationship between peasant organizations and Indian leaders was not without tension. Peasant organization was premised on class and not ethnic-based solidarity and presumed national homogeneity based on the mestizo citizen. Although land reform was a priority within peasant political organizations, territory was not. Cultural demands such as access to communication channels and bilingual education were also excluded from peasant organizations' agendas.

Scholars have been quick to categorize pan-Indian organizations as either class- *or* ethnic-based social movements, yet neither category captures the overlap between class and ethnic identity. In this book, I questioned the sharp dichotomy drawn between the peasant movements of the past and the Indian, or ethnic, movements of the present. Peasant organizations certainly did make demands for land and credit, and they understood these issues to be part of their survival—not just material survival but cultural and spiritual survival as well. In this way, peasant organizations engaged in a politics of identity. Cárdenas's advice to Kataristas "to see with two eyes" comes close to capturing the way that Indian peasants in Bolivia—and in Chiapas, Mexico—continued to be peasants, while also organizing and demanding Indian rights and autonomy. The model of multiculturalism emerging from within Indian rights organizations in Mexico, among them the CNI, combines socioeconomic demands tied to land, territory, and resources, with more "cultural" demands, such as bilingual education and access to mass communication.

During the last twenty years, countries as diverse as Colombia, Ecuador, Guatemala, Mexico, Nicaragua, Paraguay, Peru, and Venezuela all adopted or amended their constitutions to recognize the multicultural, multi-ethnic nature of their societies (Clavero 1994; Stavenhagen 1996b; Van Cott 2000a). Yet, at the same time, under neoliberal economic regimes, agricultural subsidies were slashed, communal land privatized, and agricultural goods opened to international markets. The model of multiculturalism that has emerged in Latin America in the course of the last twenty years recognizes indigenous "culture," but eliminates the material base necessary for its reproduction. One of the most formidable challenges for Latin American Indian movements today is putting pressure on political leaders to give some teeth to the constitutional reforms that have been made. As class-based organization declined in the post–cold war period, so has conversation about structural inequality and the importance of material conditions in shaping individuals' and groups' consciousness and behavior. Indian organizations must find a way to emphasize socioeconomic inequality and class solidarity, while at the same time focusing on the racism that continues to mark quotidian life and institutional structures in the region, as well as the ways in which class and ethnic discrimination reinforce one another.

In an era of tight budgets, neoliberal governments have been loath to support development projects in indigenous regions that require substantial influxes of governmental monies. Indigenous social movements, particularly in the Andean region, have turned to nongovernmental organizations and international development institutions, such as the World Bank and the Inter-American Development Bank, for assistance in financing the training of local leaders, microdevelopment projects, and a host of other initiatives. International funding institutions such as the World Bank have developed an interest in Indian rights and culture in an effort to buttress "social capital" in the region.[20] In the 1990s, international donors and funding agencies began to focus their energies—and monies—on local levels. For institutions such as the World Bank, this decision was due in part to corruption and to entrenched and intransigent national bureaucracies. The failure of neoliberal governments to improve poverty indices in the region also forced development agencies to shift strategies, involving local people in order to boost program success. "Development with identity" has become a new field within development circles in which ethnic ties and solidarity are viewed as a type of social capital that communities can build on in order to secure resources (Radcliffe 2001).

Across Latin America in the 1990s, national governments decentralized resources and control over policy to subnational units in an effort to reduce the size of bloated central governments, to make government more accountable, and to save money. Local Indian social movements, particularly in Ecuador and Bolivia, have taken advantage of decentralization, which has meant additional monies for local governments, where indigenous peoples have gained experience in governing.[21] In Ecuador and Bolivia, indigenous leaders have built on local experience in governing to consolidate regional and national movements from which Indian political leaders have emerged (see Albó 1994; Lucero 2002; Pallares 2002; Selverston-Scher 2001).

The very presence of millions of Indian peoples in Mexico and in the Americas today is testimony to the fact that assimilation has not been an unmitigated success. Mobilization around ethnic identity is not anachronistic; Indians use it to adapt to changing conditions in the present. In the highlands of Jalisco, Mexico, for example, Guillermo de la Peña found that Indian "agriculturalists . . . that take advantage of modern techniques and sell their products in national and international mercantile circuits don't lose their forms of ceremonial organization and communal symbols. In fact, the latter is reinforced as a way of establishing preferential relationships in situations of risk and uncertainty" (de la Peña n.d.: 26). Similarly, Colloredo-Mansfeld argues that indigenous culture in Otavalo, Ecuador, adapts positively to outside influences and changing material culture. Members of the Otavalo diaspora continue to produce "Indian" designs and consider themselves indigenous. Although some critics claim that tourism has reduced Otavaleño culture to a superficial commercial display, Colloredo-Mansfeld disagrees and argues that "the influence of tourist spending has, if anything, led to entirely new expressions of indigenousness" (Colloredo-Mansfeld 1999: 198).

One of the strengths of a democratic system of government is its ability to accommodate different ways of life and forms of social organization so long as these competing systems do not infringe on others' rights. The forms of social and political organization developed by Indian peoples over the years reflect not simply cultural differences, but are a response to political and historical conditions. In my view, recognition of these systems—by the Mexican state, as well as by mainstream Mexican society—will help make them more democratic. Recognizing Indian "traditions and customs" opens a dialogue between Indian and non-Indian society about democracy and the ways both groups can work to make their respective institutions and processes more democratic. Without dichotomizing the Indian and the non-Indian worlds into two separate spheres, we have much to learn from one another. At the beginning of this new millennium, millions of native peoples in Mexico, Latin America, and around the world continue to clamor for recognition of difference and for protection of their rights—both as individuals and as members of larger communities. Indians cannot be the only ones to see with two eyes. So must we.

NOTES

Preface

1. Hereafter, I will refer to San Cristóbal de las Casas simply as San Cristóbal.

2. The official dialogue between the EZLN and the Mexican government took place in two distinct phases. The first phase was held between February 1994 and January 1995. No accords were signed during this phase, and the EZLN ultimately rejected the government's proposals. The second phase began in March 1995 when the executive branch and the legislative Commission of Conciliation and Pacification (COCOPA) elaborated an "Initiative of Law for the Dialogue, Conciliation, and Dignified Peace in Chiapas," published as a formal decree on March 11, 1995 (Centro de Derechos Humanos "Fray Bartolomé de las Casas" 1999: 16).

3. The officially demarcated "zone of conflict" lies within three municipalities in eastern Chiapas: Altamirano, Las Margaritas, and Ocosingo.

4. The San Andrés Accords are the only accords on a substantial policy issue that have been signed since the conflict began.

5. The term "thick description" is Clifford Geertz's (1973).

Introduction

1. The Ejército Zapatista de Liberación Nacional (EZLN) took its name from the Indian revolutionary leader Emiliano Zapata, one of four regional leaders of the 1910 Mexican Revolution and a Náhuatl Indian from Morelos state. The leaders who came to power after the revolution claimed to incorporate Zapata's demands in Article 27 of the constitution, which established communal landholdings, or ejidos, for Mexican peasants. (These same leaders had Zapata killed in an ambush in 1919.)

2. In general terms, being Indian in Mexico means being poor, often extremely poor. One study found that as the probability of being indigenous increased (measured by the percentage of indigenous peoples living in a municipality), so does an individual's probability of being poor. For example, living in a 50-percent indigenous municipality increased the probability of a household head being poor by 24.5 percent. The author of the study concluded that living in an indigenous municipality increased the marginal probability of being poor more than any other single variable (Panagides 1994: 136).

   In this study, I use "indigenous" and "Indian" to refer to native peoples in the Americas. While "Indian" is a term that has been used historically to discriminate against and disparage indigenous peoples, it is now being used as a positive identifier by many Indian organizations.

3. The National Peasant Confederation (CNC), like the National Worker's Confederation (CTM) and the National Network of Popular Organizations (CNOP), is organized around corporatist lines and is not, strictly speaking, a class-based organization. National-level confederations link state- and local-level ones, which channel popular voices into official organizations. The class-based orientation of CNC, CTM, and CNOP greatly depends on

national-level leaders and the administration in power, but until 1982 the PRI-controlled government generally held left-of-center national political affiliations.

4. In this book, I define indigenism, or indigenismo, as state policies designed for indigenous peoples by non-Indians. Favre provides a more elaborate definition of indigenismo as "a current of thought and of ideas that is organized and developed around the image of the Indian. It is presented as an interrogation of Indian-ness by non-Indians in function of the preoccupations and ends of the latter" (cited in Barre 1983: 30).

5. Although some Mexican intellectuals and elites have held up Mexico's Indian past as a source of pride and national patrimony, the larger public has typically perceived Indians as dirty, lazy, and as impediments to national progress (see Friedlander 1975).

6. Indians in Ecuador literally shut down the capital and the surrounding region for a week in June 1990, marking the beginning of national Indian movement in Ecuador (see Pallares 2002; Selverston-Scher 2001; Zamosc 1994). In Bolivia, the 1980s witnessed the rise of the first indigenous organizations in the tropical lowlands of eastern Bolivia with the formation of CIDOB, the Indigenous Confederation of the East, Chaco, and Amazon of Bolivia (see Albó 1994). The pan-Maya movement in Guatemala got its start in the 1980s around language issues (see Fischer and Brown 1996).

7. Héctor Díaz-Polanco—anthropologist and advisor to the EZLN during the Dialogue of San Andrés—has argued that autonomy cannot be considered as just one among a list of demands indigenous peoples are making for special recognition and rights, for bilingual education, protection of cultural artifacts, and guaranteed representation in elected office. "Autonomy," he argues, "is the 'articulating demand'—the demand through which all other claims are fulfilled. Neither should we consider autonomy as merely the protection and survival of indigenous cultures. Autonomy is an explicitly political demand requiring a change in the distribution of political power and the creation of new institutions that facilitate the political participation of previously excluded groups" (Díaz-Polanco 1998: 216–17).

8. I will take up the topic of Indian autonomy at length in chapter 4. Suffice it to say here that Indian demands for autonomy, while sharing some essential characteristics, are diverse. The different uses to which the term has been put can be attributed in part to the local character of Indian autonomy practices.

9. As an ideal type, "political activist" may be defined by the number of hours an individual dedicates weekly to political activities. This proved to be nearly impossible to measure in my study. The Mexican Indian movement is in the early stages of consolidation, and few individuals have formal office space and titles. Additionally, among poor peasants in Chiapas and in Mexico more generally the lines between political and personal work are often blurred. Local leaders of Tojolabal ejido unions, for example, do much of their work by talking to people in their communities, discussing local problems and grievances, and transporting individuals in buses that the union has purchased for community use. Many of the interviews I conducted took place in open fields, during community fiestas, and on buses going to and from Comitán and Las Margaritas. It was rare for me to conduct an interview in an office setting.

10. One of the most polemical debates in Mexican academic and policy circles during the 1970s occurred between *campesinistas* and *descampesinistas*. Campesinistas viewed peasants as occupying an important and "necessary" role within the capitalist system: peasants provided a

reservoir of cheap (captive) family labor on which rested the profits and the growth of a considerable part of the modern capitalist system. Campesinistas maintained that peasants would *not* disappear as capitalism advanced. In the opposing camp, descampesinistas, such as Roger Bartra (1974), argued that peasants were linked to precapitalist modes of production and were, therefore, outside capitalism: peasants were inefficient producers exploited by retrograde commercial capital who would eventually be absorbed by capitalism.

Chapter One

1. The use of the word "corporate" here refers to a form of social and political organization within indigenous communities of highland Chiapas, which was typically hierarchical and highly structured; leadership within these communities was based on age, wealth, and service to the community.

2. Using cognitive and psychological theories of human behavior, functionalists such as George Foster (1967), Ralph Beals (1973), and Oscar Lewis (1963) later challenged the focus on harmony in functionalist anthropology by pointing out the conflict that existed within indigenous and mestizo communities.

3. Structuralism was similar in many ways to functionalism. Both camps focused on the ways in which society's different dimensions, or spheres, functioned to work together as a whole. In particular, structuralist anthropologists were interested in describing social life as a model so as to study it comprehensively.

4. In Chiapas, the term "ladino" is used to refer to non-Indians.

5. The cofradía system consists of religious brotherhoods founded to honor important patron saints (Wasserstrom 1983: 262). It has been thoroughly studied by functionalist anthropologists, who have viewed the system as a local institution fundamentally associated with maintaining the boundaries of rural communities in the face of fluctuating outside pressure toward incorporation. According to Hewitt (1985: 55), the civil-religious hierarchy was the repository of local political power, the mechanism through which status was defined within the community, and at the same time acted as an important channel for the redistribution of wealth through community service rather than accumulation for private gain.

6. The congress provided a space for Tzotzils, Tzeltals, Tojolabals, and Ch'ols to come together and discuss problems of health care, land, education, and commercialization for their products—in their own languages and on their own terms. The 1974 Indian congress was a watershed event for indigenous political and social organization in Chiapas and in Mexico. It was the first time that Indians in Chiapas came together to speak about their common problems. The organizational processes that congress participants and promoters generated broke the political monopoly that the official party had in indigenous regions.

7. Héctor Díaz-Polanco (1985), for example, viewed class identity as involving political forms of organization and specific ideological structures; he criticized fellow Marxists for focusing exclusively on narrowly defined economic components in their definition of class.

8. The political party that ruled Mexico for seventy-one years on the national level (1929–2000) underwent several name changes before it became the Institutional Revolutionary Party, or PRI, in 1946. The National Revolutionary Party (PNR) was formed in 1929, which was replaced by the Party of the Mexican Revolution (PRM) in 1938, which later became the PRI.

9. Scholars have characterized the political system set up by Lázaro Cárdenas as state corporatist (see Camp 1999: chap. 1). Although the term has been used to describe many different types of regimes, in state corporatist systems the state organizes interest groups (for example, peasants, workers, and so on) into monopolistic units with nonoverlapping domains of representation (Schmitter 1993: 198). This system of representation is tightly controlled by the state, making it unlikely that different interest groups would organize around mutual interests. State corporatism has often been contrasted to a pluralist system of representation (represented best by the United States). For more on Mexico's corporatist model, see Spalding (1981) and Sloan (1985). For a historical look at how President Cárdenas shaped Mexican corporatism, see Hamilton (1982).

10. The diocese provided literacy and leadership training to Indians as catechists, which, in a state where Indians were systematically denied civil rights, was an intensely political act. The diocese also encouraged Indians to unite to defend their rights, even if the church left the actual organization to others. It has been widely reported that in the 1970s, Archbishop Samuel Ruiz invited radical political activists from northern Mexico to organize the Indians, with the understanding that the activists would take care of the political side of the equation and the diocese would look after Indians' social and spiritual lives. By the early 1990s, however, a rift occurred between the diocese and several of the predominant political organizations active in the Lacandon jungle, chief among them the National Liberation Movement (MLN), of which subcomandante Marcos was a member (Tello 1995; see Womack 1999).

11. The most visible state presence was the police, whose forces increased during the 1980s as civil wars raged in Central America, and the Mexican government worried about possible spillover effects. In the 1990s, border patrolling increased on the southern border as the United States poured millions of dollars into Mexico's drug interdiction efforts.

12. Scholars have typically defined external self-determination as independent statehood and internal self-determination as "more meaningful participation in the political system" (Halperin and Scheffer with Small, cited in Van Cott 1996: 47).

13. In recent years at international forums and within international governmental and intergovernmental bodies, indigenous peoples have argued that they should not be treated as ethnic minorities, but as peoples, with all the rights accorded to peoples in international law. Indigenous peoples do not consider themselves to be ethnic minorities because, they claim, their ancestors were present before those who later became majorities within current nation-states (Lapidoth 1996: 17). The definition of indigenous peoples as peoples per se has been an incredibly thorny question, which remains unresolved.

14. According to Hannum, the principle of self-determination did not rise to the level of a rule of international law at the time of the United Nations Charter in 1945, nor is self-determination mentioned in the 1948 Universal Declaration of Human Rights. The UN General Assembly first took up the issue of self-determination in 1960 in its Declaration on the Granting of Independence to Colonial Countries and Peoples (Hannum 1990: 34).

15. Approximately 40 million indigenous peoples belonging to four hundred different ethnic groups live in Latin America and the Caribbean: 10 percent of Latin America's total population (Deruyttere 1994). Although estimates of indigenous populations are notoriously imprecise, the World Factbook (2001) reports that with 55 percent, Bolivia is the most indigenous

country in Latin America (in percentage terms). Following Bolivia is Peru (45 percent) and Guatemala (43 percent). Uruguay does not have an indigenous population to speak of, and small minority populations are found in Brazil (less than 1 percent), Argentina (mestizo, Amerindian, and other nonwhites comprise 3 percent), and Colombia (1 percent).

16. Although many studies of state-corporatist regimes in Latin America emphasize the strength of the state, Yashar points out that state-centralized control was compromised by "the absence of a rationalized bureaucracy, the failure to establish authority, and a lack of monopoly on the legitimate use of force" (Yashar 1999: 82). Writing about the Mexican context, Knight (1990a) and Rubin (1998) have pointed to the uneven reach of Mexican corporatism.

17. It is easier to say what social movements are *not,* than what they are. Social movements are not simply groups, yet they fall short of being revolutions or insurrections. One author defines a social movement as "a sustained challenge to power holders in the name of a population living under the jurisdiction of those power holders by means of repeated public displays of that population's numbers, commitment, unity and worthiness" (Diani, cited in Lucero 2000). Although most social movements have political goals, members of social movements typically eschew institutional or formal political activity—such as partisan proselytizing or work for political parties—in favor of less formally structured protest activity. Jelin (1986: 18) captures the noninstitutionalized character of social movements in her definition of these movements as "forms of collective action with a high degree of popular participation which use noninstitutional channels, and which formulate their demands while simultaneously finding forms of action to express them, thus establishing themselves as collective subjects, that is, as a group or social category."

18. In 1976, military or military-backed governments ruled Argentina, Chile, Brazil, Ecuador, Peru, Paraguay, Uruguay, Nicaragua, and Guatemala.

19. Not all social movement organizations that emerged in Latin America during these years were formed in response to military dictatorships. Beginning in the late 1970s and early 1980s, regional and national Indian movement organizations emerged in Ecuador (Confederation of Indigenous Nationalities, CONAIE), Venezuela (National Indian Council of Venezuela, CONIVE), and Colombia (National Indigenous Organization of Colombia, ONIC) (Van Cott 2001).

20. There is some debate in the literature over how to interpret indigenous peoples' demands for individual citizenship rights. Some authors, such as Deborah Yashar (1999), argue that indigenous demands for citizenship rights in the 1990s arose, in part, from neoliberal states' failure to protect individual rights. Others, such as Bartolomé Clavero (1994: 110), argue that indigenous demands for individual rights are linked to the exercise of collective rights, that is, membership in a wider community. See Stavenhagen (1996b) for a general discussion of the relationship between individual and collective rights.

21. In a review essay on recent trends in the study of Latin American social movements, Philip Oxhorn argues that literature emerging in the late 1990s on this theme rejected the "polarizing theoretical debates around the importance of 'strategy' versus 'identity for social mobilization'" (Oxhorn 2001: 164). Oxhorn goes on to say that today researchers are integrating work on structure, opportunities, and resources (along with norms, ideas, culture, and even individual personalities) in the study of social movements.

22. Convention 169 of the International Labor Organization (ILO) stands out as the most progressive and far-reaching single document on indigenous rights to date. Convention 169 replaced the ILO Convention 107, passed in 1957. Among international organizations, the ILO has distinguished itself in addressing the issue of indigenous rights (Hannum 1990: 77). In a nutshell, Convention 169 implies the recognition of some form of self-rule, autonomy, or internal self-determination for indigenous peoples. This self-determination refers to the right of indigenous peoples to possess a separate and distinct administrative structure and judicial system, as well as the right to retain customs, institutions, and customary laws (Assies, van der Haar, and Hoekema 2000: 3). Significantly, while Convention 169 refers to indigenous peoples as "peoples," it does not imply that Indians can exercise the rights accorded to peoples in international law. Therein lies the convention's principal limitation. The text of Convention 169 is available at the International Labor Organization's Web site, which can be found at URL: http://ilolex.ilo.ch:1567/english/convdisp1.htm.

Chapter Two

1. For a discussion of the status of the peasantry in Latin America, see Kearney (1996).

2. The EZLN uprising opened spaces within which indigenous peasants renewed their demand for land. In 1994 there were more than one thousand land takeovers in the state and in 1995, more than two thousand (van der Haar 1998: 100). Van der Haar (1998) has described the post-1994 period in Chiapas as one of "re-peasantization."

3. In the 1990s, a number of scholars of Mexico produced work that critically examined the view—quite common in the literature on Mexican politics—that the Mexican state was a Leviathan. Political scientist Jeff Rubin (1998), for example, has argued that Zapotec Indians in Juchitán, Oaxaca, actively resisted the national and state governments for decades and that the Mexican state was not as hegemonic as scholars have claimed. A text that became a point of reference in this area is Gil Joseph and Daniel Nugent's *Everyday Forms of State Formation* (1994). This volume examined, through empirical chapters on different case studies, how local societies and cultures participate in the process of state formation, even while they are also shaped by states.

4. The Echeverría administration is surpassed only by the Cárdenas (1934–40) and Díaz Ordaz (1964–70) administrations in the number of hectares distributed.

5. The Congreso Nacional de Pueblos Indígenas (CNPI) was created in 1975 in Pátzcuaro, Michoacán, and quickly became appropriated by local organizations that used the organization to launch more independent initiatives. Internal divisions and the proliferation of dissident groups within the CNPI, however, caused its influence to greatly wane after the first three years. By 1979, the more independent organizations within CNPI abandoned its ranks to join the newly formed National "Plan de Ayala" Network (CNPA) that was organized in a decentralized and semiautonomous fashion in contrast to traditional hierarchical and vertically organized confederations (Fox and Gordillo 1989: 148).

6. Arturo Luna Luján, personal interview with author, Tuxtla Gutiérrez, Chiapas, March 25, 1996.

7. Ibid.

8. Tojolabals live in five municipalities within Chiapas: Comitán, Trinitaria, La

Independencia, Altamirano, and Las Margaritas, the latter being the municipality with the largest Tojolabal population. Las Margaritas can be divided into four main geographical regions. The first is *tierra fría* (cold region), the area lying between Comitán and Altamirano, which is primarily corn producing, has the highest population density within the municipality, and is divided into ejidos and small farms. I refer to this area as the Tojolabal Canyon (Cañada Tojolabal). The second is the *montaña* (mountain) area directly east of the Tojolabal Canyon, which has historically functioned as a site of internal migration and for receipt of excess population. In the 1920s, diverse groups of Tojolabals arrived in this area to seek "national" lands on which to settle ejidos (that is, uninhabited land owned by the government). By the 1940s, however, the montaña region became saturated and began to send population farther east into the Lacandon jungle. The third subregion is heavily ladino and located in the city of Las Margaritas. Lastly, the Lacandon jungle region encompasses part of Las Margaritas and Altamirano and is located above the Euseba River and part of the Jataté. Beginning in the 1950s, this region began to receive Tojolabals that came in search of land to plant coffee (Martínez Lavín n.d.: 4–5).

9.   See chapter 1, above, for a definition of the cargo system.

10.   Since anthropologists began to visit the area in the nineteenth century, scholars have engaged in heated debates concerning Tojolabal origins and numerical estimates of the population. In an article published in 1969, Montagú put the Tojolabal population at 40,000 or more, although she admitted that her figure was much higher than the official one. She also noted that as late as 1900 mapmakers considered the region to be unpopulated (Montagú 1969: 226–27). Basauri (1990: 210), one of the earliest anthropologists to visit the region, writes that he is "sure that this tribe is no more than a fraction of the Quiche or Maya-Quiche who stayed in the region after their great empire disappeared." In the early 1960s Alfonso Villa Rojas, the renowned Mexican anthropologist, calculated the Tojolabal population in Comitán, La Trinitaria, La Independencia, and Las Margaritas at almost 10,000 and noted that "the number of Tojolabals who can express themselves in their language is markedly decreasing as the surrounding population is mestiza and speaks Spanish" (Villa Rojas 1985: 70–71). Later studies estimated the population to be between 32,000 and 33,000 in the municipalities of Comitán, La Trinitaria, La Independencia, Altamirano, and, most important, Las Margaritas (Martínez Lavín n.d.; Ruz 1993).

In an article written in 1984, Mario Humberto Ruz, a Mexican anthropologist and the leading scholar on contemporary Tojolabals, noted that scholars had written only 132 pages (when linguistic studies were discounted) on the Tojolabal Maya people. Although this dearth of scholarly information about the Tojolabals was partially ameliorated with the publication of the four-volume study edited by Ruz (1981), scholarly production about Tojolabals is scant, especially when compared with the prodigious existing literature on Tzeltal and Tzotzil Maya peoples (see Vogt 1994).

11.   The appropriation of Indian land in the mid-nineteenth century in Chiapas was facilitated by liberal legislation introduced during this period. In 1856, liberal politicians ordered that older communal land be divided up into individual plots. Ruz argues that large landowners, in the name of eliminating ecclesiastical privilege, took over indigenous community lands not belonging to the church (Ruz 1992: 142).

12. It is a common fallacy in North American formulations of ethnicity that change in culturally plural systems inevitably means "culture loss." Kay Warren suggests that this view is based on the assumption that cultural distinctiveness is culture and that national society is somehow the opposite of "the cultural." This parallels the common Western view, she claims, that third-world societies are culturally distinct, while the West transcends these particularities through economic and scientific rationality. Warren's work on Guatemala, in contrast, suggests that changes in culture provoke not loss but transformation (1992: 203).

13. Since the nineteenth century, the term *baldío* has referred to a kind of sharecropper, usually one whose lands were absorbed by the newly formed estates and who was required to work three or four days each week for the landlord (Wasserstrom 1983: 261). In Chiapas, the existence of the baldío became more widespread after state laws were passed in 1847 that dispossessed Indians of their lands and obligated them to live permanently on fincas as baldíos, exchanging their manual labor for permission to live and work on the land. In the Tojolabal region, *mozo baldío* was the term used most often to describe sharecroppers on the fincas. Gómez and Ruz (1992) note that, not surprisingly, former mozos refer to the entire time period as "el baldío" because the work was also "en balde" (in vain).

14. Several scholars have described the formation of these councils (Díaz-Polanco 1992; Hernández Castillo 2001c; Medina 1977).

15. This demand was a direct threat to the Castellanos family, powerful regional caciques and influential political actors (Absalón Castellanos Domínguez was governor of Chiapas from 1982 to 1988). Since the creation of ejidos in Las Margaritas in the 1940s and 1950s, ejido authorities have been involved in land disputes with members of the Castellanos family.

16. Harvey notes that the most important leaders of the UU were Catholic catechists and intellectuals. The catechists participated in the 1974 Indian congress, while the intellectuals were members of the Unión del Pueblo (Union of the People, UP), the post-1968 Maoist organization that came to work in Chiapas in the late 1970s (Harvey 1998: 79).

17. Historically, indigenous religious and communal rituals and celebrations were centered around the planting and harvesting of crops. Communal labor involved clearing and cleaning communal plots of land. Additionally, communities tied their continued existence to territories and plots of land they claimed to have possessed "from time immemorial."

18. Michael Kearney (1996), for example, argues that most peasants have not been self-sufficient on the land for decades—perhaps centuries—and that the term "peasant" is thus a misnomer. If we examine the question of changing earning patterns with data from the municipality of Las Margaritas we see that in 1990 peasants used 10 percent of the total land available for cultivation for the planting of corn and beans and another 10 percent for coffee. They dedicated the rest of the land to grazing. In the jungle-border region of Las Margaritas, the percentage of land used for grazing was 24 percent in 1990, while in the Lacandon jungle region the figure was 28 percent (*Censos agrícola-ganadero y ejidales,* cited in Leyva and Ascencio 1996). These 1990 figures can be compared with ones from the 1950–70 period. In 1950, 94 percent of the land under cultivation (5,890 of a total cultivated land area of 6,290 hectares) was dedicated to corn and beans. Peasants planted coffee on 2 percent of the total cultivated land, and no pasture land was recorded. In 1970, peasants utilized 45 percent of the land for planting corn and beans (13,578 hectares of 30,404 hectares cultivated). In that

year, 9 percent of the land was used for coffee (2,791 hectares) and 5 percent was reserved for grazing (1,606 hectares of cultivated land).

19. While this leader does not mention names, those responsible for the violence were most likely landowners in league with government officials. In Chiapas, landowners and politicians frequently cooperate with one another, making it difficult for observers (and victims) to separate the two groups.

Vignette One

1. PROCAMPO is a federal program that functions essentially like a subsidy to farmers producing basic foodstuffs.

2. The National Solidarity Program was President Salinas's (1988–94) pet project that funneled monies to state and municipal governments for development projects that were initiated by local communities. PRONASOL was an attempt by the federal government to bypass corporatist organizations such as the National Peasant Confederation (CNC) and go directly to "the people." As the government's voice for indigenous peoples, the National Indigenous Institute (INI) coordinates all government programs for indigenous peoples.

Chapter 3

1. Criollos were persons of Spanish descent born in the New World. Mexico's war of independence from Spain was championed by criollos, who fought against the crown and those loyal to it.

2. Notwithstanding the fact that during the nineteenth century the majority of administrations professed liberalism as their creed, liberalism, as a body of coherently articulated political beliefs, never really existed (Xavier-Guerra 1985). Brading puts it bluntly, arguing that "it is difficult to imagine an ideology [referring to liberalism] less suited for post-colonial Mexico" (Brading 1980: 109). The current of liberalism that became hegemonic in Mexico during the key years of nation-building was a type of popular or national liberalism. (For treatment of conservative liberalism in other Latin American contexts, see Viotti's [1985] work on Brazil.) One author describes these leaders "not as men who sustained an organized theory within a body of doctrines held by liberals; these popular liberals cannot be said to have had a structured liberal thought but rather a series of liberal ideas" (López Cámara 1977: 246). These "popular" liberals were men such as Gordiano Guzmán, lower-level cacique from Michoacán, and Juan Alvarez, southern cacique and ally of Vicente Guerrero. Alvarez, for example, not only seemed to have little respect for classic liberal ideas such as the defense of private property, but was known to defend Indians who attacked towns in Guerrero, arguing that the local landowners were swindlers (Brading 1980: 132–33). For a fascinating treatment of regional and local liberalisms in nineteenth- and twentieth-century Mexico, see Mallon (1995).

3. Latin American elites, comparing race relations in their countries to the racial situation in the United States, claimed that racism did not exist in Latin America. They attributed this lack of racism to mestizaje, which, they argued, prevented the racial conflict that existed in North America and Europe (see the work of Gilberto Freyre on Brazil and José Vasconcelos on Mexico).

4. Wade points out the pervasiveness of the assumption that only when racial identifications are relatively clear-cut and allied to explicit and systematic discriminations can race be socially significant, arguing that this view tends to ignore the real importance of racial identifications in Latin America (Wade 1993). According to Wade, mestizaje, as an ideology, does not exclude the possibility of racism. Wade argues that for elites, mestizaje meant that blacks and Indians may be included within the nation as non-black or non-Indian, that is, potential recruits to mixed-ness. As blacks or Indians, however, they are excluded from the nation-state. Latin American nation-states have glorified their African and Indian roots, but as Wade points out, "the future held for them [blacks and Indians] paternalistic guidance toward integration, which also ideally meant more race mixture and perhaps the eventual erasure of blackness and Indianness from the nation" (Wade 1993: 10). Behind this democratic discourse of mestizaje "lies the hierarchical discourse of *blanqueamiento* (whitening), which points up racial and cultural difference, valorizing whiteness and disparaging blackness and Indianness" (Wade 1993: 18).

5. This description is Enrique Krauze's (cited in Knight 1990b). It is interesting to note that there was much discussion during the Díaz administration about the president's Indian origins. Knight (1990b) cites additional references to Díaz's racial background, which described him as "of supposed only one-eighth Indian blood" and, in fact, "probably all white." In the historical record, Díaz seems to have undergone a process of whitening as his term wore on.

6. Administration officials continued to profess this vision as late as the Echeverría administration (1970–76)—the last administration to openly profess assimilationist goals. A 1976 INI document stated, "Our work should never be done by compulsion or coercion, but rather through persuasion and demonstration; given the small margin of security that indigenous populations have at their disposal, they are not favorably disposed to try out new ways of behaving that depart from their traditional ones. . . . In our contact with the indigenous, we should try to persuade and not to impose" (INI 1976: 41, 47).

7. The timing of INI's creation was due more to policy recommendations issued at the First Interamerican Indigenist Congress held in Pátzcuaro in 1940, in which delegates called on nation-states to develop indigenist institutions, than to President Alemán's commitment to the issue. The presence and pressure of anthropologist Alfonso Caso was instrumental in the creation of the INI in Mexico at this particular moment (INI 1978a: vii).

8. As the official government agency for indigenous affairs, INI coordinates or has a significant impact on the coordination of more than three thousand first-tier indigenous organizations. Among the most important agencies it coordinates are: the Ministry of Education; the Ministry of Health; the Ministry of Agrarian Reform; the Office of the Agrarian Comptroller; the Ministry of Social Development; the Ecology Institute; the National Commission for Human Rights; and the National Institute of Anthropology and History (Tresierra 1994: 196).

9. In theory, each CCI targets four main areas: promotion of production (agricultural aid, commercialization, and reforestation); social welfare (preventive medical and dental care); training and counseling (legal counseling, shelter system, scholarships); and the promotion of cultural heritage (development and promotion of native cultures). In practice, CCIs are organized according to available resources and typically have at least one doctor, veterinarian, lawyer, and sociologist or anthropologist.

10. After the Tzotzil-Tzeltal CCI was created in San Cristóbal in 1951, another six were developed in Chihuahua (1952), Oaxaca (1954, 1959), and Yucatán (1959). During the boom years of the Echeverría administration, sixty-eight CCIs were created in different regions of the country. In Chiapas, for example, ten of the fifteen functioning CCIs were built during the Echeverría administration. After Echeverría, the greatest level of indigenist activity occurred during the Salinas administration, when thirteen CCIs were constructed nationwide, including four in Chiapas. From the administration of Echeverría to that of Salinas, 84 percent of all CCIs were built. Today, in addition to the ninety-six CCIs dispersed throughout twenty-three states, the INI also operates fifteen radio stations, three training centers, and more than one thousand shelters for indigenous children (INI 1994: 27).

11. Medina (1977) noted that the organization of indigenous peoples into Consejos Supremos was based on officials' mistaken notion of Tarahumara political organization.

12. Gregorio Morales, First Mam Supreme Council, Mazapa de Madero, December 1994, in an interview with Hernández Castillo (2001c: 131).

13. The CNPI stated their purpose and mission: "The fundamental objectives of this new organism [CNPI] is to increase and maintain the unity of the Indian Peoples so that they can obtain their demands and fight constantly for the objectives of the Mexican Revolution that will permit the self-determination of our communities and the end to all the mechanisms that have kept us on the margins of social progress" (*Acción Indigenista* 1975a). Although the CNPI was originally created as an appendage of the CNC, it did assume some of the demands of the nation's indigenous peoples and, in some cases, promoted the development of independent Indian leaders (Hernández Castillo 2001c). By the early 1980s, the CNPI leadership had escaped state control. At this time, tensions reached a climax between those factions that fought to maintain their independence from the state and those that favored state control of the organization. In 1981, official leadership was imposed on the CNPI by top administration officials close to the CNC, and the organization itself was fully incorporated into the latter (Díaz-Polanco 1992: 153).

14. The views of these anthropologists are found in the classic work, *¿De eso que llaman la antropología mexicana?* (Bonfil et al. 1970) and in selected essays in *INI 30 Años Después: Revisión Crítica* (Instituto Nacional Indigenista 1978b).

15. This shift in INI policy was mirrored in López Portillo's general policy positions. Upon assuming office in 1976, the president publicly distanced himself from the more reformist elements in the Echeverría administration as he responded to the peso's sharp devaluation, intense capital flight, and an IMF stabilization program (Fox 1993: 136). Later in his administration, however, the balance shifted back toward reformist positions and distributive policy. This was due in part to shifting alliances, but also to a more favorable national and international environment for distributive reforms.

16. There are countless examples of the limited nature of "participatory" indigenismo on local and regional levels. Writing about the Mam-Mochó-Cakchiquel CCI in southeastern Chiapas, Aída Hernández argues that while the local Supreme Council was advised as to the location of the new CCI in the area in 1978, it was not consulted about INI development programs that were ill-suited to the particular conditions of the region. Hernández notes that the professional personnel for this new CCI came mainly from Mexico City, while the technical

staff was hired from among the mestizo population of Motozintla: only two indigenous persons joined the staff, one as a watchman and the other as a driver (Hernández Castillo 2001c).

17.   To what extent can we attribute this policy shift to pressure by grassroots organizations? After all, López Portillo entered the presidency amid growing social protest that increased over the course of his term, especially as both oil revenues and calls for redistribution to rural areas increased. Yet, ironically, signs of rural militancy slowed during the late 1970s, precisely at the time that the administration shifted toward a more reformist position. According to interviews with officials in the López Portillo administration conducted by one author, policymakers responded to *potential* rather than actual protest (Fox 1993).

18.   Carlos Saldívar Alvarado, personal interview with author, Las Margaritas, Chiapas, December 1, 1995.

19.   Mercedes Olivera, personal interview with author, San Cristóbal, Chiapas, April 27, 1996.

20.   Ibid.

21.   Ibid.

22.   Ibid.

23.   These indigenous intellectuals and professionals also came from Culturas Populares (within the Secretaría de Educación Pública), and the National Association for Indigenous Bilingual Teachers in Michoacán.

24.   Zárate argues that the Purépecha New Year celebration marks the beginning of a new strategy of collective action from direct confrontation within the framework of agrarian politics to the construction of an ethnic movement with broader goals (Zárate 1993: 33).

25.   Salinas campaigned on the promise to create PRONASOL, which he believed would help alleviate the social dislocations experienced by Mexicans in the transitional phase toward a leaner, more productive and efficient state apparatus (see Cornelius and Craig 1994: 6).

26.   In fieldwork they conducted on the northwestern Mexican border, Contreras and Bennett (1994) found that participants they interviewed had little understanding of Solidarity's organizational and participatory ideology. Their survey data suggested that only about one-tenth of the population benefiting from Solidarity programs had been personally engaged in these programs in a potentially "transformative" way.

27.   Solidarity expenditures for fiscal year 1991 were approximately U.S. $140 million. A whopping 64 percent of INI's budget in fiscal year 1991 came from Solidarity funds (Fox 1994: 188).

28.   On August 8, 1990, President Salinas inaugurated a Solidaridad fund for the Promotion of the Cultural Patrimony of Indigenous Peoples in San Felipe del Progreso in the state of Mexico. During the inaugural ceremony the president affirmed:

> Our indigenous compatriots are also demanding respect for their culture and their tradition, for their identity and their social organization. In these lie the deepest roots of our plural nation-hood, always united and in solidarity. . . . No one should impose their ideas on you, and much less tell you what you should be. You are owners and builders of your own future, of your destiny. Your culture should not be violated, it is one essential component of our national patrimony, of our collective treasure. Your rights as Mexicans protect that culture, but we will try to make this protection even more apparent, elevating it to the level of our maximum law. I reiterate my commitment of respect and I call on all to echo it. (Fondos de Solidaridad 1992)

29. Because organizations tended to see the INI as nonpartisan, INI was able to convince a wide range of organizations to participate in the Regional Funds program. Solidarity programs administered by the INI typically drew on existing constituencies already active in INI programs, rather than creating new ones.

30. The CCI-Tojolabal covers the five municipalities in the state that have Tojolabal presence: Altamirano, Comitán, Independencia, Las Margaritas, and La Trinitaria.

31. Francisco Gómez Sánchez, personal interview with author, Las Margaritas, Chiapas, February 17, 1996.

32. Carlos Saldívar Alvarado, personal interview with author, Las Margaritas, Chiapas, December 1, 1995.

Vignette Two

1. San Juan Chamula is a Tzotzil Indian community twenty kilometers from San Cristóbal. The traditional dress code for men consisted of white pants and a white woolen vest. Today, many men continue to wear the vest, typically paired with Western-style pants.

2. National totals for all thirty-three forums held were as follows: 12,000 participants; 2000 presentations; and 9,000 proposals (Memoria: Informe de resultados 19).

Chapter Four

1. Before its dismantling on May 1, 1998, Tierra y Libertad consisted of areas covering more than eleven municipalities in Chiapas: Ocosingo, Las Margaritas, La Trinitaria, La Independencia, Comalapa, Amatenango de la Frontera, Motozintla, Bella Vista, Siltepec, La Grandeza, and Villa Comatitlán. At the time it was destroyed, Tierra y Libertad was the most consolidated autonomous municipality in Chiapas.

2. In another place, Díaz-Polanco insists that activists discussed autonomy before January 1, 1994, but without the force or dynamism that the Zapatista movement generated for it:

> It was not as if the demand for autonomy was completely absent before the Zapatista uprising. There were voices and isolated groups that demanded autonomy and that rejected the imposition [of the federal government] and articulated indigenous aspirations for a better world. On some occasions indigenous organizations utilized the term, although in very few cases was it converted into the backbone of a political program that recovered, at the same time, the ethnic, the national, and the urgency of democracy. More than a clear articulation of demands, the organizations often presented laundry lists of interminable demands. But with the Zapatista uprising, the theme of autonomy acquired a national relevance, democratic vigor and a more defined profile. A multitude of small and large contributions have originated from every corner of the country, theories and practices that have been constructing the concept of regional autonomy, multi-culturalism, and inclusive democracy as a tool of justice for indigenous peoples and for the peace of the nation. (Díaz-Polanco 1996: 133)

3. EZLN advisor Héctor Díaz-Polanco estimated the number of ANIPA participants who served as advisors and guests to the Zapatistas at 50 percent or more (Héctor Díaz-Polanco, personal communication).

4. Autonomy is an inherently relative concept and will be defined here as group capacity to make decisions about means and ends internally (without external intervention [Fox and Gordillo 1989]). In this view, overt organizational independence represents one extreme along a continuum, a political choice made by grassroots groups that are highly autonomous vis-à-vis the state, although not necessarily autonomous in relation to opposition political parties (Fox and Gordillo 1989: 131–32).

5. Reforms under the Salinas administration increased this percentage from 4 percent to the current figure of approximately 5 to 6 percent (Rodríguez 1997).

6. Cuauhtémoc Cárdenas was the left-coalition candidate for president in 1988.

7. Van Cott (2000a) makes a similar argument about Convention 169 and the Bolivian and Colombian constitutions. To date, eleven Latin American countries have ratified Convention 169: Argentina (2000); Bolivia (1991); Colombia (1991); Costa Rica (1993); Ecuador (1998); Guatemala (1996); Honduras (1995); Mexico (1990); Peru (1994); Paraguay (1993); and Venezuela (2002) URL: http://ilolex.ilo.ch:1567/english/convdisp1.htm.

8. Araceli Burguete Cal y Mayor, personal interview with author, San Cristóbal, Chiapas, April 9, 1996.

9. One author called this meeting in Matías Romero "a seedbed for the birth of the current Indian movement in Mexico." More than one hundred representatives came together to exchange experiences on inequality and the violation of Indian rights (Vera n.d.: 5).

10. Araceli Burguete Cal y Mayor, personal interview with author, San Cristóbal, Chiapas, April 9, 1996.

11. Margarito Ruiz, personal interview with author, San Cristóbal, Chiapas, May 4, 1996.

12. Translation from Hindley 1996: 234.

13. The nature and extent of this authority, however, is not clear. Indigenous peoples tend to define "peoples" in ethnic, linguistic, and cultural terms. The international community, in contrast, has typically defined the term to mean the permanent population of a state (that is, a politico-territorial rather than an ethnic definition) (see Van Cott 1996). Furthermore, the international community has not supported indigenous peoples' claims to (external) self-determination based on their status as "peoples."

14. This first new paragraph is followed by five statements guaranteeing women's equality, an individual's right to health care, a family's right to dignified housing, and the rights of minors.

15. Hindley (1996: 238) points out the importance of implementing legislation: "In Mexico, constitutional mandates are statements of principle that set normative frameworks for state action." Implementing legislation provides political interpretation of these broad constitutional mandates; they define administrative structures, rules of operation and implementation, and division and scope of powers. After much delay, in 1992 the Salinas administration promised to initiate a series of consultations with indigenous groups to draw up the implementing legislation for Article 4. But the effort was dropped after the excitement surrounding the Quincentenary had died down. Again in spring 1994, the National Commission of Justice for Indigenous Peoples spearheaded a national consultation on the specifics of the implementing legislation. The consultation was called at the last minute in many areas of the country and was, therefore, highly controversial among indigenous organizations. Policymakers did not take the commission's conclusions seriously, and no

implementing law had been developed by the mid-1990s. In its absence, the state retains the prerogative to define what it means to "protect," "promote," and to "take into account" (Hindley 1996).

16. Although not underestimating the importance of these meetings for fomenting unity, Hale (1994a) has focused on their darker side, pointing to the tensions between popular groups *(populares)* and indígenas. Despite the efforts at unity at the October 1991 meeting in Guatemala—illustrated by the slogans, banners, and speeches professing *"unidad indígena y popular"* (popular and indigenous unity)—Hale argues that tensions between the two groups increased as the meeting wore on. According to Hale, the main sources of division centered around four axes: imperialism versus colonialism; national culture and mestizaje; the role of the state; and spirituality. On all four of these topics, indígenas and populares differed dramatically; indígenas spoke of the continuing colonialism of national states and linked this colonialism to mestizaje. Hale's account also points out populares' disregard for Indian spirituality and their desire to capture state power in national liberation struggles. By the end of the congress, many indígena leaders had abandoned the meetings in frustration and anger.

17. Exchanges between Indian and non-Indian intellectuals have taken place in the press, in venues such as the Mexico City daily, *La Jornada,* for example. One of the most notable exchanges took place in 1996 between Héctor Aguilar Camín and Adolfo Regino, a Mixe Indian intellectual and activist.

18. Discussion regarding municipal autonomy in Chiapas is regional in scope, due to the large size of both the official municipalities in the state as well as the rebel municipalities *(municipios en rebeldía)* created by the EZLN beginning in December 1994.

19. Gilberto López y Rivas, one of the EZLN's principal advisors and longtime participant in the Indian movement, stated this position in a talk given at the forum "Chiapas in the Nation" held in San Cristóbal in June 1996.

20. Indian organizations in Oaxaca have been pioneers in pressuring the state government to modify its electoral law to protect the exercise of Indian "traditions and customs" in the election of political representatives. In Oaxaca's Code of Political Institutions and Electoral Proceedings, Volume 4, Article 112 ("Of the Renovation of State Government Positions in the Municipalities through Election by Uses and Customs") it states that "the communities referred to here, respecting their uses and customs, may register their candidates directly, without the intervention of any political party or through any political party" (*Código de Instituciones y Procedimientos Electorales de Oaxaca, Instituto Estatal Electoral,* October 1995). This law has been in force since September 1995.

21. The Mexican House of Representatives (Cámara de Diputados) has five hundred members, three hundred of whom are elected in single-member districts and two hundred who are elected in five national districts, or circunscripciones.

22. One of the government's strategies from the beginning of the conflict was to reduce its scope, insisting that the EZLN was a local and not a national movement and that the EZLN's demands required local, and not national, solutions. Over time, however, it became increasingly difficult for the government to paint the Zapatistas as a local movement, given their use of Mexican national heroes, the constitution, and the national flag. On February

22, 1994, during the first round of peace negotiations that took place between the government and the EZLN, comandante Ramona, a diminutive Tzotzil woman, offered a Mexican flag to the government's representative, Manuel Camacho, as Marcos asked him, "We want to ask you if there is another way of living under this flag, another way of living with dignity and justice under this flag. You all have told us that there is; you have spoken with true words, you have spoken these words to our hearts. Give us an opportunity for peace" (Méndez and Romero 1996).

23. A number of politicians, intellectuals, and political analysts in Mexico view the restructuring of political and economic power under an ethnic autonomy regime as an unacceptable threat to the status quo. Although the government diluted the potential for increased political power and control over natural resources that indigenous peoples would exercise within autonomous regions by limiting the exercise of autonomy to local levels, even that is seen by some observers as ceding too much. According to Fernando Escalante, a noted sociologist and general director of academic programs at the renowned Colegio de México, the EZLN is, in effect, "asking that discrimination be legalized . . . that the laws make a distinction on the basis of ethnic origin; they are supporting discrimination by demanding that there is one law for indigenous peoples and another for non-indigenous" (Correa and Corro 1996: 25).

24. The principal romería sites for Tojolabals are Santo Tomás de Oxchuc, San Mateito de Guatemala, Padre Eternito de Trinitaria, Santa Margarita in Las Margaritas, San Bartolomé in Carranza, and San Pedro en los Regadios. Several Tojolabal regional leaders told me that the traditional practice of romerías helped to explain regional identification among the Tojolabal people, something, they said, not seen among Tzeltals and Tzotzils.

25. Ruz argues that a functioning, indeed flourishing, regional economy was present in the Tojolabal region during the eighteenth and nineteenth centuries: "The social actors participating in these historic processes were in constant and direct contact notably among themselves but also with the inhabitants of other regions. . . . The comings and goings of traders (in addition to the occasional interventions of conquistadors and expeditionaries to the Lacandon jungle area) added to the intense traffic of temporary laborers attracted to the flourishing regional economy" (Ruz 1992: 347).

26. In the Tojolabal Canyon, ejido communities range in size from 30 families to 150 (approximately 150 to 750 persons). Ejido assemblies typically elect the municipal agent and other local officials. Minor crimes are resolved within the community and region without having to go to the municipal judge in Las Margaritas; punishments are set by the communities; and most have their own jails.

27. Reports on the extent of integration and consolidation of the RAP project within the Tojolabal region differ greatly depending on the person speaking. In an interview published in *La Jornada* (Mexico City daily newspaper) on November 4, 1995, Luis Hernández, secretary general of CIOAC-Chiapas and Tojolabal leader, affirmed that thirty-seven communities in the CIOAC (border) region were part of the regional autonomy movement: fourteen from Pueblos Tojolabales; ten from Yajk'achil B'ej and thirteen from Tierra y Libertad (Morquecho and Rojas 1994a).

28. Comment made by Antonio Hernández Cruz in a session held on Indian autonomy and rights during the 1995 ANIPA congress held in San Cristóbal in December 1995.

29. Since 1994, activists within the national Indian movement have engaged in a debate over the degree to which organizations should put their limited resources into strengthening communal forms of autonomy, on the one hand, and the extent to which they should expend resources on campaigns for legislative change, on the other. Although these two activities are not diametrically opposed, they do represent different political positions. The San Andrés Accords on Indian Rights and Culture signed by the government and the EZLN in February 1996 reflect the comunalista position. As mentioned above, the bulk of support for the comunalista camp comes from Oaxaca. Activists associated with this camp are Martínez Luna, Floriberto Díaz, Adelfo Regino Montes, Joel Aquino, and ethnic intellectuals/activists Luis Hernández Navarro and Gustavo Esteva. Comunalista advocates tend to focus more on Indian spirituality, community rituals, and how to build strong Indian governments from the grassroots level.

The other main camp within the national Indian movement is most strongly associated with legislative change and regional autonomy. This camp overlaps substantially with ANIPA leadership. The camp's most prominent advocates include Antonio Hernández, Margarito Ruiz, Carlos Beas Torres, and ethnic intellectuals Araceli Burguete, Héctor Díaz-Polanco, Gilberto López y Rivas, and Consuelo Sánchez.

30. In the early 1980s in the Sierra Juárez region of Oaxaca, Floriberto Díaz, Mixe anthropologist and political activist, created the Comité de Defensa y Desarrollo de los Recursos Naturales y Humanos Mixes, or CODREMI. CODREMI is a good example of the growing trend toward regionalization of the Indian movement during the 1980s. The organization's demands included land reform, transport, and the commercialization of local products (Luis Hernández Navarro, personal communication, April 21, 1997). In addition, CODREMI demanded "absolute respect for communal self-determination of lands, natural resources, and autochthonous forms of organization as original inhabitants." CODREMI has also called for respect for community organization and life, indigenous languages, calendars, and intercommunity exchange of goods (Mejía and Sarmiento 1987: 96). In addition to his participation in the formation of CODREMI, Díaz was instrumental in creating a conservatory for young Mixe musicians (Centro de Capacitación Musical), the largest of its kind in the country. This project was part of a larger effort by Mixe communities to rescue the Mixe language, that is, to encourage its use and to disseminate Mixe philosophy. In the same region in 1978, the Asamblea de Autoridades Mixes united Mixe municipal presidents and traditional leaders in a regional association. In the late 1980s, Servicios del Pueblo Mixe (SER) was created to address ethnically based demands; SER emphasized cultural mechanisms and traditions that distinguish the Mixe people, such as communal work and local forms of justice (Stephen 1996: 12). One area of particular interest to SER has been the relationship between Indian law and national, positive law. In the 1990s, Adelfo Regino Montes, one of Díaz's students, became one of the most visible and eloquent supporters of the comunalista position within the national Indian movement.

31. In the Mexican context, Indians' desire for state recognition is not only a question of dignity and authenticity. Because the Mexican state controls a disproportionate amount of

resources—compared to Western European and North American states—Indians have little choice other than to solicit monies from state officials.

Vignette Three

1. El Camerón was referred to as "The Shrimp" because of his pale skin, relative to other Tojolabal Indian people.

2. Misunderstandings existed between the director of the CCI-Margaritas, Gilberto González Estrada, and government officials in the capital, Tuxtla Gutiérrez. González promised NAT leaders that state security forces would not evict them by force, but the state's secretary of the Ministry of the Interior gave orders to send police to oust them from the premises. The appearance of the state police, not surprisingly, caused mistrust and suspicion on the part of Cruz and NAT members, who continually referred to this gap between INI promises and state action during the negotiation process.

3. INI officials found themselves in the position of having to enforce the accords signed in February 1996, despite the fact that the accords are not legally binding. To further complicate the situation, the government delegation to the peace talks on Indian Culture and Rights did not invite the INI to participate as advisors or invited guests after the first (of three) rounds of discussion on this topic. Observers have suggested that the government did not invite INI advisors back for the second round of talks in November 1995 because of their demonstrated sympathy with EZLN proposals and demands during the first round. The government delegation, then, in the final two rounds of discussion on Indian rights and culture negotiated with the EZLN without the presence of the state's experts on the topic, the National Indigenist Institute (INI)!

4. To briefly summarize the functions of each council, the plural council of consultation would decide on programming, diffusion, and administration of the radio station; the centers of radio production would be responsible for taping programs of general community interest to air on the radio; and the community correspondents, consisting of volunteers from the community, would give their opinions on programs they would like to hear on the radio as well as assist in making general programming decisions.

5. Since 1951 (when the INI arrived in Chiapas), the institute has occupied an awkward position between indigenous community organizations and conservative state governments in Chiapas. In a state historically governed by powerful landowning interests, the INI is viewed as a "radical" political organization, and many state leaders perceive the INI as working to empower indigenous organizations. For example, during the administration of Patrocinio González Garrido (1988–93), the governor attempted to buy the station and to make it part of the state government broadcasting network. In order to keep the station in the hands of INI, station directors had to watch their programs more carefully and restrict broadcasting opportunities for many independent peasant organizations who had used this medium (Hernández Castillo 2001c). Although independent Indian organizations tend to see the INI as a representative of a hostile state, within the state apparatus the INI is commonly viewed as a radical governmental agency gone "native."

Chapter Five

1. The other three themes that were to form part of the dialogue between the EZLN and the Mexican government were social welfare and development, democracy and justice, and women's rights in Chiapas.

2. The official, or legal, name of the municipality is San Andrés Larraínzar.

3. The EZLN delegation maintained its base in San Andrés as did the first and most important working group: community and autonomy.

4. The term *coleto* refers to ladino or non-Indian inhabitants of San Cristóbal who perceive themselves as racially and culturally superior to Indians living in surrounding villages.

In an interview with Saul Landau, subcommander Marcos compared the racism of ladinos against Indians in Chiapas to apartheid in South Africa:

> The racism used against the indigenous Chiapans is very similar to apartheid in South Africa. It's just less acknowledged here. Until 1993 a chicken, a hen, was worth more than the life of an indigenous person. Until not long ago, the indigenous in San Cristóbal couldn't walk on the sidewalk; they had to walk in the street, and they were scorned. They were despised simply because they looked Indian. Anybody not able to speak proper Spanish—meaning able to get proper schooling, besides being dark-skinned, short-statured, and dressed in a particular way—couldn't go into certain places. They were treated like animals. And according to what the landowners say, not even like an animal because an animal is worth more. (Marcos, cited in Landau 1996: 27)

5. The Comisión de Concordia y Pacificación (Commission of Conciliation and Pacification, COCOPA) was created by law in March 1995 in an effort to restart the dialogue after the federal army entered Zapatista territory in a failed attempt to capture the EZLN high command in February 1995. The COCOPA was charged with assisting both parties in setting the bases for dialogue, including the designation of meeting places, providing adequate security for both parties, and setting the rules that would govern these meetings. The COCOPA consisted of six federal senators and eight deputies from the four main political parties, PRI, PAN, PRD, and PT, as well as one representative each from the executive branch and the Chiapas state congress. The Comisión Nacional de Intermediación (National Commission of Intermediation, CONAI) was created during the first phase of dialogue that began in February 1994 in the Cathedral of San Cristóbal.

From April to early October 1995, representatives from both sides, with the COCOPA and the CONAI, set out rules that would govern the dialogue process. One of the most difficult issues was security. The Mexican Red Cross was primarily responsible for getting the EZLN representatives from the Lacandon jungle to the dialogue site for the duration of the talks. Volunteer citizens, who literally made a human chain *(cinturón de seguridad)* around the dialogue site, both in San Cristóbal and in San Andrés Larraínzar, provided round-the-clock security for the delegation. Volunteers from "civil society" also made and served food for these hundreds of volunteers, who were mostly indigenous.

6. There was a conscious attempt by the EZLN to include indigenous organizations from around the country on its guest list. Also notable is the large number of non-Indians whom the EZLN invited to participate as guests and serve as advisors. Although the strong

mestizo presence, particularly among the advisors, demonstrates the EZLN's commitment to ethnic inclusiveness, it also continues a long tradition in Mexico of mestizo advisors to popular organizations. This has been particularly true within both official and independent peasant and indigenous organizations. Within the national Indian movement, however, this trend is beginning to shift as the movement consolidates itself at the national level and as an increasing number of young and middle-aged indigenous leaders take leadership roles within the National Indigenous Congress (CNI).

7. The overwhelming majority of the guests and advisors present at all the phases of the Dialogue of San Andrés came at the EZLN's request.

8. After the second round during which EZLN supporters dominated the discussion, the government reinvited some of their advisors from the INI back during the final round of negotiations.

9. Significantly, at the time of the signing of the accords in February 1996, not one of Mexico's political parties called for this type of reform in their official issue platforms—including the left-of-center Party of the Democratic Revolution (PRD). For more on the relationship between Mexico's political parties and Indian rights, see Burguete (2000).

10. EZLN advisors who had the CCRI's ear during the negotiations and who were opposed to the regional model included Gustavo Esteva and Luis Hernández Navarro, among others. The regional autonomy model, as expressed by its proponents, proposed a fourth level of government within Mexico's federal system. Recall that shortly before, in the Fourth Declaration of the Selva Lacandona, EZLN repudiated struggles for political power, which, in effect, debilitated the regional model's chances of being included within the accords (personal communication by e-mail, Araceli Burguete, June 29, 2000).

11. In Spanish, "pueblo" may be used both to signify "people" and "town."

12. The EZLN and the government both promised to accept the COCOPA's proposal without making additional changes to it.

13. The COCOPA's proposal, which was presented to President Zedillo on November 29, 1996, included the following provisions:

1. Indian peoples "have the right to self-determination and, as an expression of this right, to autonomy as part of the Mexican State, to decide how to organize themselves internally within social, economic, political, and cultural spheres.

2. The right to apply indigenous normative systems in the regulation and solution of internal conflicts, respecting individual rights, human rights, and, in particular, the dignity and integrity of indigenous women, their procedures, judgments, and decisions will be validated by the juridical authorities of the state.

3. To elect their authorities and to exercise mechanisms of internal governance in agreement with indigenous norms in the ambit of autonomy, guaranteeing the participation of women in conditions of equality.

4. To strengthen their political participation and representation in accordance with cultural specificities. Collective access to the use and enjoyment of natural resources from their lands and territories, understood as the totality of the habitat that indigenous peoples use and occupy, save those whose direct dominion corresponds to the nation.

5. To preserve and enrich their languages, knowledge of all the dimensions that comprise their culture and identity, and acquire, operate, and administer their own means of communication.

6. The Federation, the states, and the municipalities should, in the area of their respective competencies, and in consultation with indigenous peoples, promote equitable and sustainable development, as well as bilingual and intercultural education. In the same manner, these governmental entities should promote the respect and the knowledge of the diverse cultures that exist in this nation and combat all types of discrimination" (Correa 1996: 33–34).

14. I am indebted to Guillermo Trejo for these observations (August 2000).

15. Many months later in a conference held in January 1999, members of the governmental delegation, reflecting on the suspension of the dialogue during the fall of 1996, confessed to a lack of political will at that particular point in the dialogue process. They claimed that because a parallel discussion was being negotiated in Congress over similar issues of democracy and state reform during the fall of 1996, they could not, in good faith, participate simultaneously in both (see Arnson and Manaut 2000).

16. In the final hours before these local elections, the Zapatista supreme command (CCRI) issued orders to its followers to abstain from voting. In the days leading up to the election, the PRD was highly favored to wrest dozens of municipalities from the PRI's hands. With a rate of abstention upward to 100 percent in much of the jungle region, however, the PRI held on to mayoral seats in the crucially important municipal head towns of Ocosingo and Las Margaritas. The EZLN explained its boycott of the election by claiming that security conditions in northern and eastern Chiapas—where the bulk of its supporters live—made elections impossible.

17. FZLN members were present in large numbers at a national forum convened by the EZLN on state reform in June 1996. My observations of and interactions with FZLN members at that forum led me to conclude that FZLN members were deeply skeptical about electoral democracy.

18. Scholars working within the New Social Movement (NSM) paradigm in Latin America have been the most optimistic about the positive links between civil society and democratization (see Ellner [2001] for a cogent review essay on Latin American democracy in the "postconsolidation" literature).

19. Linz and Stepan (1996: 7) define civil society as "that arena of the polity where self-organizing groups, movements, and individuals [social movements as well as civic associations from all social strata], relatively autonomous from the state, attempt to articulate values, create associations, and solidarities, and advance their interests." Linz and Stepan contrast civil to political society, which includes political parties and governmental officials. See Hagopian (1998) and Oxhorn and Ducatenzeiler (1998) on the role of civil society in the democratic consolidation phase.

20. The literature on juridical pluralism in Latin America is rapidly expanding. For a general overview of the central issues at stake in the Latin American context, see Stavenhagen and Iturralde (1990). A comprehensive Web site devoted to legal pluralism in Latin America can be found at URL: http://www.alertanet.org. On legal pluralism in Bolivia and Colombia,

see Van Cott (2000b) and Alvarez and Vacaflor (1998). On Mexico, the exercise of "traditions and customs" in Oaxaca has been well documented: see de León (2001). On elections and "usos y costumbres" in Oaxaca, see Recondo (1999) and González and Martínez (2002).

21.   Some intellectuals have openly and publicly expressed racist ideas with respect to Indian political practices and autonomy. For example, Ignacio Burgoa Orihuela, the judge Zedillo sought out in 1996 for his opinion on the constitutionality of the signed San Andrés Accords, warned that if the San Andrés Accords were signed into law, Mexico may return to a period of "human sacrifice" *(sacrificios humanos)* (cited in Hernández Castillo 2001b: 147). Liberal intellectuals such as Juan Pedro Viqueira have taken a different tack in arguing against the accords. Viqueira, for example, maintains that Indian "traditions and customs" should not be legalized because they are based on an inaccurate, culturally deterministic view of Indian peoples and their local practices (Viqueira 2001: 32).

22.   The recognition of Indian peoples as subjects of "public law," in effect, recognizes Indian peoples as subjects with rights and obligations. The demarcation of Indian peoples as subjects of "public interest," as stated in the Senate version of the reforms, suggests that Indians are subjects of public assistance, granting them a lower juridical status than in the former.

23.   The final votes were tallied on July 18, 2001, and the reforms were promulgated on August 14, 2001. The nineteen states approving the reforms were Aguascalientes, Campeche, Chihuahua, Coahuila, Colima, Durango, Guanajuato, Jalisco, Michoacán, Nayarit, Nuevo León, Puebla, Querétero, Quintana Roo, Tabasco, Tlaxcala, Sonora, Veracruz, and Baja California. The state legislatures of Guerrero, Hidalgo, San Luis Potosí, Baja California Sur, Chiapas, State of Mexico, Oaxaca, Sinaloa, and Zacatecas rejected the reforms. Two states, Yucatán and Tamaulipas, never voted; in Morelos, the vote was suspended (López Bárcenas et al. 2002: 128–31).

24.   The possibility of submitting constitutional controversies is a fairly recent event in Mexican judicial history, beginning only in 1996.

25. Municipal officials in the state of Oaxaca submitted the majority of the controversies.

Vignette Four

1.   The name of the workshop was "The Rights of Women in our Customs and Traditions," and it was held on May 19–20, 1994, in San Cristóbal. The epigraph was translated by Elizabeth Manrique and can be found in Rojas (1995).

2.   Elizondo drew his examples from Rodolfo Vázquez's *Liberalismo, Estado de Derecho y Minorías.* Elizondo is not alone in pointing to natives' "barbaric" treatment of their women to justify the need for enlightened Western rule. This practice was quite common in colonial and neocolonial contexts. West (1997: xvii) describes how, in India, the British pointed to *satidaha* (immolation of widows) "as an example of the 'unworthiness' of Indian customs and traditions, which necessitated embracing the 'modernization' of colonialism."

3.   ANIPA is the largest single organization within the National Indigenous Congress (CNI), comprising approximately 60 percent of CNI membership.

4.   "El Despertador Mexicano" 1994: 45–46.

5.   Recall that in 1992, President Salinas pushed through Congress an amendment to Article 4 of the constitution, which, in effect, declared the Mexican nation multicultural.

Conclusion

1. Ethnic autonomy has become an important political question and the subject of much debate (and bloodshed) in dozens of countries throughout the world. Although it is not my purpose to address the question of ethnic autonomy outside the Latin American context, readers interested in this topic should consult two excellent general works on autonomy: Hannum (1990) and Lapidoth (1996). For those interested specifically in ethnic conflict, see Gurr (2000) and Stavenhagen (1996a).

2. Five Latin American countries have constitutionally codified ethnically defined autonomy regimes: Colombia, Ecuador, Nicaragua, Panama, and Venezuela (see Van Cott 2001).

3. Van Cott argues that there are two distinct negotiating sites for such a discussion: an armed conflict negotiating site (Nicaragua [1984–87] and Panama [1925–38]) or a constitutional reform negotiating site (Colombia [1991], Ecuador [1998], and Venezuela [1999]).

4. Indigenous peoples comprise approximately 4 percent of the country's total population (Barry 1990: 83). The most numerous, the Guaymí with 54,000 members, are located in western Panama. The Chocó people, with 25,000 members, live in the Pacific lowlands. Small numbers of Teribe and Bokota peoples inhabit the western mountain range. The Kuna, with some 30,000 members, have been most successful in defending their autonomy and achieving legal recognition. This is due largely to the relative remoteness of the San Blas Islands, which has allowed them to keep outside influence to a minimum (Barry 1990: 87). Second to the Kuna, the Guaymí have organized to protect their land and culture, demanding their own autonomous comarca (reserve) in the 1980s.

5. In addition to Colombia, Ecuador and Venezuela also successfully codified ethnic autonomy regimes within the context of constitutional reform (Van Cott 2001). In the summer of 1990, after leading a national mobilization that shut down the country for a week, the CONAIE (Confederation of Indigenous Nationalities of Ecuador), the country's largest and most influential national-level indigenous organization, initiated its demand for territorial autonomy. This represented a shift from previous demands for land distribution to demand for territories and control of natural resources on those territories. During the course of the 1990s, indigenous organizations in Ecuador grew in political maturity and influence. In 1997 after the CONAIE led other civil society organizations in a movement to oust President Abdalá Bucaram, a constituent assembly was convened (Van Cott 2001: 45). Three indigenous delegates, along with four nonindigenous delegates who sympathized with movement demands, participated in the seventy-member assembly. All seven delegates represented the Plurinational Pachakutik Unity Movement (MUPP), which was founded by the CONAIE and other social movements before the 1996 elections (Van Cott 2001: 47).

Like Colombia, Venezuela's indigenous population is miniscule in number, comprising some 1.5 percent of the country's population. Venezuela was late to officially recognize its cultural and linguistic plurality, which it did only recently when indigenous peoples gained historic rights in Venezuela's new constitution written in 1999 (Giordani and Villalón 2002: 44). Chávez's government reserved three delegate positions for indigenous peoples in the National Constituent Assembly (ANC), convened during the summer of 1999. The new constitution acknowledges the existence of indigenous peoples and their communities, as well as their social, political, and economic systems of organization (Giordani and Villalón 2002: 45).

6. The resguardo and cabildo, administrative-territorial units that had been legally recognized governing councils dating to the colonial era, were not swept away with liberal reforms of the mid-nineteenth century in Colombia, as occurred throughout Latin America (Van Cott 2000a: 45).

7. Although indigenous peoples in Colombia have historically been treated as second-class citizens, they have organized nationally since the early 1980s, holding the First National Indigenous Congress in 1982. This congress led to the formation of the National Organization of Colombian Indigenous Peoples (ONIC), which, according to one observer, provided an institutional base for the election of Lorenzo Muelas, ONIC's director, to the National Constitutional Assembly in 1991 (Urrego 2001: 174).

8. The Constituent Assembly consisted of seventy-four total delegates.

9. Héctor Díaz-Polanco, a scholar and advocate of regional autonomy regimes in the continent, highlights the importance of the 1991 changes in the Colombian constitution, noting that "indigenous territories" are identified as part of the organization of the state, and these "territorial entities possess autonomy in the negotiation of their interests" (Article 287, cited in Díaz-Polanco 1997: 148). Indigenous people living in these autonomous territories have the right to (1) be ruled by their own authorities, (2) exercise the corresponding competences, (3) administer the resources and establish the taxes necessary for the fulfillment of their functions, and (4) share in the national income. Díaz-Polanco also notes that the Colombian constitution establishes that competences will be distributed between the nation and the territorial entities and that "indigenous territories will be governed by councils and regulated according to the habits and customs of their communities." These councils have broad functions detailed in the constitution itself (Article 330, cited in Díaz-Polanco 1997: 148).

10. In both the Panamanian and Nicaraguan cases, indigenous peoples participated directly in negotiations with the government. Also in both cases, the U.S. government played a significant role in supporting indigenous peoples' demands for ethnic autonomy vis-à-vis central governments' resistant to such demands (Van Cott 2001; for more detailed information on the Nicaraguan case, see Díaz-Polanco 1997: 119–25; on Panama, see Howe 1998).

11. The Mexican state is relatively weak in remote rural areas of Mexico, such as Chiapas (see Stephen 2002). However, even there, the Mexican state asserts itself through the army and through social welfare programs administered by state officials and institutions.

12. See Viqueira and Sonnleitner (2000) on the debate concerning political parties and indigenous peoples in highland Chiapas. They argue that political parties should not be seen as "foreign" structures that have been imposed on indigenous communities. Rather, in many highland indigenous communities, political parties have been fully integrated into local political life.

13. Members of many Protestant organizations do not contribute monetarily to or participate in community rituals, such as the annual fiesta in honor of a village's patron saint. Many Protestants also refuse to participate in community work, often done on Sunday, a day in which work is proscribed.

14. The information documented by the press during the dismantlement of the municipal center of Tierra y Libertad (Amparo Aguatinta) confirmed that the autonomous municipality consisted of: a) public buildings; b) an office for the president or Autonomous

Council; c) an office for the exercise of justice; d) an office of civil registry that registered births, marriages, and deaths; and e) a jail. Additional commissions, such as those of health, supplies, and education, were housed in private homes (Burguete 2002a).

15. In Mexico, remunicipalization cannot be decreed at the national level, but is controlled by state congresses.

16. The seven new municipalities created in 1999 were: Aldama, Benemérito de las Américas, Maravilla Tenejapa, Marqués de Comillas, Montecristo de Guerrero, San Andrés Duraznal, and Santiago El Pinar (Burguete 2002a).

17. For an analysis of the electoral results by district and municipality, see the Center for Economic and Political Studies in Community Action (CIEPAC) article entitled "Resultados Electorales en Chiapas" (2000).

18. To be fair, Salazar has defended his inaction by claiming that until there is national-level legislation passed on Indian rights, he will not push forward legislation on the state and local levels in Chiapas.

19. See Aída Hernández Castillo (2001b) for a discussion of ethnic essentialism within the National Indigenous Congress. In this article, Hernández argues that indigenous women within the National Indigenous Congress have been vocal in their criticism of ethnic essentialism.

20. Portes and Landolt (2000: 532) define social capital as "the ability to secure resources by virtue of membership in social networks or larger social structures." My argument here builds on their assertion that social capital, regardless of how strong, is no substitute for material capital and cannot replace the provision of credit, material infrastructure, and education. Portes and Landolt argue that the most social capital can do is "to increase the 'yield' of such resources by reinforcing them with the voluntary efforts of participants and their monitoring capacity to prevent malfeasance" (Portes and Landolt 2000: 146).

21. I am not suggesting that decentralization programs significantly undercut the power of national governments or that national governments are suddenly out of the policy-making loop. The international financial institutions funding decentralization projects, such as the World Bank, work through national governments. NGOs working at local levels must also cooperate with the state. Examining ethno-development projects in the Andean region (which profess administrative and political decentralization as a goal), Radcliffe, Laurie, and Andolina (2002: 12) argue that coordination around said projects has resulted in an emerging pattern of development administration in Latin America in which "actors who historically would have operated in distinct spheres—the state, grassroots organizations, non-governmental organizations—are now coming together in new quasi-state institutions." The power of the state, they argue, is not diminished, but reconstituted in new ways.

WORKS CITED

Acción Indigenista, Boletín del Instituto Nacional Indigenista. 1975a.
Lineamientos de política indigenista según el Plan Básico de Gobierno: 1976–
1982. No. 269 (November). México, D.F.: Instituto Nacional Indigenista.
———. 1975b. Resultado del Primer Congreso Nacional de Pueblos Indígenas.
No. 268 (October). México, D.F.: Instituto Nacional Indigenista.
Aguayo Quesada, Sergio. 1998. *1968, Los archivos de la violencia*. México, D.F.:
Grijalbo; Reforma.
Aguirre Beltrán, Gonzalo. 1967. *Regions of refuge*. México, D.F.: Instituto
Indigenista Interamericano.
———. 1976. *Aguirre Beltrán: Obra polémica*. Ed. Angel Palerm. México, D.F.:
Centro de Investigaciones y Estudios Superiores en Antropología Social;
Instituto Nacional de Antropología e Historia.
Albó, Xavier. 1994. And from Kataristas to MNRistas? The surprising and bold
alliance between Aymaras and neoliberals in Bolivia. In *Indigenous peoples and
democracy in Latin America,* ed. Donna Lee Van Cott, 55–81. New York: St.
Martin's Press.
Alvarez Melgar, José Antonio, and Jorge Luis Vacaflor Gonzáles, eds. 1998.
*Memoria seminario internacional de administración de justicia y pueblos
indígenas*. La Paz, Bolivia: Ministerio de Desarrollo Sostenible y Planificación,
Viceministerio de Asuntos Indígenas y Pueblos Originarios, Servicio de
Asistencia Jurídica para Pueblos Indígenas y Originarios.
Arnson, Cynthia, and Raúl Benítez Manaut, eds. 2000. *Chiapas: Los desafíos de la
paz*. México, D.F.: ITAM; Porrúa.
Asamblea Nacional Indígena Plural Por la Autonomía (ANIPA). 1996. Proyecto
de iniciativa de decreto que reforma y adiciona los artículos 3, 4, 14, 18, 41, 53,
73, 115, and 116 de la constitución política de los Estados Unidos Mexicanos
para la creación de las regiones autónomas. V National Assembly, Chilapa,
Guerrero. April 29–May 1.
Assies, Willem, Gemma van der Haar, and André J. Hoekema, eds. 2000. *The
challenge of diversity: Indigenous Peoples and Reform of the state in Latin
America*. Amsterdam: Thela Thesis.
Bailey, John. 1994. Centralism and political change in Mexico: The case of national
solidarity. In *Transforming state-society relations in Mexico: The national solidarity
strategy,* ed. Wayne A. Cornelius, Ann L. Craig, and Jonathan Fox, 97–119. La
Jolla: Center for U.S.-Mexican Studies; University of California, San Diego.

Balboa, Juan. 1996. Elorriaga y Entzin, libres. *La Jornada* June 7. URL: http://www.jornada.unam.mx.

Barre, Marie Chantal. 1983. *Ideologías indigenistas y movimientos indios*. México, D.F.: Siglo XXI.

Barry, Tom. 1990. *Panama: A country guide*. Albuquerque, N.M.: The Inter-hemispheric Education Resource Center.

Bartra, Armando. 1985. *Los herederos de Zapata: Movimientos campesinos posrevolucionarios en México, 1920–1980*. México, D.F.: Ediciones Era.

Bartra, Roger. 1974. *Estructura agraria y clases sociales en México*. México, D.F.: Ediciones Era.

————. 1993. *Agrarian structure and political power in Mexico*. Baltimore, Md.: Johns Hopkins University Press.

Basauri, Carlos. 1990 [1940]. *La población indígena de México*. Vol. II. Rpt., México, D.F.: Instituto Nacional Indigenista.

Beals, Ralph. 1973 [1946]. *Cherán: A Sierra Tarascan village*. New York: Cooper Square Publishers.

Bonfil Batalla, Guillermo et al. 1970. *De eso que llaman la antropología mexicana*. México, D.F.: Nuestro Tiempo.

Brading, David. 1980. *Los orígenes del nacionalismo mexicano*. México, D.F.: Ediciones Era.

Brysk, Allison. 1996. Turning weakness into strength: The internationalization of Indian rights. *Latin American Perspectives* 23, no. 2 (spring): 38–57.

————. 2000. *From tribal village to global village: Indian rights and international relations in Latin America*. Stanford, Calif.: Stanford University Press.

Burguete Cal y Mayor, Araceli. 1998. Remunicipalización en Chiapas: Los retos. *Cemos Memoria* (August): 14–25.

————. 2000. Partidos políticos y pueblos indígenas en México: Crónica de desencuentros. In *Indigenismos, reflexiones críticas*, ed. Natividad Gutiérrez, Marcela Romero, and Sergio Sarmiento, 145–76. México, D.F.: National Indigenist Institute.

————. 2002a. Procesos de autonomías de facto en Chiapas. Nuevas jurisdicciones y gobiernos paralelos en rebeldía. In *Tierra, libertad, y autonomía: Impactos regionales del zapatismo en Chiapas*, ed. Shannan L. Mattiace, Rosalva Aída Hernández, and Jan Rus. México, D.F.: CIESAS.

————. 2002b. Remunicipalization in Chiapas: Reorganización territorial inconclusa. *CEMOS Memoria* no. 157 (March). URL: http://www.memoria.com.mx/157/Burguete.htm.

————. n.d. Chiapas: Cronología de un etnocidio reciente (Represión política a los indios, 1974–1987). Academia Mexicana de Derechos Humanos A.C.

Burton, Michael, Richard Gunther, and John Higley. 1991. Introduction: Elite transformations and democratic regimes. In *Elites and democratic consolida-tion in Latin America and southern Europe,* ed. John Higley and Richard Gunther, 1–37. New York: Cambridge University Press.

C169 Indigenous and Tribal Peoples Convention. 1989. International Labor Organization. URL: http://ilolex.ilo.ch:1567/english/convdisp1.htm.

Camp, Roderic Ai. 1999. *Politics in Mexico: The decline of authoritarianism.* 3d ed. Oxford: Oxford University Press.

Campbell, Howard. 1994. *Zapotec renaissance: Ethnic politics and cultural revival-ism in southern Mexico.* Albuquerque: University of New Mexico Press.

Cancian, Frank. 1992. *The decline of community in Zinacantán: Economy, public life, and social stratiWcation, 1960–1987.* Stanford, Calif.: Stanford University Press.

Cardoso, Fernando Henrique. 1986. Democracy in Latin America. *Politics and Society* 15, no. 1: 23–42.

Centro de Derechos Humanos "Fray Bartolomé de las Casas." 1999. *Presunta justicia.* San Cristóbal de las Casas: Centro de Derechos Humanos "Fray Bartolomé de las Casas."

CIEPAC (Centro de Investigaciones Económicas y Políticas de Acción Comunitaria). 2000. Resultados electorales en Chiapas. *Chiapas al Día,* no. 212 (September 15). URL: http://www.ciepac.org/bulletins/200–300/bolec212.htm.

Clavero, Bartolomé. 1994. *Derecho indígena y cultura constitucional en América.* México, D.F.: Siglo XXI.

Código de Instituciones y Procedimientos Electorales de Oaxaca. 1995. Oaxaca Instituto Estatal Electoral.

Collier, George, with Elizabeth Lowery Quaratiello. 1994. *Basta! Land and the Zapatista rebellion in Chiapas.* Oakland: The Institute for Food and Develop-ment Policy.

Colloredo-Mansfeld, Rudi. 1999. *The native leisure class: Consumption and cultural creativity in the Andes.* Chicago: University of Chicago Press.

Comaroff, John, and Jean Comaroff. 1992. *Ethnography and the historical imagination.* Boulder, Colo.: Westview Press.

Congreso Nacional Indígena. 2001. Resolutivos of third meeting of the National Indigenous Congress held in Nurío, Michoacán, 2–4 Mar. 2001: Declaración por el reconocimiento constitucional de nuestros derechos colectivos. May 9. National Indigenous Congress. August 16, 2001. URL: http://www.laneta.apc.org/cni/.

Contreras, Oscar F., and Vivienne Bennett. 1994. National solidarity in the northern borderlands: Social participation and community leadership. In *Transforming state-society relations in Mexico: The national solidarity strategy,* ed. Wayne A. Cornelius, Ann L. Craig, and Jonathan Fox, 281–305. La Jolla: Center for U.S.-Mexican Studies; University of California, San Diego.

Cook, Maria Lorena. 1996. *Organizing dissent: Unions, the state, and the democratic teachers' movement in Mexico.* University Park: Pennsylvania State University Press.

Cornelius, Wayne A., Ann L. Craig, and Jonathan Fox. 1994. Mexico's national solidarity program: An overview. In *Transforming state-society relations in Mexico: The national solidarity strategy,* ed. Wayne A. Cornelius, Ann L. Craig, and Jonathan Fox, 3–26. La Jolla: Center for U.S.-Mexican Studies; University of California, San Diego.

Correa, Guillermo. 1996. Guerra y Narro, de la COCOPA: El dilema de Zedillo es que debe decidir sobre un documento que no conocía. *Proceso* no. 1050 (December 15): 32–35.

———. 1997. El fracaso de la COCOPA, atribuible a la "cerrazon del gobierno": Juan N. Guerra. *Proceso* no. 1082 (July 27): 34–36.

Correa, Guillermo, and Salvador Corro. 1996. El debate por los indígenas. *Proceso* (December 8): 22–27.

Dandler, Jorge E. 1999. Indigenous peoples and the rule of law in Latin America: Do they have a chance? In *The (un)rule of law and the underprivileged in Latin America,* ed. Juan Mendez, Guillermo O'Donnell, and Paulo Sergio Pinheiro. South Bend, Ill.: University of Notre Dame Press.

Davis, Diane E. 1994. *Urban leviathan: Mexico City in the twentieth century.* Philadelphia, Pa.: Temple University Press.

Declaración de las Representaciones del Comité Ejecutivo Nacional y el Grupo Parlamentario del PRD sobre el Diálogo con la Comandancia General del EZLN. 1996. Unpublished document. San Cristóbal de las Casas, Chiapas, July 1.

De la Peña, Guillermo. n.d. Proyecto nacional y resistencia etnica en América Latina. Unpublished Manuscript.

De León Pasquel, Lourdes, ed. 2001. *Costumbres, leyes, y movimiento indio en Oaxaca y Chiapas.* México, D.F.: CIESAS and Porrúa.

Deruyttere, Anne. 1994. The indigenous peoples' fund: An innovative mechanism in support of the ethnodevelopment of the indigenous people of Latin American and Caribbean. Inter-American Development Bank, Sustainable Development Department: Indigenous Peoples. *Working Paper* ENP108. May. URL: http://www.iadb.org/sds/publication/publication_350_e.htm.

Díaz-Polanco, Héctor. 1985. *La cuestión etnico-nacional.* México, D.F.: Editorial Linea.

———. 1987. *Etnia, nación y política.* México, D.F.: Juan Pablos Editor.

———. 1992. El estado y los indígenas. In *El nuevo estado mexicano: Estado, actores y movimientos sociales,* vol. III, ed. Jorge Alonso et al. Guadalajara: Universidad de Guadalajara; México, D.F.: Nueva Imagen.

———. 1996. Las voces de la autonomía regional en México (1994–1995) (recopilacion). *Boletín de Antropología Americana* 27: 133–45.

———. 1997. *Indigenous peoples in Latin America: The quest for self-determination.*

Trans. Lucía Reyes. Boulder, Colo.: Westview Press.

———. 1998. La autonomía, demanda central de los pueblos indígenas: Significado e implicaciones. In *Pueblos indígenas y estado en América Latina*, ed. V. Alta et al. Quito: Universidad Andina Simon Bolivar.

Di Palma, Giuseppe. 1990. *To craft democracies: An essay on democratic transitions.* Berkeley and Los Angeles: University of California Press.

Dresser, Denise. 1991. *Neopopulist solutions to neoliberal problems: Mexico's national solidarity program.* Current Issue Brief Series, no. 3. La Jolla: Center for U.S.-Mexican Studies; University of California, San Diego.

Edelman, Marc. 1999. *Peasants against globalization: Rural social movements in Costa Rica.* Stanford, Calif.: Stanford University Press.

"El Despertador Mexicano," Organo Informativo del EZLN, México, no. 1, diciembre de 1993. 1994. In *EZLN: Documentos y comunicados, 1 de enero/8 de agosto de 1994.* Prólogo de Antonio García de León Crónicas de Carlos Monsivais y Elena Poniatowska. México, D.F.: Ediciones Era.

Elizondo, Carlos Mayer-Serra. 2001. Hay culturas superiores? Editorial. *Reforma,* June 8, p. 13A.

Ellner, Steve. 2001. Latin American democracy in "post-consolidation" literature: Optimism and pessimism. *Latin American Politics and Society* 43 (spring).

Ewen, Alexander. 1994. Mexico: The crisis of identity. *Akwe: kon (All of Us): A Journal of Indigenous Issues* XI, no. 2: 28–40.

EZLN Documentos y Comunicados 15 de agosto de 1994/29 de septiembre de 1995. 1994. Prólogo de Antonio García de León Crónica de Carlos Monsivais y Elena Poniatowska. Vol. II. México, D.F.: Ediciones Era.

Favre, Henri. 1973. *Cambio y continuidad entre los Mayas de México.* México, D.F.: Siglo XXI.

Fischer, Edward F., and R. McKenna Brown, eds. 1996. *Maya cultural activism in Guatemala.* Austin: University of Texas Press.

Fondos de Solidaridad para la Promoción del Patrimonio Cultural de los Pueblos Indígenas de México. 1992. México, D.F.: Instituto Nacional Indigenista.

Foster, George. 1967. *Tzintzuntzan: Mexican peasants in a changing world.* Boston: Little, Brown & Company.

Foweraker, Joe. 1995. *Theorizing social movements.* London: Pluto Press.

Foweraker, Joe, and Ann L. Craig, eds. 1990. *Popular movements and political change in Mexico.* Boulder, Colo.: Lynne Rienner Publishers.

Fox, Jonathan. 1993. *The politics of food in Mexico: State power and social mobilization.* Ithaca, N.Y.: Cornell University Press.

———. 1994. Targeting the poorest: The role of the National Indigenous Institute in Mexico's solidarity program. In *Transforming state-society relations in Mexico: The national solidarity strategy,* ed. Wayne A. Cornelius, Ann L. Craig, and Jonathan Fox, 179–216. La Jolla: Center for U.S.-Mexican Studies; University of California, San Diego.

Fox, Jonathan, and Gustavo Gordillo. 1989. Between state and market: The campesinos' quest for autonomy. In *Mexico's alternative political futures,* ed. Wayne A. Cornelius, Ann L. Craig, and Jonathan Fox, 131–72. La Jolla: Center for U.S.-Mexican Studies; University of California, San Diego.

Freyre, Gilberto. 1946. *The masters and the slaves (casa grande y senzala): A study in the development of Brazilian civilization.* Trans. Samuel Putnam. New York: Alfred A. Knopf.

———. 1959. *New world in the tropics: The culture of modern Brazil.* New York: Alfred A. Knopf.

Friedlander, Judith. 1975. *Being Indian in Hueyapan: A study of forced identity in contemporary Mexico.* New York: St. Martin's Press.

Gabriel, John. 1994. Initiating a movement: Indigenous, black and grassroots struggles in the Americas. *Race & Class* 35, no. 3: 1–17.

Gamio, Manuel. 1960 [1916]. *Forjando patria.* Rpt., México, D.F.: Editorial Porrúa.

García Barrios, Ana. n.d. La pérdida de la tradición. San Cristóbal de las Casas. Instituto de Estudios Indígenas, Universidad Autónoma de Chiapas.

García de León, Antonio. 1985. *Resistencia y utopía: Memorial de agravios y crónica de revueltas y profecías acaecidas en la provincia de Chiapas durante los últimos 500 años de su historia.* 2 vols. México, D.F.: Ediciones Era.

Geertz, Clifford. 1973. *The interpretation of cultures; Selected essays.* New York: Basic Books.

Gilly, Adolfo. 1971. *La revolución interrumpida: Mexico, 1910–1920.* México, D.F.: El Caballito.

Giordani, Lourdes, and María Eugenia Villalón. 2002. An expansion of citizenship in Venezuela. *NACLA Report on the Americas* XXXV, no. 6 (May/June): 44–45.

Gómez, Antonio Hernández, and Mario Humberto Ruz. 1992. *Memoria baldía: Los Tojolabales y las fincas testimonios.* México, D.F.: Universidad Nacional Autónoma de México; Tuxtla Gutiérrez: Universidad Autónoma de Chiapas.

González Oropeza, Manuel, and Francisco Martínez Sánchez. 2002. *El derecho y la justicia en las elecciones de Oaxaca.* 2 vols. Oaxaca: Tribunal Estatal Electoral.

Gurr, Ted Robert. 1970. *Why men rebel.* Princeton, N.J.: Princeton University Press.

———. 2000. *People versus states: Minorities at risk in a new century.* Washington, D.C.: United States Institute of Peace Press.

Gutiérrez, Natividad. 1999. *Nationalist myths and ethnic identities: Indigenous intellectuals and the Mexican state.* Lincoln: University of Nebraska Press.

Hagopian, Frances. 1998. Democracy and political representation in Latin America in the 1990s: Pause, reorganization, or decline? In *Fault lines of democracy in post-transition Latin America,* ed. Felipe Aguero and Jeffrey Stark, 99–141. Coral Gables, Fla.: North-South Center Press.

Hale, Charles R. 1991. "Miskitu" revolution in the revolution. *NACLA Report on the Americas* 25, no. 3 (December): 24–28.

———.1994a. Between Ché Guevara and the Pachamama: Mestizos, Indians and identity politics in the anti-quincentenary campaign. *Critique of Anthropology* 14, no. 1: 9–39.

———. 1994b. *Resistance and contradiction: Miskitu Indians and the Nicaraguan state,* 1894–1987. Stanford, Calif.: Stanford University Press.

———. 1997. Cultural politics of identity in Latin America. *Annual Reviews of Anthropology* 26: 567–90.

Hamilton, Nora. 1982. *The limits of state autonomy: Post-revolutionary Mexico.* Princeton, N.J.: Princeton University Press.

Hannum, Hurst. 1990. *Autonomy, sovereignty, and self-determination: The accommodation of conflicting rights.* Philadelphia: University of Pennsylvania Press.

Hart, John M. 1987. *Revolutionary Mexico: The coming and process of the Mexican revolution.* Berkeley and Los Angeles: University of California Press.

Harvey, Neil. 1994. *Rebellion in Chiapas: Rural reforms, campesino radicalism, and the limits to Salinismo.* Center for U.S.-Mexican Studies at the University of California, San Diego, Transformation of Rural Mexico, no. 5, Ejido Reform Research Project. La Jolla: Center for U.S.-Mexican Studies; University of California, San Diego.

———. 1998. *The Chiapas rebellion.* Durham, N.C.: Duke University Press.

Hernández Castillo, Rosalva Aída. 1994. Reinventing tradition: The women's law. *Akwe: kon (All of Us): A Journal of Indigenous Issues* 11, no. 2: 67–70.

———. 1995. De la comunidad a la convención estatal de mujeres: Las campesinas chiapanecas y sus demandas de género. In *La explosión de comunidades en Chiapas,* ed. June Nash et al. Copenhagen: International Work Group on Indigenous Affairs (IWGIA). (English-language edition: From community to women's state convention: The Chiapas campesinos and their gender demands. 1995. In *The explosion of Communities in Chiapas,* ed. June Nash et al., 53–63. Copenhagen: IWGIA Document No. 77.)

———. 2001a. Between civil disobedience and silent rejection: Differing responses by Mam peasants to the Zapatista rebellion. *Latin American Perspectives* 28, no. 117: 98–119.

———. 2001b. Entre el esencialismo étnico y la descalificación total: La política de identidades en México y las perspectives de las mujeres. *CEMOS Memoria* (May): 20–25.

———. 2001c. *Histories and stories from Chiapas: Border identities in southern Mexico.* Trans. Martha Pou. Austin: University of Texas Press.

Hernández Cruz, Antonio. 1999. Autonomía Tojolab'al: génesis de un proceso. In *México: Experiencias de autonomía indígena,* ed. Araceli Burguete Cal y Mayor. Copenhagen: IWGIA.

Hernández Navarro, Luis. 1992. Las convulsiones sociales. In *Autonomía y nuevos sujetos sociales en el desarrollo rural,* ed. Julio Moguel et al. México, D.F.: Siglo XXI.

———. 1994. The Chiapas uprising. Trans. William Rhett-Mariscal. In *Rebellion in Chiapas,* ed. Neil Harvey. Center for U.S.-Mexican Studies at the University of California, San Diego, Transformation of Rural Mexico, no. 5, Ejido Reform Research Project. La Jolla: Center for U.S.-Mexican Studies; University of California, San Diego.

———. 1997. Ciudadanos iguales, ciudadanos diferentes: La nueva lucha india. *Este País,* February, pp. 30–40.

Hewitt de Alcántara, Cynthia. 1985. *Anthropological perspectives on rural Mexico.* London: Routledge & Kegan Paul.

Hindley, Jane. 1996. Towards a pluricultural nation: The limits of indigenismo and Article 4. In *Dismantling the Mexican state?* ed. Rob Aitken et al., 225–43. New York: St. Martin's Press.

Howe, James. 1998. *A people who would not kneel.* Washington, D.C.: Smithsonian Institution Press.

Instituto Nacional Indigenista. 1976. *Seis años de acción indigenista, 1970–1976.* México, D.F.: INI.

———. 1978a. Bases para la acción, 1977–1982 (Guía para la Programación). México, D.F.: INI.

———. 1978b. *INI 30 años después: Revisión crítica.* México, D.F.: INI.

———. 1982. *Memoria de actividades, 1976–1982.* México, D.F.: INI.

———. 1994. Instituto Nacional Indigenista: 1989–1994. México, D.F.: INI; SEDESOL.

Jelin, Elizabeth. 1986. Otros silencios, otras voces: El tiempo de la democratizacion en la Argentina. In *Los movimientos sociales ante la crisis,* ed. F. Calderón G. Buenos Aires: Universidad de las Naciones Unidas.

Joseph, Gilbert M., and Daniel Nugent, eds. 1994. *Everyday forms of state formation: Revolution and the negotiation of rule in modern Mexico.* Durham, N.C.: Duke University Press.

Karl, Terry Lynn, and Philippe C. Schmitter. 1991. Modes of transition in Latin America, southern and eastern Europe. *International Social Science Journal* 128 (May): 269–84.

Kearney, Michael. 1996. *Reconceptualizing the peasantry: Anthropology in global perspective.* Boulder, Colo.: Westview Press.

Keck, Margaret, and Kathryn Sikkink. 1998. *Activists beyond borders: Advocacy networks in international politics.* Ithaca, N.Y.: Cornell University Press.

Knight, Alan. 1986. *The Mexican revolution.* 2 vols. New York: Cambridge University Press.

———. 1990a. Historical continuities in social movements. In *Popular movements and political change in Mexico,* ed. Joe Foweraker and Ann L. Craig, 78–102. Boulder, Colo.: Lynne Rienner Publishers.

———. 1990b. Racism, revolution, and indigenismo: Mexico, 1910–1940. In *The idea of race in Latin America,* ed. Richard Graham, 71–113. Austin: University of Texas Press.

Landau, Saul. 1996. In the jungle with Marcos (Chiapas, Mexico; Zapatista revolt leader subcomandante Marcos) (Interview). *Progressive,* March, pp. 25–30.

Lapidoth, Ruth. 1996. *Autonomy: Flexible solutions to ethnic conflicts.* Washington D.C.: United States Institute of Peace Press.

Lewis, Oscar. 1963 [1951]. *Life in a Mexican village: Tepoztlán restudied.* Rpt., Urbana: University of Illinois Press.

Leys Stepan, Nancy. 1991. *"The hour of eugenics": Race, gender, and nation in Latin America.* Ithaca, N.Y.: Cornell University Press.

Leyva Solano, Xóchitl. 2001. Regional, communal, and organizational transformations in Las Canadas. *Latin American Perspectives* 28, no. 117: 20–44.

Leyva Solano, Xóchitl, and Gabriel Ascencio Franco. 1996. *Lacandonia al filo del agua.* México, D.F.: Fondo de Cultura Económica.

Linz, Juan J., and Alfred Stepan. 1996. *Problems of democratic transition and consolidation: Southern Europe, South America, and post-communist Europe.* Baltimore, Md.: John Hopkins University Press.

López Bárcenas, Francisco et al. 2002. *Los derechos indígenas y la reforma constitutional en México.* México, D.F.: Centro de Orientación y Asesoría a pueblos Indígenas; Ce-Acatl; ediciones Casa Vieja; Redes.

López Cámara, Francisco. 1977. *La génesis de la conciencia liberal en México.* México, D.F.: Facultad de Ciencias Politicas y Sociales, UNAM.

Lucero, José Antonio. 2000. On feuds, tumults, and turns: Politics and culture in social movement and theory, review article. *Comparative Politics* 32, no. 2: 231–49.

———. 2002. Arts of unification: Political representation and indigenous movements in Bolivia and Ecuador. Ph.D. Dissertation, Princeton University.

Mallon, Florencia. 1995. *Peasant and nation: The making of postcolonial Mexico and Peru.* Berkeley and Los Angeles: University of California Press.

Martínez Lavín, Carlos. n.d. Los Tojolabales: Una tentativa de aproximación sociológica. Unpublished manuscript.

Martínez Luna, Jaime. 1993. ¿Es la comunidad nuestra identidad? In *Movimientos indígenas contemporáneos en México,* ed. Arturo Warman and Arturo Argueta, 157–70. México, D.F.: CIIH; Porrúa.

McAdam, Doug. 1982. *Political process and the development of black insurgency, 1930–1970.* Chicago: University of Chicago Press.

McAdam, Doug, John D. McCarthy, and Mayer N. Zald. 1996. Introduction: Opportunities, mobilizing structures, and framing processes—toward a synthetic, comparative perspective on social movements. In *Comparative perspectives on social movements: Political opportunities, mobilizing structures, and cultural framings,* ed. Doug McAdam, John D. McCarthy, and Mayer N. Zald, 1–20. Cambridge: Cambridge University Press.

McCarthy, John D., and Mayer N. Zald. 1977. Resource mobilization and social movements: A partial theory. *American Journal of Sociology* 82, 6: 1212–41.

Medina, Andrés. 1977. Los Indios. In *Siete ensayos sobre indigenismo,* ed. Salomón Nahmad et al., 5–27. México, D.F.: INI.

———. 1982. Presentación. In *¿Existe una antropología Marxista? Escritos exploratorios,* ed. Andrés Medina. México, D.F.: Universidad Nacional Autónoma de México.

Mejía Piñeros, María Consuelo, and Sergio Sarmiento. 1987. *La lucha indígena: Un reto a la ortodoxia.* México, D.F.: Siglo XXI; UNAM.

Melucci, Alberto. 1989. *Nomads of the present: Social movements and individual behavior in contemporary society.* Minneapolis: University of Minnesota Press.

Memoria: Informe de resultados de la consulta nacional sobre derechos y participación indígena. 1996. Unpublished manuscript, May.

Méndez B., Luis H., and Miguel Angel Romero. 1996. Chiapas: Semblanza de un conflicto, enero de 1994 febrero de 1996. *El Cotidiano* 76: 1–40.

Mexico. 2000. Instituto Nacional de Estadística, Geografía e Informatica. *XII Censo General de Población y Vivienda 2000.* Tabulados básicos y síntesis de resultados de los Estados Unidos Mexicanos. Pp. 21–23, 30. June 28. URL: http://www.inegi.gob.mx.

Moguel, Julio. 1992. Crisis del capital y reorganización productiva en el medio rural (Notas para la discusión de los pros, contras y asegunes de la apropiación del proceso productivo). In *Autonomía y nuevos sujetos sociales en el desarrollo rural,* ed. Julio Moguel et al. México, D.F.: Siglo XXI.

Montagú, Roberta. 1969. The Tojolabal. In *Handbook of middle American Indians.* Vol. VII. Austin: University of Texas Press.

———. 1986 [1957]. La ranchería de Yocnahab (primer libro de notas de 1957). In *Los legítimos hombres: Aproximación antropológica al grupo Tojolabal,* ed. Mario Humberto Ruz, 125–236. Vol. IV. México, D.F.: Universidad Nacional Autónoma de México.

Montemayor, Carlos. 2000. *Rehacer la historia: Análisis de los nuevos documentos del 2 de octubre de 1968 en Tlatelolco.* México, D.F.: Planeta.

Morales Bermúdez, Jesus. 1992. El congreso indígena de Chiapas: Un testimonio. In *Anuario de cultura e investigación.* Tuxtla Gutiérrez: Instituto Chiapaneco, Departamento de Patrimonio Cultural del Estado de Chiapas.

Morquecho Escamilla, Gaspar. 2002. Pablo Salazar y otros actores sociales a un año de gobierno en Chiapas. *CEMOS Memoria* no. 157 (March). URL: http://www.memoria.com.mx/.

Morquecho Escamilla, Gaspar, and Rosa Rojas. 1994a. Nuestras voces escondidas hasta el primero de Enero. *La Jornada,* November 4, p. 16.

———. 1994b. Ratifica la CIOAC la creación de una región autónoma en Chiapas. *La Jornada,* October 18, p. 16.

Nahmad Sitton, Salomón. 1977. Gobierno indígena y sociedad nacional. In *Siete ensayos sobre indigenismo,* ed. Salomón Nahmad et al., 5–27. México, D.F.: INI.

Nash, June et al. 1995. *The explosion of communities in Chiapas.* Copenhagen: IWIGA.

Oberschall, Anthony. 1993. *Social movements: Ideologies, interests, and identities.* New Brunswick, N.J.: Transaction Publishers.

O'Donnell, Guillermo. 1989. Transitions to democracy: Some navigation instruments. In *Democracy in the Americas: Stopping the pendulum,* ed. Robert Pastor, 62–75. New York: Holmes and Meier.

Olson, Mancur. 1965. *The logic of collective action: Public goods and the theory of groups.* Cambridge, Mass.: Harvard University Press.

Ortner, Sherry B. 1996. Resistance and the problem of ethnographic refusal. In *The historic turn in the human sciences,* ed. Terrence J. McDonald, 281–304. Ann Arbor: University of Michigan Press.

Oxhorn, Philip D. 2001. From human rights to citizenship rights? Recent trends in the study of Latin American social movements. *Latin American Research Review* 36, no. 3: 163–82.

Oxhorn, Philip D., and Graciela Ducatenzeiler, eds. 1998. *What kind of democracy? What kind of market? Latin America in the age of neoliberalism.* University Park: Pennsylvania State University Press.

Pallares, Amalia. 2002. *From peasant struggles to Indian resistance: The Ecuadorian Andes in the late twentieth century.* Lincoln: University of Nebraska Press.

Panagides, Alexis. 1994. Mexico. In *Indigenous people and poverty in Latin America: An empirical analysis,* ed. George Psacharopoulos and Harry Anthony Patrinos, 127–63. Washington, D.C.: The World Bank.

Pérez Castro, Ana Bella. 1982. Movimiento campesino en Simojovel, Chiapas, 1936–1978. *Anales de Antropología* 2, no. 19.

Portes, Alejandro, and Patricia Landolt. 2000. Social capital: Promise and pitfalls of its role in development. *Journal of Latin American Studies* 32: 529–47.

Pozas, Ricardo, and Isabel Pozas. 1971. *Los indios en las clases sociales de México.* México, D.F.: Siglo XXI.

Pronunciamiento Conjunto que el Gobierno Federal y el EZLN Enviarán a las Instancias de Debate y Decisión Nacional. 1996. Documento 1 de los acuerdos alcanzados sobre Derechos y Cultura Indígena. January 16. Unpublished document.

Los Pueblos Indígenas de México ante La Suprema Corte de Justicia de la Nación. 2002. Ed. José Luis Castro González and Luiz Irene del Carmen Montes Lara. April. Tract.

Radcliffe, Sarah. 2001. Indigenous municipalities in Ecuador and Bolivia: Transnational connections and exclusionary political cultures. Paper presented at Princeton University, Princeton, N.J., March 2.

Radcliffe, Sarah, Nina Laurie, and Robert Andolina. n.d. Indigenous people and political transnationalism: Globalization from below meets globalization from above? *Transnational Committees Programme, Working Paper* WPTC-02-05. URL: http://www.transcomm.ox.ac.uk/working%20papers/WPTC-02-05%20Radcliffe.pdf.

Recondo, David. 1999. "Usos y costumbres," y elecciones en Oaxaca. Los dilemmas de la democracia representativa, en una sociedad multicultural. *Trace* (December): 85–101.

Redfield, Robert. 1941 [1930]. *The folk culture of Yucatán.* Rpt., Chicago: University of Chicago Press.

Regino Montes, Adelfo. 1996. Los derechos indigenas, en serio. *La Jornada,* October 22, p. 22.

———. n.d. Autonomia y derecho indígena. Unpublished manuscript.

Reyes, Jorge. 2002. Proponen diputados ajustar Ley Indígena. *Reforma.* February 18. URL: http://www.reforma.com/nacional/articulo/169852/default/htm.

Rodríguez, Victoria E. 1997. *Decentralization in Mexico: From reforma municipal to solidaridad to nuevo federalismo.* Boulder, Colo.: Westview Press.

Rojas, Rosa, ed. 1995. *Chiapas, ¿y las mujeres qué?* México, D.F.: Ediciones del Taller Editorial La Correa Feminista; Centro de Investigacion y Capacitacion de la Mujer A.C.

Ross, John. 2000. *The war against oblivion: Zapatista chronicles, 1994–2000.* Monroe, Maine: Common Courage Press.

Rubin, Jeffrey W. 1990. Rethinking post-revolutionary Mexico: Popular movements and the myth of the corporatist state. In *Popular movements and political change in Mexico,* ed. Joe Foweraker and Ann L. Craig, 247–67. Boulder, Colo.: Lynne Rienner Publishers.

———. 1996. Decentering the regime: Culture and regional politics in Mexico. *Latin American Research Review* 31, no. 3: 85–126.

———. 1998. *Decentering the regime: Ethnicity, radicalism, and democracy in Juchitán, Mexico.* Durham, N.C.: Duke University Press.

Rubio, Blanca. 1987. *Resistencia campesina y explotación rural en México.* México, D.F.: Ediciones Era.

Ruiz, Margarito. 1990. Los 20 mil obstaculos. *México Indígena,* no. 7: 14–16.

———. 1994. El frente independiente de pueblos indios. *Revista Mexicana de Sociología* 2: 117–32.

Rus, Jan. 1977. Antropología social en los altos de Chiapas. *Apuntes de Lectura,* no. 3.

———. 1994. The "comunidad revolucionaria institucional": The subversion of native government in highland Chiapas, 1936–1968. In *Everyday forms of state formation: Revolution and the negotiation of rule in modern Mexico,* ed. Gilbert M. Joseph and Daniel Nugent, 265–300. Durham, N.C.: Duke University Press.

Rus, Jan et al. 1986. *Abtel ya pinka/Trabajo en las fincas.* San Cristóbal de las Casas, Chiapas: INAREMAC.

Ruz, Mario Humberto. 1992. *Savia india, floración ladina: Apuntes para una historia de las fincas comitecas (siglos XVIII y XIX).* México, D.F.: Consejo Nacional para la Cultura y las Artes.

———. 1993 [1984]. Los Tojolabales. In *La población indígena de Chiapas,* ed. Victor Manuel Esponda Jimeno. Rpt., Tuxtla Gutiérrez: Gobierno del Estado de Chiapas; DIF.

———. 1994. Los Tojolabales. INI monograph. México, D.F.: INI.

———, ed. 1981. *Los legítimos hombres: Aproximación antropológica al grupo Tojolabal.* 4 vols. México, D.F.: Centro de Estudios Mayas de la UNAM.

Schmitter, Philippe C. 1993. Corporatism. In *The Oxford companion to politics of the world,* ed. Joel Krieger. Oxford: Oxford University Press.

Secretaría de Gobernación y Gobierno del Estado de Chiapas. 1988. *Los municipios de Chiapas.* México, D.F.: Talleres Gráficos de la Nación.

Selverston-Scher, Melina. 2001. *Ethnopolitics in Ecuador: Indigenous rights and the strengthening of democracy.* Miami, Fla.: North-South.

Servicios del Pueblo Mixe, A.C. 1996. La autonomía: Una forma concreta de ejercicio del derecho a la libre determinación y sus alcances. Adelfo Regino Montes, coordinador general. Presented at Mesa 1, Foro Nacional Indígena, San Cristóbal de las Casas, Chiapas, January 3–8.

Sierra, María Teresa. 1995. Indian rights and customary law in Mexico: A study of the Nahuas in the Sierra de Puebla. *Law & Society Review* 29, no. 2: 227–54.

Silverts, Henning. 1969. Ethnic stability and boundary dynamics in southern Mexico. In *Ethnic groups and boundaries: The social organization of culture difference,* ed. Fredrik Barth, 101–16. Boston: Little, Brown, and Co.

Sloan, John W. 1985. The Mexican variant of corporatism. *Inter-American Economic Affairs* 38 (spring): 3–18.

Smith, Gavin. 1989. *Livelihood and resistance: Peasants and politics of land in Peru.* Berkeley and Los Angeles: University of California Press.

Spalding, Ruth. 1981. State power and its limits: Corporatism in Mexico. *Comparative Political Studies* 14 (July): 139–64.

Stavenhagen, Rodolfo. 1989 [1980]. *Problemas étnicos y campesinos*. Rpt., México, D.F.: Instituto Nacional Indigenista; Dirección General de Publicaciones del Consejo Nacional para la Cultura y las Artes.

———. 1996a. *Ethnic conflicts and the nation-state*. New York: St. Martin's Press.

———. 1996b. Indigenous rights: Some conceptual problems. In *Constructing democracy: Human rights, citizenship, and society in Latin America*, ed. Elizabeth Jelin and Eric Hershberg, 141–59. Boulder, Colo.: Westview Press.

———. 1999. Prólogo: Hacia el derecho de autonomía en México. In *México: Experiencias de autonomía indígena*, ed. Araceli Burguete, 7–20. Copenhagen: IWGIA.

———. 2001. *La cuestión étnica*. México, D.F.: El Colegio de México.

Stavenhagen, Rodolfo, and Diego Iturralde, eds. 1990. *Entre la ley y la costumbre: El derecho consuetudinario indígena en América Latina*. México, D.F.: Instituto Indigenista Interamericano; San José, Costa Rica: Instituto Interamericano de Derechos Humanos.

Stephen, Lynn. 1996. Redefined nationalism in building a movement for indigenous autonomy in Mexico: Oaxaca and Chiapas. Paper presented at the annual meeting of the American Anthropological Association, San Francisco, Calif., November 20–24.

———. 2002. *¡Zapata lives! Histories and cultural politics in southern Mexico*. Berkeley and Los Angeles: University of California Press.

Tarrow, Sidney G. 1994. *Power in movement: Social movements, collective action, and politics*. Cambridge: Cambridge University Press.

Tax, Sol. 1943. *Notas sobre Zinacantán, Chiapas*. Chicago: University of Chicago Press.

Tello Díaz, Carlos. 1995. *La rebelión de las Cañadas*. México, D.F.: Cal y Arena.

Touraine, Alain. 1988. *Return of the actor: Social theory in postindustrial society*. Minneapolis: University of Minnesota Press.

Tresierra, Julio C. 1994. Mexico: Indigenous peoples and the nation-state. In *Indigenous peoples and democracy in Latin America*, ed. Donna Lee Van Cott, 187–210. New York: St. Martin's; Inter-American Dialogue.

Urrego, Miguel Angel. 2001. Social and popular movements in a time of cholera, 1977–1999. In *Violence in Colombia 1990–2000: Waging war and negotiating peace*, ed. Charles Bergquist, Ricardo Penaranda, and Gonzalo Sánchez G., 171–78. Wilmington, Del.: Scholarly Resources.

Van Cott, Donna Lee. 1996. Prospects for self-determination of indigenous peoples in Latin America: Questions of law and practice. *Global Governance* 2: 43–64.

———. 2000a. *The friendly liquidation of the past: The politics of diversity in Latin America.* Pittsburgh: University of Pittsburgh Press.

———. 2000b. A political analysis of legal pluralism in Bolivia and Colombia. *Journal of Latin American Studies* 32: 207–34.

———. 2001. Explaining ethnic autonomy regimes in Latin America. *Studies in Comparative International Development* 35, no. 4: 30–58.

———, ed. 1994. *Indigenous peoples and democracy in Latin America.* New York: St. Martin's Press.

Van der Haar, Gemma. 1998. La campesinización de la zona alta tojolabal: El remate zapatista. In *Espacios disputados: Transformaciones rurales en Chiapas,* ed. María Eugenia Reyes Ramos, Reyna Moguel Viveros, and Gemma van der Haar, 99–113. México, D.F.: UNAM; San Cristóbal de las Casas: El Colegio de la Frontera Sur.

Vasconcelos, José. 1976. *La raza cósmica: Misión de la raza iberoamericana, Argentina y Brazil.* 4th ed. México, D.F.: Espasa-Calpe.

Vázquez Soto, Luz Idolina. 1983. Organización campesina Tojolabal: Instancias organizativas y sus luchas. B.A. thesis. Universidad Autónoma de Chiapas.

Vera Herrera, Ramón. n.d. Foro nacional indígena: Las fibras de un fuerte tejido invisible. Unpublished manuscript.

———. 1995. Las fronteras de la enormidad. *Ojarasca* (October–November): 37–43.

Vértiz, Columba. 2001. La propuesta zapatista de medios de comunicación, insuficiente. *Proceso* 1270, Mar. 4, 2001. September 25. URL: http://www.proceso.com.mx/1270/1270n03.html.

Victoria, Carlos San Juan. 1996. La novedad de los antiguos: Promesas y retos del resurgir de los pueblos como actores politicos. *El Cotidiano,* no. 76: 34–41.

Villa Rojas, Alfonso. 1985 [1965]. *Estudios etnológicos de los Mayas.* Rpt., México, D.F.: Universidad Nacional Autónoma de México.

Viotti, Emilia da Costa. 1985. *The Brazilian empire: Myths and histories.* Chicago: University of Chicago Press.

Viqueira, Juan Pedro. 1995. Los altos de Chiapas: Una introducción general. In *Chiapas, los rumbos de otra historia,* ed. Juan Pedro Viqueira and Mario Humberto Ruz, 219–36. México, D.F.: Centro de Estudios Mayas del Instituto de Investigaciones Filológicas, UNAM.

———. 2001. Los usos y costumbres en contra de la autonomía. *Letras Libres* (March): 30–34.

Viqueira, Juan Pedro, and Willibald Sonnleitner, eds. 2000. *Democracia en tierras indígenas: Las elecciones en los altos de Chiapas (1991–1998).* México, D.F.: CIESAS; El Colegio de México; Instituto Federal Electoral.

Vogt, Evon Z. 1994. *Fieldwork among the Maya: Reflections on the Harvard Chiapas Project.* Albuquerque: University of New Mexico Press.

Wade, Peter. 1993. *Blackness and race mixture: The dynamics of racial identity in Colombia.* Baltimore, Md.: Johns Hopkins University Press.

———. 1997. *Race and ethnicity in Latin America.* London: Pluto Press.

Warman, Arturo. n.d. Políticas y tareas indigenistas [1989–1994]. Unpublished manuscript.

Warren, Kay B. 1992. Transforming memories and histories: The meanings of ethnic resurgence for Mayan Indians. In *Americas: New interpretive essays,* ed. Alfred Stepan, 189–219. New York: Oxford University Press.

———. 1993. Introduction: Revealing conflicts across cultures & disciplines. In *The violence within: Cultural and political opposition in divided nations,* ed. Kay B. Warren, 1–23. Boulder, Colo.: Westview Press.

———. 1998. *Indigenous movements and their critics: Pan-Maya activism in Guatemala.* Princeton, N.J.: Princeton University Press.

Wasserstrom, Robert. 1983. *Class and society in central Chiapas.* Berkeley and Los Angeles: University of California Press.

West, Lois A., ed. 1997. *Feminist nationalism.* New York: Routledge.

Wolf, Eric R. 1957. Aspects of group relations in a complex society: Mexico. *American Anthropologist* 58, no. 6.

———. 1959. *Sons of the shaking earth.* Chicago: University of Chicago Press.

———. 1982. *Europe and the people without history.* Berkeley and Los Angeles: University of California Press.

Womack, John. 1999. *Rebellion in Chiapas: An historical reader.* New York: New Press.

World Factbook 2001. URL: http://www.cia.gov/cia/publications/factbook/.

Xavier-Guerra, François. 1985. *México: Del antiguo régimen a la revolución.* 2 vols. México, D.F.: Fondo de Cultura Económica.

Yashar, Deborah. 1998. Contesting citizenship: Indigenous movements and democracy in Latin America. *Comparative Politics* 31, no. 1: 23–42.

———. 1999. Democracy, Indian movements, and the postliberal challenge in Latin America. *World Politics* 52, no. 1: 76–104.

Zamosc, León. 1994. Agrarian protest and the Indian movement in the Ecuadorean highlands. *Latin American Research Review* 21, no. 3: 37–69.

Zárate Hernández, José Eduardo. 1993. *Los señores de utopía: Etnicidad política en una comunidad Phurhépecha: Ueamuo-Santa Fé de la Laguna.* Zamora: El Colegio de Michoacán; México, D.F.: CIESAS.

Zepeda, Jorge. 1993. No es lo mismo agrario que agrio ni comuneros que comunistas, pero se parecen: La UCEZ en Michoacán. In *Perspectivas de los movimientos sociales en la región centro-occidente,* ed. Jaime Tamayo. Guadalajara: Universidad de Guadalajara; México, D.F.: UNAM.